A POETICS OF PERFORMANCE

A POETICS OF PERFORMANCE

THE ORAL–SCRIBAL AESTHETIC IN ANGLOPHONE CARIBBEAN FICTION

Carol Bailey

THE UNIVERSITY OF THE WEST INDIES PRESS
Jamaica • Barbados • Trinidad and Tobago

The University of the West Indies Press
7A Gibraltar Hall Road, Mona
Kingston 7, Jamaica
www.uwipress.com

© 2014 by Carol Bailey
All rights reserved. Published 2014

A catalogue record of this book is available from the National Library of Jamaica.

ISBN: 978-976-640-495-6 (print)
978-976-640-538-0 (Kindle)
978-976-640-542-7 (ePub)

Cover illustrations by Erold Bailey
Cover design and book design by Robert Harris
Set in Scala 10.25/15 x 27
Printed in the United States of America

FOR EROLD, NATHARA AND MANDISA, AND
IN LOVING MEMORY OF MY MOTHER, MINA

Contents

Acknowledgements / ix

Introduction / 1

1

Opening Acts: Scholarly and Literary Precursors to Performing Fiction / 22

2

(Re)membering: The Power of Stories in *The Colour of Forgetting* and *Unburnable* / 37

3

Inter-Performance and the Woman-Centred Poetics in *The Wine of Astonishment* and *The Book of Night Women* / 75

4

Affirming the Female "Subject Person": Rereading Gender Discourses in *The Dragon Can't Dance* / 119

5

Globalizing Yard in "Joebell and America" and "How to Beat a Child the Right and Proper Way" / 141

Afterword / 173

Notes / 183

Selected Bibliography / 201

Index / 215

Acknowledgements

"Turn T'anks"

THIS BOOK IS A capstone of my many years of education, and so I thank all the people who have, at some point in my educational journey, taught, mentored and encouraged me. For ushering in my sojourn into tertiary education I thank all my teachers at Sam Sharpe Teachers' College. I deeply appreciate the work of my professors at the University of the West Indies, where the ideas for this project broke ground and where much of my earlier learning was both consolidated and deeply enriched. So maximum respect to Carolyn Allen, Edward Baugh, Victor Chang, Nadi Edwards, Earl McKenzie, Mervyn Morris, David Williams, Curdella Forbes and Maureen Warner-Lewis. Thank you for being the backbone of a first-rate Department of Literatures in English. And to the multiple other influential people, such as Mary Gray, who have been so nurturing during my time at the University of the West Indies, many thanks. I am especially indebted to Professor Warner-Lewis for introducing me to the field of orature and for providing such a stellar example of scholarly excellence in the field. This project began as a Master of Philosophy, which I started at the University of the West Indies. I am grateful for the work of my first committee from the Department of Literatures in English. In addition to those named above, I thank Michael Bucknor; and Carolyn Cooper, thanks for your inspiring and pioneering work, for caring and for always asking, "How the book going?" My classmates and study partners at the University of the West Indies have played a special role in shaping my academic trajectory. Thank you all.

A special thanks to the Department of English at Clark University, particularly my advisor, John Conron, and the late Winston Napier for providing me with a space to begin my graduate work and explore some of the ideas developed here, and for being exceedingly generous.

I completed my graduate studies at the University of Massachusetts Amherst, where my work was facilitated and supported by Stephen Clingman, Laura Doyle, Jenny Spencer, Nick Bromell, Suzanne Daly, Joseph Skerrett, James Young and others. Thanks to Stephen Olbrys Gencarella and Donal Carbaugh from the Department of Communications, who also supported my work, and Rhonda Cobham-Sander, who served on my dissertation committee. I am grateful for the support my committee members have offered beyond the dissertation and with this work.

I am grateful to Andrea Rushing, Rhonda Cobham-Sander, Anita and Orlando Patterson, and others for facilitating opportunities that have contributed to my successful completion of this project.

The Five College Fellowship Program allowed me time to complete the dissertation project that led to this book. I am especially grateful to Smith College and the Department of Afro-American Studies, particularly Anne Ferguson, Paula Giddings and Kevin Quashie, for their support and mentorship.

I have had the privilege of teaching in a number of institutions, each of which has embraced my work, allowing me room to test my ideas in different courses. For such opportunities, I thank Amherst College, Harvard University, Keene State College, Rhode Island College, Smith College, the University of Massachusetts and the University of the West Indies. My current institution, Westfield State University, has offered me release time to complete this project. I thank Elizabeth Preston for granting me that time; many thanks to colleagues in the Department of English and Regina Smialek for their warm support. My chair, Emily Todd, has also been particularly supportive. A special thanks to Marilyn Sandidge and Vanessa Holford Diana, who enthusiastically helped me to track down references. Many thanks to other faculty and staff at Westfield State University, particularly Ryan at the copy centre. I am grateful for the community and research support that the Five College Women's Studies Research Center offered long before this project was anything close to a book.

For their generosity and astute comments on drafts, for patiently listening to my questions and ideas, and for all their advice, I thank Curdella Forbes and Cathy Schlund-Vials. Thank you, Karen Cardozo, Nicole Aljoe, Rowland Abiodun, Meg Hart, Keguro Macharia, Rachael Mordecai, Lauren

Rosenberg, Bill Doreski, Silvio Torres-Saillant and Michael Niblett, Ifeoma Kiddoe Nwankwo for reading and providing such helpful feedback. I am also grateful for the valuable comments I received from Michelle Stephens and Paulette Bell in the early years of the project, and to Merle Hodge and Funso Aiyejina for signalling to me early on that these ideas were worth pursuing. Many thanks to Rosie Pearson for her invaluable editorial and research assistance and for her investment in my work.

Thank you to my faithful friends Carol Brown, Carlene Edie, Keisha-Khan Perry, Carmeneta Jones, Denia Fraser, Ricka Dawkins and Merlene Soares for your love and unwavering support, encouragement and insistence. Many thanks to so many important people not named here.

My sincere gratitude to my family: to Nigel and Letha for their steadfast all-round support; Keel and Kora for their enthusiasm; and my sisters Joan, Annette, Salome, my brother-in-law Allan, Kahlia and my other nieces and nephews for their support, sheer joy and affirmation. My gratitude to my in-laws, the Baileys, for their various contributions. Nathara and Mandisa kept me going with their love and inspiration. Thank you for allowing me recess time, for the numerous summer days you sacrificed so I could be in the library. And to Erold, I cannot thank you enough for your steady and enduring support and encouragement – for your unwavering confidence and for reading drafts and providing honest, incisive and gentle feedback. For all the times you took charge of the domestic, extended family and other responsibilities so I could devote time to this work, I am truly grateful.

I am honoured and grateful that Linda Speth and the editorial board of the University of the West Indies Press accepted this project for publication. The reviewers provided excellent feedback, which has strengthened this work. I appreciate the meticulous work of the Press's editorial team, as well as the contribution of other staff who faciliatated the publication of this book.

A portion of chapter one appeared under the title "Destabilizing Caribbean Critical Orthodoxies: Interrogating Orality in Marie-Elena John's *Unburnable*" in *Caribbean Quarterly* (59, no. 1 [2013]: 31–49). I thank *Caribbean Quarterly* editor Kim Robinson-Walcott for her role in helping me refine that essay.

Much gratitude to my circle of friends in Amherst and elsewhere on whom I rely for so much, and to all friends and associates not named here, no disrespec', thank you.

Introduction

> The sound bubbled up
> through a cistern one night
> and piped its way into
> the atmosphere,
> and decent people wanted
> to know
> "What kind of ole nayga music is that
> playing on the Government's radio?"
> But this red and yellow and dark green
> sound,
> stained from traveling underground,
> smelling of poor people's dinners
> from a yard dense as Belgium,
> has the healing.
> More than weed and white rum healing.
> More than bush tea and fever grass cooling
> and it pulses without a symphony conductor
> all it need is a dub organizer.
> – Lorna Goodison, "Jah Music"

THE POEM ABOVE, LORNA Goodison's "Jah Music", was published in 1986, in Goodison's second collection, *I Am Becoming My Mother*. Goodison, one of the Caribbean's most critically acclaimed poets, has been lauded for, among other accomplishments, her dexterous deployment of Caribbean language and other local expressive resources in her literary creations. Goodison dedicates this poem to Michael "Ibo" Cooper, a well-known Jamaican musician, Rastafarian and founding member of the Jamaican international reggae band

Third World. "Jah Music" was published more than two decades after the formation of reggae music in Jamaica, after the music had achieved relative local mainstream acceptance and international recognition. The poem's validation of this folk-generated performance mode, as well as the inroads that reggae music has made into mainstream society, locate this work within postcolonial conversations about the legitimacy of the cultural creations of the underclass.

The journey of reggae music from its roots in Kingston's inner city to what the poem refers to as the "atmosphere" instantiates the movement of the folk and inner-city performance culture into creative writing and critical discourse, and into mainstream acceptance. Goodison's poetic rendering of the twists and turns taken by reggae music functions as a staging ground for broader conversations about facets of Caribbean culture that have been simultaneously marginalized and recuperated, even as the poem chronicles the irrepressible character of these cultural modes.

"Blood in the north, blood to come in the south, and the blue crying red in between" is the opening line of Merle Collins's second novel, *The Colour of Forgetting* (1995). Appearing multiple times throughout the novel, this phrase functions as the work's primary leitmotif and structuring device. Significantly, too, the warner woman, one of the main characters in *The Colour of Forgetting* and its prophetic voice, stages the novel's opening performance with these words. The inclusion of this phrase at the beginning of the novel and its appearance throughout mark another example of the way in which disavowed performance modes have penetrated the literature. Long before reggae and calypso became the kinds of working-class performance genres that official society actively sought to suppress, "warning" was among the discounted performances.[1] Warner women belong to a centuries-old oral tradition associated with Afro-Caribbean spiritual and religious traditions such as Pocomania. These local prophets customarily marched through rural communities at dawn with a prophecy of impending disaster.

Published just under a decade after Goodison's "Jah Music", *The Colour of Forgetting* therefore follows in that tradition of interrogating age-old cultural prejudices and privileging the folk/working-class–generated performance modes. This early inclusion of the warner woman's cry and Collins's integration of her as one of the novel's primary narrators showcases how Caribbean writers have tapped into the oral-performance tradition to elicit both the means and the subject of their discourses about cultural legitimacy and various other concerns. By naming the warner woman Carib, Collins signals her alignment with an indigenous and virtually forgotten culture, thereby reaching beyond colonial history for her fictive tools. And like Goodison's poem, Collins's novel epitomizes the inward turn, one of the central structuring ideas of this work.

A *Poetics of Performance* shares a discursive and cultural space with Goodison's "Jah Music" and Collins's *The Colour of Forgetting*. These texts are emblematic of how Caribbean writers deploy the cultural products of the underclass to interrogate assumed boundaries and highlight the interdependence between written and oral-performance traditions. This book engages in an intensive exploration of the intersections and tensions between anglophone Caribbean literary and performance cultures through a theorization of a particular kind of fiction that I refer to here as "performing fiction". I use this term to describe West Indian novels and short stories that employ specific kinds of orature – such as songs, stories, proverbs, gossip and speeches – as their central mode of narration. I distinguish between written fictions that *include* forms of orature (and may even do so extensively), and those in which orature is the primary organizing frame and narrative strategy. These works illustrate a close inter-performative relationship between writing and the live oral-aesthetic culture that extends beyond literature that merely "borrows" from oral-aesthetic forms. In light of the synergies between orature and this category of fiction, I theorize performing fiction through an elucidation of the stylistic and thematic synergies that mark these hybrid fictions.

In ascribing the nomenclature "performing fiction" to these works, I am also suggesting that they adopt a poetics of performance.[2] That is to say that their formal structure, their recuperations of voice and body, and their themes are fundamentally shaped by performance, with its proclivities towards improvisation, incompleteness and responsiveness to audience. My use of the term "poetics of performance" also acknowledges the integral place of West Indian performance modes in these fictions. Thus, inscribed on these pages are not only particular oral forms such as songs, stories and proverbs, but also the communal spaces (yards, verandahs, village squares, friend and family gatherings, political meetings, demonstrations, dancehalls, churches, carnival parades) where performances are staged. In such spaces, these forms of orature also function as markers of belonging and as vehicles of political engagement and protest. Thus, in recovering these forms of orature, writers simultaneously encode the extensive gamut of meanings and discursive possibilities of their performative contexts. And it follows that in addition to integrating specific performance modes as part of their form, these written fictions also show how performance functions as a discursive space where Caribbean ideologies and cultural traditions are scrutinized, challenged and reinforced. Further, by making performance itself a subject of critical inquiry, performing fictions are also engaged in a meta-performative discourse in the way in which they foster and are engaged in a reflection on the nature of writing, speaking, voice and performance.

This book uses and distinguishes between two related key terms: *orality*, the general term for all kinds of utterances, and *orature*, the artistic use of orality. Maureen Warner-Lewis's definitions of orality as "an umbrella term for all forms of verbal communication" and orature as "words artistically crafted in an oral medium" are helpful here.[3] And building on Ugandan linguist Pio Zirimu's initial definition of orature as "the use of utterance as an aesthetic means of expression", Ngũgĩ wa Thiong'o defines orature as "verbal artistic production".[4] Therefore, the term *orature*, with its evocation of the performative more accurately and specifically – rather than the general term *orality* – describes the forms that shape these fictions. And the emphasis on artistry in definitions of orature shows the clear links between orature and performance.[5] The intricate incorporation of aesthetics of orature into the scribal text therefore creates a hybrid form of prose fiction: it retains features that are associated with British novels and short stories, but these are overlaid by Caribbean performance modes.

Performing fictions tap into the novel's inherent propensity towards experimentation, which was theorized by Mikhail Bakhtin in his famous work *The Dialogic Imagination*.[6] The novels and short stories under consideration here take on a specifically Caribbean character; the writers remain true to their forms in terms of experimentation, but also expand those forms by creating West Indian works undergirded by the orature-performance of the Caribbean. Sylvia Wynter has highlighted the paradoxical nature of the novel, noting how it is a product of a capitalist economy yet also functions as "the critique of the very historical process which has brought it to such heights of fulfilment".[7] Therefore, writers' turns to the culture of the folk and urban poor for their fictive tools illustrate both the improvisational orientation of the novel and its capacity to critique itself and the context out of which it is created.

Because of the participatory implications of orature and performance, the term "performing fiction" also implies the presence of an audience, beyond the way in which we typically think of readers as audiences for other kinds of written fiction. The gerund "performing" also connotes the live, active process-orientation and incompleteness inherent in performances. Thus, the analyses of the performing fictions under consideration here demonstrate how these characteristics that are endemic to performance constitute the structures of these oral-literary works. Given the extensive use of performance as literary aesthetic in the fictions analysed in this work, *A Poetics of Performance* makes a case for a critical practice that is attentive to performance as a primary, analytical approach to this kind of prose fiction.

Mervyn Morris's explication of the term "performance poem" as a poem "designated for presentation to an audience rather than for private perusal by an isolated reader" provides a helpful context within which performing fiction might be understood. Morris's further articulation of performance poems as constituting "voices that insist on being sounded"[8] is especially applicable to these fictions, in which the narrative voices often appear as those of storytellers, singers and interlocutors. An active, involved audience is therefore an essential component of engagement with performing fictions, a feature which signifies upon the Caribbean context, in which audiences are especially active – almost always operating within the call and response tradition. In performing fictions, the conventional reader is thus refashioned as an interlocutor.

I use the term "performing fiction" to mean performing *in* fiction, which describes the enactment of particular performances on the written page, akin to what Richard Schechner describes as 'restored behaviour". Schechner defines restored behaviour as "strips of behaviour" that performers of all types recover, rearrange and reconstruct in the act of performance.[9] While Schechner's characterization refers to the live reenactment of performances, this theorization of performing fictions is attentive to writings that constitute a "restoration" or "recovery" of live performance as narrative strategy in written works. It is the recovery or restoration of orature and its related performances through the crafting of narrators as singers, storytellers or actors that creates these hybrid fictions that straddle the written and oral-performative systems.

Performing *in* fiction also expresses the written stories' reenactment of specific performance modes associated with Caribbean people's self-definition and their resistance to hegemonic institutions such as slavery, colonialism and various brands of neocolonialism. Thus, these writers' choice of orature-performance as a mode in which to write stories that engage with current debates illustrates a rootedness in a long tradition of deploying performance as a tool of critical engagement and as a challenge to various ideological and stylistic imperatives. Historically, Caribbean peoples have used a variety of performance styles as vehicles for self-expression and resistance.[10] Events such as carnival and Christmas parades offered blacks and free coloureds in the post-emancipation period an opportunity to mock the establishment and assume "socially superior" roles, which emphasized their self-assertion. While this study is attentive to such resistance to new and enduring manifestations of colonialism, it also moves beyond the ways in which performance facilitates confrontation with colonial structures. This book focuses on how this tradition of using performance as a discursive tool and site of resistance continues but is reconstituted in performing fictions, through writers' utilization of performance modes as the vehicle of critical discourse.

The term "performing fiction" also designates fictions that perform. Because they use the words on the page to tell stories, all fictions are, at some level, inherently engaged in performance. This intrinsic performativity of Caribbean fiction, particularly its carnivalesque orientation, has been addressed by Benítez-Rojo.[11] In this work, the emphasis is on what the novel and short story *do* as a result of the overlaying of performances in these works. In other words, this book also explores what the texts are posing as or purporting to be when they explicitly straddle writing and orality, even as they bear the traditional scribal names and ostensible forms of novels and short stories.

Writers of performing fiction engage in what I term an "inward turn", a profoundly significant political-ideological element of a literary poetics grounded in Caribbean orature-performance. My use of "inward turn" here describes these writers' deep and extensive engagement with the Caribbean itself: that is to say, talking to the self rather than talking back to the metropole. This study includes works by Vic Reid, Samuel Selvon and Earl Lovelace, authors who have in some ways engaged with the early anti-colonial "writing back" that characterized Caribbean literature. However, these writers' use of the expressive resources, their groundbreaking creation of a literary aesthetic that draws on the cultural practices of the folk and urban poor, marks a strong, burgeoning and sustained self-directed impulse and the charting of a new literary and critical course.

This kind of discursive turning in also necessarily includes challenging some of the Caribbean's most cherished ideals and practices, including those that have already been accepted and promoted as counteractive to colonial and neocolonial paradigms. Marie-Elena John's interrogation of orality exemplifies this kind of critical, self-directed gaze. My use of "inward turn" in this way acknowledges but de-emphasizes the contestation of colonial discourses; it departs from the "writing back" to the empire that inevitably preoccupied an earlier generation of Caribbean writers, and instead pivots to collective self-scrutiny.

Significantly, A Poetics of Performance is attentive to the ways in which these textual performances actively engage with the live culture, particularly how they seek to bridge the inevitable gap between the material culture and literary representations of the latter. The formal shifts, conversations and interactions I highlight among the texts analysed in this book are indicative of the histories, discursive turns and political developments in the Caribbean and its diaspora over the last seven decades.

Another important component in these multiple textual performances is that a narrative mode – orature – which started as an articulation of nationalist sentiment and an expression of decolonizing efforts has endured and re-emerged as a way of addressing current issues such as transnationalism, postnationalism and diaspora. Marlon James's *The Book of Night Women* (2009), Marie-Elena John's *Unburnable* (2006) and Colin Channer's "How to Beat a Child the Right and Proper Way" (2006), fictions written in diasporan and metropolitan settings in the beginning of the twenty-first century, retain or rekindle a commitment to the national within the global through a return to orature. These stylistic inward turns in some ways call into question the idea of a global melting pot, in which national boundaries are collapsed through psychic migrations or postmodern cosmopolitanism. While none of these texts asserts a static nationalism, they do illustrate the enduring relevance of nationalism in new and renewed ways. Their textual performances retain a West

Indian nationalist ethos while they simultaneously reconstitute themselves in ways that are relevant to new locales and responsive to new exigencies. Not surprisingly, then, in these fictions, performance as subject, literary aesthetic and discursive tool engages many of the key concerns of Caribbean writing over the last few decades. I outline below those that are most germane to my discussion in this book.

Questions related to gender are essential to any consideration of orature-performance in the Caribbean context. Further, because many of the orature-performance modes recuperated in performing fictions are associated with women, *A Poetics of Performance* also makes the case that a woman-centred poetics is a central component of these works.[12] It posits that this performative voice is most often "feminine", and that this discussion engages the relationship between style and the authors' foregrounding of perspectives that might be referred to as "female" or "feminine". This inevitable centrality of female perspectives brings to the fore not only women's integral role in shaping the expressive culture of the Caribbean, but also their distinguished presence in intellectual discourses and their long history as freedom workers, particularly in decolonization efforts.

This work is especially attentive to male writers' execution of female voices in their primary narrative roles. With the exception of a few studies – notably, Curdella Forbes's *From Nation to Diaspora* (2005), which examines gender in the work of Samuel Selvon and George Lamming, and Belinda Edmondson's *Making Men: Gender, Literary Authority, and Women's Writing in Caribbean Narrative* (1999), which includes a discussion of works by major male West Indian writers – critical conversations that address women and womanist-feminist concerns in literature tend to centre on female-authored works. In its theorization of gender, *A Poetics of Performance* fills an important gap through its exploration of male writers' recuperation of performance modes associated with women as central discursive resources in their fictional accounts of Caribbean experiences and critical contemplations.

A Poetics of Performance explores how Earl Lovelace's initial, subtle and tentative "feminized" performing fiction prefigures Channer's and James's bolder, more explicit "womanized" performing fiction. It addresses the cultural and political shifts that may account for the differences between Channer's and James's "woman-centred" performance poetics and Lovelace's earlier renditions of a female narrator. Lovelace, one of the Caribbean's best-known contemporary authors, is among the first writers to invest in orature and performance in the extensive ways that this book suggests. I have thus selected *The Wine of Astonishment* (1984) and *The Dragon Can't Dance* (1979), the two works in which Lovelace's poetics of performance is firmly established, as two of the primary texts on which this book's engagement with gender constructions and ideologies is based. Lovelace's embedded female-centred discourse anticipates Marlon James's *The Book of Night Women*, in which a bold-faced womanist-feminist poetics emerges. The historical foundations of James's slave narrative reveals the creole genealogy of West Indian performance poetics, grounded in the region's plantation beginnings and the local landscape. Yet this work evinces strong resonances with Lovelace's nationalist commitment, which is deeply rooted in African spiritual retentions. Lovelace and James take up the question of citizenship, particularly women's citizenship, as central to nationalist debates that are often read or presented as gender-neutral engagements. Although James's novel is set in a historical context in which questions of nationhood and citizenship were not being explicitly debated, his recovery of women as essential workers in emancipation struggles emphasizes women's enduring activism in claims to personhood, citizenship and belonging. James's recourse to an aggressive brand of "feminine" performance further highlights women's roles as participants and leaders in Caribbean peoples' quests for liberation.

This work also discusses Lovelace's short story "Joebell and America", from *A Brief Conversion and Other Stories* (1988), which, when brought into dialogue with Channer's "How to Beat a Child the Right and Proper Way", extends a shift in current discourse on migration in such a way that hegemonic migrant locations are decentred. The undermining power of the two stories in conversation is accentuated by the ironies of their locations: Joebell goes to America without going there; in Channer's story, Jamaica goes to America, travelling in a channel through the body-voice of its verbose narrator, Ciselyn. The manner in which space and place are treated in these two works, in which the Caribbean location is privileged both physically and psychically, evinces fresh and exciting characterizations of home and citizenship.

Merle Collins's *The Colour of Forgetting* takes up the problem of representation, one of the ongoing thorny issues that animate Caribbean scholars. In its choice of performative narrative voices and its meta-performative explorations, this novel addresses key questions regarding what stories get told as well as the means of their telling, and further, the ways in which the choice of rhetorical tool decides not simply how stories are told but also which stories emerge and which ones are suppressed.[13] *The Colour of Forgetting* is essential to these debates because of its important place within the larger body of Caribbean women's writing. The novel, at the time it was published, signalled a shift away from the focus on writings by canonical male writers such as Wilson Harris, George Lamming, V.S. Naipaul, Vic Reid and Derek Walcott in conversations about representations of the past. Also of crucial import is the particular way in which *The Colour of Forgetting* addresses a neocolonial problem of the very recent past: the United States' invasion of Grenada. Collins explores the experience of what she refers to in the poem "Shame Bush" as a shaming of national pride. This national shame resulted in a deliberate forgetting, and selective remembering. The inward turn that I address in this work is especially evident in *The Colour of Forgetting* as Collins's narrative performers turn away from Euro-American versions of historical events in favour of the warner woman's voice and the voices of other ordinary speakers whose family stories shape and constitute Grenadian history.

The self-reflexivity of *The Colour of Forgetting* – that is, the way in which storytelling functions as both meta-discourse and narrative strategy – anticipates further literary explorations of how orality itself is implicated in the problem of historical representation. Therefore, placing Marie-Elena John's problematized representation of orality in *Unburnable* in conversation with *The Colour of Forgetting* simultaneously foregrounds the significance of oral stories in challenging representations of the past, and radically moves the discourse away from a valorization of orality as the representational counterpoint to written history. In a real sense, John's novel marks a turning point in the interpretation of orality in West Indian literature: specifically, it illustrates a movement away from the tendency to view orality as a liberating force in literature, and an effort to subject it to critique in the same way that the preoccupation with certain scribal modes has been called into question in West Indian literary debates. The setting of the novel between the United States and the Caribbean, and the ostensible protagonist's position as a returnee from the diaspora in search of her family stories, extends the discourse in another direction: her return home for records that she hopes will correct stories she already knows takes her to other oral versions that have their own political and representational problems.

My concern with a performance-based literary aesthetic in these selected works is apparent in the ongoing conversations about the nature of Caribbean literature, specifically what features make literature from and about this region distinctive. *A Poetics of Performance* makes the case that what is distinctive about performing fictions is that Caribbean orature-performance shapes these works in a comprehensive way. This is not to say that the inclusion of orature is an essential quality that makes these texts Caribbean, nor am I suggesting that writers of performing fictions are the only writers from the region creatively exploiting the expressive tools from the region. Indeed, this turn to performance – rooted first in rural folk orature and later in a wider repertoire including musical and other expressions of the urban poor – is a characteristic feature of Caribbean literature even where orature-performance does not constitute the overarching structure, as it does in these performing fictions. Instead, this book focuses on a pattern, a "repeating" performance-driven aesthetic, so to speak, that is inherent in the literature.[14]

This distinction and intersection between fictions where orature-performance is the core aesthetic and Caribbean fiction as a whole, which inherently intersects with the local expressive culture, is an issue that Kamau Brathwaite wrestled with in his essays on "nation language". Brathwaite articulated a vision of a Caribbean literature grounded in the creole and Afro-based linguistic and performative resources of Caribbean autochthonous culture. Brathwaite's important essay "Jazz and the West Indian Novel"[15] is especially noteworthy as a seminal theorization of the influence of a particular performance genre on West Indian fiction. Similarly, Édouard Glissant addresses the oral-scribal tension and intersection in his assertion that a Caribbean national literature must be crafted at "the edge of writing and speech".[16]

Kwame Dawes's use of a reggae aesthetic to describe Caribbean literature illustrates a recognition of this relationship between orature and literature. Similarly, Antonio Benítez-Rojo characterizes the Caribbean and its literary and cultural expressions as carnivalesque performance. Benítez-Rojo's use of terms such as "polyrhythmic dance" and walking "in a certain kind of way" underscores the significance of inscribing the performance, voice and bodily presence that have come to define performing fiction.[17] With regard to gender and literary aesthetics, Evelyn O'Callaghan views women's literature in relation to men's writing as "dub" and "version", and Marlene NourbeSe Philip theorizes Caribbean migrant women's writing in terms of voiced silence and kinopoetics.[18]

The writers mentioned in the foregoing paragraph are engaged in a broader conversation with others, such as Carolyn Cooper, Mervyn Morris, Maureen Warner-Lewis and Funso Aiyejina, who have, in various ways, focused significant critical attention on oral-scribal crossings. Scholarship on Caribbean cultures has firmly established that performance is a fundamental, integral part of Caribbean experiences. However, there are no full-length studies that explore orature-performance as the structuring device in fiction. Kwame Dawes's *Natural Mysticism: Towards a New Reggae Aesthetic in Caribbean Writing* (1999) is to date the only book-length study that argues for a direct relationship between Caribbean writings and performance traditions. But Dawes's study explores Caribbean writing more generally and emphasizes the reggae-based sources of this literary aesthetic rather than the literary texts they influence.

Several other studies include prose fiction as part of a more general engagement with the interplay between the oral-performative culture and the literary tradition. Among the most notable examples is Carolyn Cooper's *Noises in the Blood: Orality, Gender, and the "Vulgar" Body of Jamaican Popular Culture* (1994), which explores the simultaneous distinctiveness of and interdependency between Jamaican oral and written cultures. Cooper's study is especially significant because of the voice/sound/body/performance image it sets up, which recurs in all the essays in the work. *Noises in the Blood* is also marked by an attentiveness to performance, which is evident in Cooper's treatment of "performance poetry" and the various non-verbal components of orality. Through her inclusion of gender in this study, Cooper also explores the subversive nature of writing in which orality is central.

Notable among essays that reflect on works significantly shaped by orature-performance are Gordon Rohlehr's seminal work on Selvon's fiction and Funso Aiyejina's insightful writings on the calypso aesthetic in Earl Lovelace's fiction. Aiyejina's use of the term "novelypso" to describe Lovelace's fiction is a significant marker of the kind of performance-based language that Caribbean critics have used to address the profound impact of orature-performance on the literature. Rohlehr's observations about Samuel Selvon's work underscore not only the extensive way in which Selvon's fiction is shaped by orature-performance but also the importance of adopting critical approaches that move beyond the traditionally literary. Rohlehr states: "When [Selvon's works] are read aloud to a group, and there is an interplay between narrator and audience, they yield up ironies and subtleties which one can miss when simply reading the words on the page.... Criticism of works which are meant to be performed can never be purely literary criticism, although it may borrow some of the methods of literary criticism."[19] Yet despite Rohlehr's acknowledgement – with a few exceptions, such as Maureen Warner-Lewis's discussion of linguistic performance, which she terms "linguistic extravaganza", in Samuel Selvon's work and Aiyejina's essay on Lovelace's "novelpso" – a performance-centred approach is still mostly peripheral to critical engagements with these fictions in which orature is so influential.[20]

Maria Grazia Sindoni's *Creolizing Culture: A Study on Sam Selvon's Work* (2006) is a significant book that explores, in part, the intersections between orality and writing as a central feature of post-1950s Caribbean literary aesthetics. In her attentiveness to the impact of orality on Selvon's oeuvre, Sindoni contextualizes Selvon's fictions as part of a broader shift in Caribbean literary aesthetics. Noting that Selvon's works illustrate the Bakhtinian, carnivalesque proclivities of the novel form, Sindoni's primarily linguistic analysis characterizes Selvon's turn to Caribbean orality as part of an anti-colonial response, "a writing back to the empire" and to the "Western literary canon".[21]

These various articulations indicate critics' recognition of this intersection of orature and literature in varying degrees. Undoubtedly, these studies provide important groundwork for the study of a direct relationship between these decades-old written forms and the centuries-old performance tradition that shapes them. By engaging a sustained discussion of selected writers' extensive use of Caribbean performance in ways that change the shape of fiction from the region, the following chapters seek to advance this conversation that wrestles with the complexities of oral-scribal intersections in Caribbean literature. With its attention to the way in which orature has changed the architecture of anglophone Caribbean prose fiction, and a focus on the self-directed gaze of the writers who create it, this work also advances the conversation about the necessity for an incorporation of this performance-driven aesthetic in critical analyses of performing fiction.

The adoption of a poetics of performance raises a number of theoretical and hermeneutical questions, all of which, at their core, ultimately relate to the nature of literature, literary inquiry and, more broadly, representation. These include: What constitutes literature? What are the implications of writers' formal choices for how we classify, study and write about literary works? Through a reading of selected works, *A Poetics of Performance* asks, more specifically: What happens to the genre of prose fiction, both novels and short stories, when stories are told through orature – that is, when the narrating voice is that of a performer in a specific form of orature? How does such a stylistic choice change the nature of literature and literary representation? Can one even speak about these works as prose when performance is such a prominent part of their structure?

This heightened attention to performance as means and subject, along with its prominence in these written fictions, demands another kind of criticism. A shift in focus to the performativity of these works makes exploration of the aesthetic features of such performance intrinsic to any basic reading of them, and therefore an incorporation of some of the critical approaches and tools of performance studies is especially useful. Because of the overwhelming presence of the speaking voice and the dialogic interaction within the texts, engagement with them involves an increased demand on the audience to imagine live performances and, at times, to imagine the self as the interlocutor to whom the stories are being told.

The premise of this book is that the shared creole performance tradition that has resulted from the intermingling of African, Asian and European cultures has, since the 1950s, served as the primary structuring frame for the work of a significant number of anglophone Caribbean writers.[22] Therefore, the inscription of specific types of Caribbean performances onto the written page has created fictions that reverberate with the distinctive performance styles that continue to flourish in these locales. This book is attentive to how writers enter and continue a tradition in which various forms of performance have been the bedrock of survival in the struggles for freedom and personhood in the colonial and postcolonial contexts of the Caribbean. The various forms of orature, including proverbs, songs, stories and gossip

– the indigenous creations of Caribbean creole cultures, with their strong African influence – that shape performing fictions, were the primary means of ensuring survival on the plantation and in post-slavery societies. Peter Roberts points out that this oral-performance tradition that was so critical to enslaved, formerly enslaved and indentured peoples has, as a means of communication and cultural transmission, endured the tyranny of formal education.[23] The writers' choice of a poetics of performance as a primary narrative strategy is therefore of crucial political and ideological import because this choice of narration is directly related to knowledge, knowledge systems and subalternity. All modes of communication and performance that have developed and been shaped by Caribbean creole culture are simultaneously marginal and central. They are central because they are the creations and tools of the majority but they are also marginal because of the hovering European culture that comprises the prevailing worldviews and ideals. Among the imperatives of this dominant, formal culture is an expressive system that decides the language and other communicative modes that are declared acceptable, and which would render their users "decent people" akin to those referred to in Goodison's poem.

Explicitly, then, the works on which the theorization of performing fiction is based are situated on the outskirts of the Euro-determined expressive culture, while at the same time being part of an established literary canon. As a result, these works and the discussion of them here participate in a broader conversation about the slippages, overlaps and meeting points between dominant and marginalized cultures. Walter Mignolo's notion of "border thinking" as generic to marginalized cultures is a useful point of entry for this broader conversation. Border thinking, with its emphasis on knowledge and knowledge systems that have been, in Mignolo's words, "subalternized", and its reliance on Michel Foucault's theory on the "archeology of knowledge", focuses on ways of knowing functioning within, yet disavowed by, Western thought and institutions.[24]

In his elaboration of border thinking, Mignolo argues that this concept is "unthinkable without understanding of colonial difference"; he further describes it as "the recognition of colonial thinking from subaltern perspectives".[25] While this distinction constitutes the nucleus of knowledge systems in the Caribbean, such a dichotomy does not fully describe the complex and multi-layered Caribbean context, where the differences between these systems and modalities are less distinct. This work therefore expands the concept of border thinking in order to account for the dynamic overlaps, accommodations and tensions between the expressive culture and epistemology of the literary genre and that of orature-performance. The tensions between orality and writing which this theorization of performing fiction explores are as much about separation and hierarchization, and a contentious intersection or interaction of modes of communication, as they are about the cultures and knowledge systems that these modes represent.

Therefore, this book is also about the different knowledge systems that coexist and contend with each other in the Caribbean, each of which is aligned with different experiences and worldviews, whether creole or European. By arguing that creole-generated modes of representation comprise the structure of these fictions, *A Poetics of Performance* must necessarily explore and privilege the devalued epistemological systems that these performances represent, and which have come to constitute a literary poetics. Forms of orature rooted in Caribbean creole cultures, which are the oral sources of the works discussed here, illustrate a stylistic turning away from European and colonially imposed knowledge systems and modes of representation (even as they simultaneously embrace them in some ways), evidencing a turn towards "subjugated knowledges".[26] While a wholesale acceptance of Caribbean performance modes as subjugated knowledge does not accurately represent the force and prevalence of these forms in the cultural fabric of the Caribbean, in a society in which formal education, writing, books and Euro-derived knowledge systems are promoted as progress, a turn to these locally derived forms for the means to write stories is an unequivocal validation of subjugated knowledge, or what Toni Morrison terms "discredited knowledges". Thus, by writing the orature of primarily the Caribbean underclass, Collins, Channer, James, John and Lovelace have produced works that undermine the very notion of books as symbols of colonial-modern hegemonic knowledge systems. These writers inscribe the voices, bodies and spirits of the Caribbean underclass, whose expressive tools and worldviews simultaneously intersect with and depart from that of the dominant culture.[27]

Chapter 1, "Opening Acts: Scholarly and Literary Precursors to Performing Fiction", takes a retrospective look at one of the defining moments in the integration of Caribbean orality in fiction from the region. The chapter examines Samuel Selvon's *The Lonely Londoners* (1956) and V.S. Reid's *New Day* (1949), as well as the critical conversations about these works. These two novels, recognized for their landmark extensive use of the Caribbean speaking voice as their narrative voice, started a trend that has been expanded and almost institutionalized as a defining feature of West Indian prose fiction. I explore how, as literary instigators, *The Lonely Londoners* and *New Day* do not merely initiate an innovative trend in novelistic representation; they boldly address the search for form that Anthony Boxill, Reinhard Sander and others have suggested was one of the fundamental issues of pre-1950s West Indian writing.[28] As two of the most significant writers to bridge the pre- and post-1950s literary epochs, Reid and Selvon carved out stylistic identities grounded in Caribbean vernacular and performance culture. This chapter also examines how the early critical emphasis on language usage in Reid's and Selvon's novels, though useful in signalling a shift in West Indian literary aesthetics, has obscured the pioneering centrality of orature as the structuring device, particularly in *New Day*. In its use of oral storytelling as the mode of narration, this work, more than any other, inaugurates a turn to performance culture for the expressive tools of literature.

Chapter 2 theorizes the problematics of representation through an analysis of Merle Collins's second novel, *The Colour of Forgetting*, and Marie-Elena John's debut novel, *Unburnable*, two works that demonstrate most explicitly the issues around representation that underpin all the other chapters of the book. These two texts also engage a metanarrative discourse and demonstrate how both written and oral stories are susceptible to distortions. In *The Colour of Forgetting*, Collins brings to the surface the simmering oral-scribal tension through recourse to Edward Baugh's notions of "the West Indian writer's quarrel with history".[29] She presents an alternative history, one that combines the stories embedded in her characters' memories with the historical methods of written history. This analysis of *The Colour of Forgetting* takes into account the critical conversation about the tensions between history and memory and illustrates how collective memory is central to the recuperation of oral stories that both contest and complement written history. Collins clearly validates oral stories and a reliance on the memories of ordinary people, those traditionally excluded from official history, and for whom monuments such as those erected in La Paz are never built. Simultaneously, this novel engages a metanarrative discourse about stories, storytelling and representation.

While *The Colour of Forgetting* valorizes oral representations as a counteraction to the distorted written versions, *Unburnable* interrogates orality. In her incorporation of gossip, hearsay, storytelling and other oral modes, John grounds this novel in orature-performance, but she also turns away from the familiar celebration of Caribbean oral traditions in which the power of written discourse is undermined by orality. In this way, *Unburnable* breaks fresh ground, because in this work orality is, like colonial or colonially oriented writings, scrutinized and interrogated. By disrupting the taken-for-granted sense of orality as a corrective mode of representation, *Unburnable* offers new possibilities for engaging the oral tradition in literature, and more broadly the nature of narrative representations.

In chapter 3, I address the claim for a woman-centred poetics in performing fictions with an analysis of Singing Sandra's calypso "Die with My Dignity" (1987) and Queen Ifrica's "Nuh Bwoy" (2009) alongside Lovelace's *The Wine of Astonishment* and James's *The Book of Night Women*. This chapter argues that Lovelace presents a female-sensitive perspective by deploying Eva's speech and perspective as the narrative structure, while James foregrounds women through his execution of female-centred performances and in his focus on women's roles in emancipation struggles. I place Lovelace, an established nationalist writer well known for his preoccupation with men and masculinity, in conversation with James, a twenty-first-century novelist who centres women and a female-oriented poetics, to show how the enlightened constructions of womanhood initiated in Lovelace's 1988 novel are less equivocally projected in James's representation. The focus on the inter-performative relationship between performing fiction, reggae and calypso shows how these oral-scribal texts written by men locate themselves in the debates about definitions of Caribbean womanhood – presenting it as dynamic, inclusive and negotiable. To a large extent, both Lovelace's and James's representations can be and have been read as forms of male political expediency in the context of the challenging roles and voices of women in the nationalist debate and at a time of increased attention to women's perspectives and representations of women in literature. Bringing these two male writers' renditions of female-centred poetics into conversation with those of the two female artistes helps to highlight the (gendered) political spaces in which orality is constructed in both the culture and its artistic products.

Chapter 4 offers a revisionary reading of Lovelace's popular novel *The Dragon Can't Dance*. I read Lovelace's classic calypso novel against the grain of critical responses to the author's preoccupation with Caribbean men. The central argument of this chapter is that in this novel that is apparently concerned with the lives and responsibilities of Caribbean men in postcolonial constructions of nations, Lovelace also addresses and advocates for the personhood of women. In fact, *The Dragon Can't Dance* embeds a "womanist-feminist" perspective similar to that of *The Wine of Astonishment*. However, my greater interest here is how Lovelace's use of a carnival poetics in *The Dragon Can't Dance* functions in his exploration of the quest for personhood and his advancement of an ideology of leadership that moves beyond the region's colonial legacy. The chapter examines an attentiveness to womanhood in this novel as part of Lovelace's broader nationalist concern.

While migration, diaspora, and transnational identities and negotiations have been among the core concerns of Caribbean literature since the 1950s and remain compelling subjects in literary and scholarly conversations, a focus on the performative dimensions of such fictions remains an untapped area of exploration. Through readings of Colin Channer's short story "How to Beat a Child the Right and Proper Way", which is structured around Jamaican yard storytelling forms, and Earl Lovelace's "Joebell and America", written in the style of Trinidadian picong, chapter 5 addresses how the work of orature-performance in transnational literary negotiations problematizes the notion of Caribbean migration. Recent works on diasporic and transnational Caribbean literature, such as Kezia Page's *Transnational Negotiations in Caribbean Diasporic Literature* (2011) and Alison Donnell's *Twentieth-Century Caribbean Literature* (2006), call our attention back to the significance of writers' engagement with Caribbean locations in late-twentieth- and early-twenty-first-century literature. This chapter extends the discussion by showing how fiction writers keep the Caribbean in sharp focus by recuperating orature-performance from the region. Lovelace's and Channer's stories intervene in these conversations about Caribbean locations and locatedness by presenting "Caribbeanness" as a cultural value system and Caribbean identity as that which is claimed, enacted and (temporarily) discarded through performance.

Framed by the calypso and reggae of the Mighty Chalkdust and Tinga Stewart respectively, this chapter theorizes "yard" and makes the case for performing fiction that resists Euro-American domination through its espousal of a West Indian cultural economy from which it derives a set of valuables that are essential for both survival in Western capitalist economies and the attainment of cultural equilibrium. In each story, the extent of the main characters' rootedness in community is manifested in the kind of performances they adopt. It is in their choice of particular performance modes that both writers advance a kind of model West Indian migrant who understands the purchasing power of yard culture.

Channer's appropriation of Caribbean storytelling captures the assertiveness of Jamaican yard culture and female agency that the story projects. In "How to Beat a Child the Right and Proper Way", a kind of yard performance that is usually reserved for feminized domestic spaces is transferred to the public performance space of the classroom, a site of formal education and Western knowledge systems. Through this strategy, Channer's character stages a kind of takeover, a cultural imposition that displaces the male professor and the Western hegemony he represents. The chapter demonstrates how in this work the critical view that the local is evoked through its absence from discourse is challenged, since in and through her performance, Channer's character Ciselyn places Jamaica at the centre of her discourse on cultural valuables. By locating his "Joebell and America" within Trinidad's picong tradition, I show how Lovelace's recovery of a centuries-old performance culture unmasks Joebell as an anti-hero and in that way calls attention to the folly of opting out of yard culture.

In the afterword, I underscore the validity of some of the book's claims by highlighting some pivotal literary moments in the development of a performance-centred poetics in a number of fictions similar to the ones analysed in this book. Here I consider how our reading strategies may, and should, be impacted by our sense of Caribbean fictions as hybrid entities in which writing, orality and performances converge. I take a reflective look at my own reading strategies, interrogating how and if they are consistent with, and depart from, standard textual analysis. This discussion also takes a critical look at some of my own claims about reader-text interactions. These closing reflections are underpinned by several questions: What are some ways in which the heretofore reader has had to reorient her- or himself in interactions with performing fiction? Does the creative use of a performative speaking voice fundamentally change how we read this kind of West Indian literature? Does the term *read* adequately describe the nature of interactions with these texts? And what happens to the body of the text that is itself so embodied and infused with the energy of specific performance modes? These inquiries ultimately lead to one of the overarching questions that underpins this study: How has the reincarnation of nineteenth-century English novels and short stories in Caribbean creole societies changed those forms and our interactions with them?

Finally, a note regarding terminology: The authors of the novels and short stories analysed in this book are all from the English-speaking Caribbean; therefore, I use the term "West Indian" when referring to the body of texts I am analysing, "Caribbean" in reference to the larger sociocultural space and "anglophone Caribbean" to highlight some aspects of the West Indies in relation to this larger regional space. I use "orality", the general term for all spoken communication, including orature, in reference to a wide variety of oral forms. "Orature", "performance" and "performance genres" are used variously in reference to the songs, stories and other oral-performance modes that the book addresses. "Orature-performance" is used exclusively in reference to the poetics of performing fiction that I also characterize as "oraliterary performances".

ONE

Opening Acts
Scholarly and Literary Precursors to Performing Fiction

CRITICAL CONVERSATIONS ABOUT ORALITY and writing consistently turn towards how these forms intersect with and depart from each other, as well as how colonial encounters and domination have shaped oral-scribal relationships.[1] Not surprisingly, these discussions have necessarily attended to how orality in general, and orature in particular, impact fiction. In the Caribbean context, discussions about fiction published in the first half of the twentieth century have centred primarily on language usage. That is, there has been substantial interest in how fiction writers navigate the creole languages of most daily interactions and the official English language in their novels and short stories. This attentiveness to language is logical, since the break from literary forms rooted in the British tradition manifested earliest, and initially most extensively, in the use of creole for dialogue and, later, as the language of narration.

In this chapter, I examine how some of the early studies that focus on language usage in Vic Reid's *New Day* and Samuel Selvon's *The Lonely Londoners* demonstrate the ways in which these novels instantiate and initiate the pivotal turn to the kind of literary aesthetics for which I argue. These two works, and the conversations about them, opened space for a theory of Caribbean fiction grounded in the intersection of oral-performative modes and the scribal tradition. Yet though the critical attention to the linguistic innovations in these novels has been useful, the emphasis on language usage in both texts has obscured the groundbreaking primacy of orature as the structuring device in *New Day*. While there has been extensive discussion of orality in *The Lonely Londoners*, critical conversations about Reid's *New Day* have overwhelmingly centred on the author's use of creole as his language of narration. The critical attention that these two novels have garnered marks them as important literary harbingers – and further, by fundamentally changing conversations about Caribbean literary aesthetics, they have stirred the move towards acknowledging a poetics of performance as the driving force of Caribbean fiction. Undoubtedly, Reid's and Selvon's novels are momentous, not only because of their revolutionary turns towards stylized creole languages as their language of narration, but also because, in the way they shape their novels, these writers signal a poetics of performance and herald a new kind of Caribbean fiction, that which I refer to in this work as performing fiction.

New Day is, as Ramchand has noted, told as an oral story, and as Mervyn Morris observes, "*New Day* was the first West Indian, and remains the only Jamaican, novel written in which the language of narration is dialect."[2] Given this and other critical acknowledgements of the groundbreaking stylistic shift that this novel began, I would argue that *New Day*, more than any other work – including *The Lonely Londoners* – establishes what is now a defining oral mode of literary representation in anglophone Caribbean fiction: like the fictions I analyse in this book, it relies on storytelling for its overarching structure. *New Day*, then – despite the stylistic shortcomings to which critics have consistently drawn attention – serves as a literary forerunner, if not inspiration, for *The Lonely Londoners*, a book that critics have agreed is a much more accomplished and elegant example of a book featuring an invented West Indian creole as literary language. Because of the significant critical attention that *The Lonely Londoners* has received, I have devoted more of the ensuing discussion to both an analysis and critical reception of *New Day*. Yet because both novels offered something new and are such important literary milestones, they both provide a useful starting point for a discussion of a style of written fiction that became more prevalent after the 1950s.

The critical consensus is that it was the entry of local West Indians into creative writing that began a trend in which the creole languages would become a mainstay in fiction from the region. Scholars mark a clear shift in language usage between nineteenth- and twentieth-century fiction. In his 1978 essay "Dialect in West Indian Literature", R.B. Le Page provides support for the claim that there had been a break from more extensive use of standard English in his observation that "I think we have now passed the phase which West Indian writers were going through when I first arrived in Jamaica in 1950. Then there was still writing, a school of authors who drew their inspiration and their language from the literature of England rather than from life."[3] "Life", in this context, is most likely a West Indian speech culture that comprises multiple creole languages and diverse forms of orature. Similarly, Kenneth Ramchand, one of the first critics to explore in detail language usage in West Indian fiction, argues that "West Indian literature seems to be the only substantial literature in which the dialect-speaking character is the central character"; he also notes that "West Indian writers have turned the dialect to . . . literary account".[4] Substantiating Ramchand's early observation, Merle Hodge, in a 2011 essay entitled "Language Use and West Indian Literary Criticism", writes, "West Indian writers have been able to build a single literary tradition which straddles the indigenous language (English-lexicon Creole) and the official language (Standard English)."[5] I have included these characterizations to show how in each instance, the critic notes an increasing presence of creole languages, and therefore orality, in literature from the region. While Le Page marks a movement away from British-inflected writing, Ramchand focuses on the significant presence of creole-speaking characters. Hodge takes the conversation much further to argue for a "literary tradition" built around creole languages.

Although there has been some caution about charting a chronological development of the creole voice in West Indian fiction, there are some identifiable phases and shifts in the trend towards the West Indianization of the voice(s) in literature.[6] Commenting on the early experimentations with creole languages, Maureen Warner-Lewis notes, "The assignation of vernacular or English to characters on the basis of author-character distance or rapport is a dominant tendency in the literature of the first four decades of the twentieth century."[7] Hodge makes a similar observation but identifies a shift in the extent of language usage and the manner in which creole languages appear in the period Warner-Lewis references. Hodge writes, "In the early phases of West Indian fiction ... writers maintained a stark separation between the two codes.... A new breed of writers would emerge from the underclass, and unlike earlier writers of colour, they would embrace and affirm their roots, eventually installing the West Indian peasant and labourer at the centre of West Indian literature."[8] A survey of fiction written between the 1930s and the present bears out Hodge's claim, as readers will note a tentative and sparing inclusion of creole voices in works from the early to mid-twentieth century, and again later in the emergence of texts such as those I analyse in later chapters, in which the creole speaker is the voice of narration. Yet as Hodge herself has noted, many writers of this time period, such as V.S. Naipaul, maintain a distance between the language of narration and that used for dialogue, while others, such as Jamaica Kincaid, deploy virtually no creole at all in their fiction. Certainly, Naipaul and Kincaid may have different motivations for their choice of language. Because Naipaul has explicitly distanced himself from West Indian culture, it is more conceivable that his decisions are ideological. On the other hand, Kincaid's choices seem more complicated and may be more driven by her audience, publisher and market, since United States publishers have only recently started accepting West Indian fiction written in vernacular languages. Furthermore, although Kincaid's oeuvre shows a mostly English register, creole rhythms are audible in "Girl" and a few of her other works. In "Girl", while the diction is English, Kincaid keeps the West Indian speaking voice central through her insertion of terms such as *doukano* and *benna*, which are not marked in any way. And the last sentence, *"you mean to say that after all you are really going to be the kind of woman who the baker won't let near the bread?"* (emphasis mine), begins in creole.[9] When read aloud, the entire story has a distinctly creole sound. These examples from Kincaid illustrate the range of possibilities for language and the subtlety with which creole expressions and voices have come to shape West Indian fiction, to the point where readers can miss some usages. Although there is a general trend towards substantial use of creole for both narration and dialogue, there still remains a range of attitudes regarding language usage, in addition to other exigencies that may determine the language of narration for post-1950s West Indian fiction.

It is within this context of a clear shift in how the creole voice is represented in fiction from the mid-twentieth century onward that Reid's and Selvon's novels are celebrated as landmark texts. A decade and a half before Kenneth Ramchand's extensive discussion of language in West Indian fiction, in which V.S. Reid's *New Day* is presented as a groundbreaking linguistic experiment, Stuart Hall named Reid's *New Day* as a critical post-war work. The frame within which Hall locates his discussion of *New Day* gives a sense of the extent of the value he and others place on that work. In Hall's view, "the process of creating an independent cultural ethos in the West Indies must involve the evolution of new creative forms and institutions. We create nothing except we also create the means whereby to find expression."[10] Edward Baugh, in his 1987 tribute to Reid, characterizes *New Day* as "part of a political and cultural awakening, the nationalist fervor, which [Jamaica] experienced in the thirties and early forties". Baugh also notes that "like the poet George Campbell, or the painter Albert Huie, or the potter Cecil Baugh, or the sculptress Edna Manley, or like his fellow novelist Roger Mais, [Reid] gave imaginative expression to the spirit of that time". Baugh further suggests that Reid's "delight in words, in language, was a delight in his, in our particular linguistic heritage".[11] By placing such significance on the means of creative expression within the context of a more general avowal of Caribbean creole cultures, both Hall and Baugh underscore the centrality of *New Day* within a larger context of postcolonial nationalist and creative momentum. In doing so, these critics address one of the central questions that has animated Caribbean literary and cultural critics and which also drives this book: What is the political and ideological import of a poetics inspired by local vernacular resources, particularly within the context of nation formation? In declaring *New Day* emblematic of early texts in which Caribbean expressive resources are the structuring device by asserting that "few novels have caught this sense of discovery with such poignancy as Vic Reid's *New Day*",[12] Hall suggests that the publication of this novel marks a milestone in the formation of a locally driven Caribbean literary tradition.

The significance that Hall attributes to *New Day* derives not just from the fact that this work uses a version of Jamaican creole – referred to by most early critics as "dialect" – nor is it merely because of sustained and extensive use of stylized Jamaican as its language of narration. Writers who attempt to deploy creole languages as their primary language of narration wrestle with orthography, because in general, there is no standardized writing system for creole languages. Thus, there was the challenge of devising a way to write a systematized representation of languages that were only oral. In this regard, *New Day* is especially significant because as Le Page, Ramchand, Morris and others have pointed out, it is one of the first novels in which the writer develops a modified creole, what Le Page refers to as "an amalgam between standard English and dialect".[13]

In one of the first critical responses to *New Day*, P.M.S.'s 1949 review in *Caribbean Quarterly* posits the following observation about Reid's linguistic innovations:

> But how are these country folk to be presented so that they will be natural and yet intelligent to those who do not know their dialect? Here was a technical problem of the first importance. . .Victor Reid has found a solution which may have been inspired by books like *How Green is My Valley* but which is nonetheless original. . . . He has created a form of speech which is natural to the characters, which is easily understood, and which has extraordinary beauty. Reid has actually created a form of language which enables him to rise above the limitations of dialect.[14]

Here, the reviewer illustrates a challenge that might very well have been a major deterrent to writers' use of creole-speaking voices in their works, particularly as the language of narration: making the characters both credible and intelligent, while still keeping the story accessible. Although the "limitations" to which the reviewer refers may at first glance suggest his own inadvertent prejudices, this remark might speak more to the genuine challenge Caribbean writers encountered as they sought to create a literary voice from the (solely oral) creole languages in a postcolonial context in which writing was synonymous with standard English.

Commenting on Reid's work, Ramchand notes,

> The use of a dialect-speaking narrator by V.S. Reid in the novel *New Day* and by John Hearne in a short story, "At the Stelling", reminds us that few West Indian authors reproduce dialect precisely in their works. In these two cases, invention is more obvious than in most. . . . Because the story is told orally by the reminiscing man, Reid is able to make a credible show of narrating in dialect. But what he actually does is push the West Indian Standard and dialect even closer together in the narrating voice of John Campbell.[15]

Yet Reid's innovations, which do indeed show the teething pains of a burgeoning, locally driven literary language, have also been variously characterized as stilted. As he examines the "technical problems" encountered by West Indian writers who seek to develop a creative language grounded in local creoles, Le Page calls Reid's "amalgam between standard English and dialect somewhat unsuccessful".[16] Likewise, despite crediting Reid with bringing "Jamaican language forcefully to the attention of the international literari", Michael Cooke compares him unfavourably with later writers: "But to some ears Campbell's idiom sounds far less deep and true than, say, Samuel Selvon's speakers or Erna Brodber's characters."[17] However, in all instances in which critics, especially earlier ones, deem Reid's linguistic inventions "unsuccessful" or flawed, such criticism is counterbalanced by the acknowledgement that Reid, in the words of Edward Baugh, tried "something new with language".[18]

In one of the most detailed and nuanced assessments of Reid's contributions as well as the challenges he encountered, Maureen Warner-Lewis names him as the writer whose work best illustrates the struggle to find a balance of languages that simultaneously foregrounds creole and makes the novel accessible to a wide audience. She writes:

> Unlike the novelists of the 1930s, [Reid] speaks from within a culture that bridged the perspectives of the black peasantry and of the black middle class. . . . [In *New Day*, Reid] forge[s] an artificial composite: to blend Jamaican Creole structures, vocabulary, and imagery with elements of Burns's Scots English and Synge's Irish English and to add to this a Biblical phrasing that would suggest the dominant literary influence among the Jamaican folk. . . . Reid's sortie into linguistic invention comes from a deliberate shunning of vernacular resources and indicates that he felt more at home with Standard English.[19]

Warner-Lewis's explanation here is important for a number of reasons. It goes beyond a passing evaluative comment regarding English-creole fusion – "this is good" or "this does not work" – to outline the conundrum that Reid faced as he wrote *New Day*.[20] By presenting Reid as a writer caught between his ideological commitment to local expressive resources – and, further, whose novel is now lauded for its celebration of folk insurgency – and his preference for, and comfort level with, English, Warner-Lewis lays out the high stakes of developing and claiming a literary form that draws its material from local expressive traditions. In this way, she speaks directly to one of the central ideas of this book – that the poetics of performance evinces a nationalism that signals a kind of coming into one's own, not just creatively, but also ideologically.

Warner-Lewis's outlining of the other English-language variations – such as Scottish and Irish – that constitute, along with creole, the language of narration in *New Day* introduces other anti-colonial orientations and possibly the motivations for Reid's overall linguistic choices. That Reid chose dialects of English from outside England, but which might be more internationally recognizable than his invented version of Jamaican, may be indicative of an alignment with other colonized groups and therefore part of a larger rejection of the dominant English ways of being. At the same time, this choice locates Reid's ideologically driven aesthetics within a larger creole, rather than Afro-Caribbean, culture. Erna Brodber's call for research that attends to the role that "secondary whites" played in the formation of creole societies in Jamaica and elsewhere in the Caribbean acknowledges the cultural mergings that have shaped Caribbean culture in general and the expressive culture in particular.[21]

These discussions of Reid's linguistic experimentation and its ideological import necessarily allude to Caribbean orality, since he writes in the language that is only used for informal speech, and that is nourished by various other oral modes. However, attention to a broader oral poetics has been tepid and tacit because for the most part, discussions of *New Day* hardly move beyond Reid's use of creole. The ways in which Reid's creative experimentation draws on a wider range of orality has therefore received only negligible critical attention. For example, Ramchand describes *New Day* as "an oral performance by the reminiscing man".[22] He also notes the presence of "repetition, monosyllabic rhythm, and personification imagery" drawn from the oral tradition as features of the narrative voice in John Hearne's short story "At the Stelling". Indeed, Ramchand asserts that "it would be impossible to feel the full effect of the [representative passages] unless we imagine a speaking West Indian voice".[23] The move of Ramchand's focus from language to speaking voice, and even more so his mention of performance, introduce to the discussion formal features grounded in orality, but he does not pursue these oral elements to the extent that he and others pursue language. Ramchand's brief statement here exemplifies the kind of passing mention of orature that characterizes discussions of Reid's stylistic innovation. Given the inventiveness Reid showed by using a creole-speaking voice and local vernacular as the language of narration as early as 1949, it is not surprising that the linguistic component of his turn to the oral tradition is what has preoccupied critics. However, the "something new" and the "giv[ing] of imaginative expression to the spirit of that time" that Baugh ascribes to Reid extend beyond a radical shift in linguistic register to include a more overarching shaping of the novel around specific performative modes.

Despite the warranted critical attention that Reid has received for his dramatic turn to Jamaican creole as his language of narration, most critics argue that it is in the work of Samuel Selvon that we see the first successful linguistic experimentations. Ramchand writes that "although both Reid and Hearne . . . come close to making a modified form of dialect to do the work of both narration and dialogue, it is in Samuel Selvon's works that the language of the implied author boldly declares a dialect differing little from the language of characters".[24] In a 1957 review of Selvon's *The Lonely Londoners*, Bruce Hamilton suggests that this novel "is written in a language of the Trinidadian streets, a strange tongue which will be unfamiliar to most Barbadian and nearly all English men and Americans".[25] The "strange tongue" to which Hamilton refers is only one aspect of Selvon's formal innovations that garnered critical attention. Ramchand notes that *The Lonely Londoners* is generally regarded as the book that most comprehensively embodies the language that West Indians speak.[26] Whereas conversations about style in *New Day* virtually stop at a discussion of its linguistic features, critical response to Selvon's early oeuvre in general, and *The Lonely Londoners* in particular, focuses on formal experiments that changed the shape of the novel more radically than any West Indian novel before it.

That Selvon has compelled critics of *The Lonely Londoners* to see beyond language is apparent even in the early, brief review of the novel quoted above. In his statement that Selvon deploys in this work a vernacular style, Hamilton gestures towards the idea that *The Lonely Londoners* marks a new turn in the Caribbean literary tradition, that a more extensive expressive system informs this work. His further description of the book gets even closer to naming this as a new kind of novel. He writes, "Structurally this book is not quite organized as a novel . . . only Mr Selvon knows if he will continue to do this special sort of thing, which he does well."[27] Because there have been similar formal experiments in other literary traditions, Hamilton is most likely thinking of the English novel, which most of the Caribbean readership at the time construed as the standard novel form. This "special sort of thing" that engenders both intrigue and uncertainty on Hamilton's part is that turn away from the English-style novel towards one more West Indian in form, sound and texture. What provokes wonder in Hamilton about the future of Selvon's literary output is declared by Ramchand as a major formal shift in West Indian novelistic techniques. Ramchand argues that *The Lonely Londoners* 'is also the book in which narrating techniques, devices of continuity, author-reader relationships, and rhythms associated with orality and oral narratives impact most tellingly *upon the form of the inherited novel*" (emphasis mine).[28] Here Ramchand isolates some key elements of a poetics of performance in his association of novelistic techniques with orality and oral narrative. His use of the term "oral narratives" is especially insightful, as it goes beyond a mere observation of varied oral forms to point out more defined formal features associated with specific types of orature – oral narratives.

In his discussion of the relationship between drama and prose fiction, Gordon Rohlehr extends Ramchand's gesture towards a discussion of the performative elements of Selvon's writing, which most critics argue were established in *The Lonely Londoners*. Rohlehr states that "when [Selvon's works] are read aloud to a group, and there is an interplay between narrator and audience, they yield up ironies and subtleties which one can miss when simply reading the words on the page".[29] These critics thus move the discussion of Selvon's stylistic innovation beyond one of language and elements of style; they begin a conversation that establishes *The Lonely Londoners* within a performance-driven tradition of written fiction. The assertion that the works "yield up ironies and subtleties" when they are treated as performative texts suggests that these fictions transcend the conventions of fiction writing and are shaped by performance modes.

But like most critics who write about this novel's stylistic breakthroughs, Ramchand does not characterize *The Lonely Londoners* as a work of fiction shaped by a particular oral-performative genre. Instead, he identifies various features such as "rhythms associated with oral narrative" and "devices of continuity". Similarly, Rohlehr speaks of the novel's performative elements but does not name a specific type of performance that shapes it. Making a similar point, Sindoni includes idioms, riddles, tall tales and characters associated with oral performances, such as the trickster and the "man of words", among the multiple ways in which orature-performance is recuperated in Selvon's fiction.[30] In her description of *The Lonely Londoners* as "a text of verbal musics", Curdella Forbes names a specific performance mode, drawn from the local Caribbean culture that shapes this novel.[31] Interestingly, Forbes's specific and very useful nomenclature, "verbal musics", takes a plural form and is followed by a list of musical formats that serve as examples. Yet there is a virtual absence of a name for the "special sort of thing" that Hamilton mentions in his 1957 review. What this demonstrates, however, is not a lack of insight on the part of critics; rather, it illustrates precisely this novel's structural elusiveness. It is shaped by a collection of sounds, forms and linguistic modes, and this inclusion of multiple forms prevents the naming of its oral counterpart.

Despite their shared stylistic innovations, *The Lonely Londoners* is a different kind of novel from *New Day*. *The Lonely Londoners* is unmistakably performative and varied in its performativity. *New Day*, on the other hand, takes a single form of orature – storytelling – and shapes the entire novel around it, while folding in multiple oral modes that storytellers or creole speakers would include in their performances and interactions. Therefore, it is in Reid's *New Day* that we see the beginning of the kind of fiction that I theorize in this book, one that, in its entirety, is shaped by a particular form of orature.

By describing *New Day* as "an oral performance by the reminiscing man", Ramchand intimates that this novel's contribution extends beyond linguistic experimentation, particularly in its use of a creole-speaking narrator. Ramchand calls attention to the fact that this narrative voice does not just speak in creole; it is a voice engaged in direct oral storytelling or a conversation between an immediate audience and a speaker who deploys multiple storytelling strategies. The result is an entire novel structured as an oral story being told to various audiences.

The conversational tone of the novel is established at its opening: "Tomorrow I will go with Garth to the city to hear King George's man proclaim from the square that Jamaica-men will begin to govern themselves.... Eh, but now I am restless tonight.... Aie – Garth remembers all the old things I ha' told him. ... But God O! Look what my eyes ha' lived to see!" For the first few pages of the novel, it is uncertain who constitutes John Campbell's audience, and it appears he is talking to himself. In these early pages he also addresses a deliberately imagined audience, mostly the dead. "Then, now! Pa John and Ma Tamah . . . and my brethren Emanuel, David, Samuel, Ezekiel, Ruth, Naomi, are you hearing. . . ? And you too bloody Governor Eyre and your crow Provost-Marshal Ramsey . . . Then now all you dead hundreds." Then Campbell switches back to the old man talking to himself: *"Aie* – me, John Campbell, youngest o' Pa John Campbell . . . I hear the singing now. Our party people are coming."[32]

Despite these suggestions of multiple audiences at the beginning of the novel and at different moments throughout, the speaker's tone is generally that of of someone telling a story to an immediate audience. But it is not just *listeners* John Campbell is engaging with; as the following statements illustrate, Reid's narrative techniques cue in the reader to the presence of an interlocutor: "I ha' no told you of Garth? Eh, I am running too fast" (255); "And I will tell why later" (256); "'Member I told you my mind knew her face?" (356). These examples suggest that the speaker is responding to a query from his listeners; thus, that sense of active engagement, the back-and-forth between speaker and audience, that characterizes performing fiction is a defining feature of this novel. In addition to the interactive features illustrated above, Reid includes an extensive range of stock storytelling phrases such as "so then" and "now then", which John Campbell consistently uses to punctuate the scenes he describes and the history that he recalls.

Significantly, too, Reid's innovations include his use of John Campbell's memory as the structuring device for this story. Of course, this is not to say that this is original in and of itself; readers need only to recall the modernist fictions of Virginia Woolf, James Joyce and others to find instances of such narrative techniques. What distinguishes Reid's use of memory in this work is his creative exploration of the memory of a creole-speaking Jamaican man who recalls details of the past in the ways rural country folk tend to do: through their ways of speaking, which are grounded in an oral tradition created on sugar plantations. In other words, the revolutionary turn in *New Day* emerges from the way the memory of the subaltern is tapped to recall a past in which the underclass takes the reign of power and charts a new political course in post-emancipation Jamaica. Thus, the idea of performing fiction as a way of "speaking" the nation into being, for which I make a case in the introduction, had some of its creative stirrings in Reid's groundbreaking novel. *New Day* established what Maureen Warner-Lewis refers to as a "national self-confidence",[33] one that turns to the creole cultures for the means of expressing the experiences and values of that nation.

Analyses of *New Day* and *The Lonely Londoners* have focused on style as well as meaning, although these two elements have mostly been discussed separately. But attentiveness to Reid's treatment of Jamaica's political history and his use of language and orature allows for a broader discussion of this writer's contribution to a Caribbean poetics. Similarly, Selvon's exploration of immigrant experiences and his stylistic innovations signal a formative Caribbean poetics. Taking the position of consensus that both novels, in varying degrees, have offered something new in terms of artistry, and that they explore some key issues in Caribbean critical conversation, I am suggesting that *New Day* and *The Lonely Londoners* represent the coming together of West Indian worldviews and modes of expression grounded in Caribbean orature. In other words, these works do not merely anticipate a poetics of performance, but they also evince the kernel of it in the formation of a new kind of prose fiction, one that has seen significant expansion in the latter half of the twentieth and the twenty-first centuries.

Stuart Hall's assertion that *New Day* "engages the past"[34] captures the critics' assessments of the thematic focus of this work. What John Campbell, Reid's central character and the story's narrator, offers is an engagement with the past that not only recounts a series of events in Jamaican freedom struggles, but also presents the local, marginalized version of events; in so doing, it offers the subaltern perspective and centres black working-class Jamaicans as the key figures in the Morant Bay rebellion and the dawning of a new political system. As Baugh observes, Reid "wrote to give his people a nurturing sense of their own history, to set over [and] against those distortions of history by which others had sought to shackle their minds. He wrote *New Day* to correct the view that Gordon and Bogle were traitors and criminals."[35] Baugh's choice of the term "nurturing" is noteworthy, as it highlights the healing of a trauma or wound that novels shaped by revisionary history, a prominent genre in postcolonial writing, continue to address. Baugh therefore places Reid among the earliest literary advocates of this kind of corrective discourse.

At the same time, those citizens whom the history books present as part of the nameless masses – focusing instead on Governor Eyre, George William Gordon, Paul Bogle and a few others as the "central" figures – are brought to life in *New Day*. Reid places the emphasis on their contribution to the laying of the groundwork for a new system of governance that is the novel's primary subject. This is the kind of revisionary history that, as I argue later in this work, characterizes novels by Collins, James and other contemporary Caribbean writers. Thus, what Reid presents in *New Day* is a new way of engaging the past, one that challenges official history through the expressive resources of the subalterns, who emerge as the makers of history in this work and many others that follow it.

Reid's aesthetic choices and overall poetics also reveal the nuanced and multilayered involvement of Jamaicans in the struggles for political independence. In *New Day*, he follows the line of the Campbell family; one of them, who emerges as a "man of the people" figure (Garth, who many agree is a thinly veiled Norman Manley), is the novel's hero. These choices may betray Reid's investment in middle-class leadership as the means of ushering Jamaica into a new political epoch. Yet Reid's inclusion of grassroots involvement in the uprisings, and, even more, his choice of performance modes – storytelling and several other oral forms, especially conversations, or what Michael Bucknor terms "grung" or "grounded" poetics – evidence the active participation of the underclass in the process of nation formation.[36] Reid's own articulation of folk involvement is among the most compelling depictions of a mass movement that *New Day* details. For Reid, the nationalist awakenings "brought guys into *thinking*. Suddenly it was no longer listening to 'Five-foot-two, eyes of blue', and go dance to Bertie King's orchestra. . . . People began talking, and you go a man yard and you knock little domino and you start discuss politics, discuss world situations."[37] As the inclusion of different class groups in *New Day* demonstrates, political awareness and activism captured the attention and involvement of Jamaicans and Caribbean people of varying colour and class groups.

With a few exceptions – for example, Curdella Forbes's rereading of *The Lonely Londoners*, which includes a discussion of Tanty, the novel's strong and vocal female character who represents how immigrants also assertively transform migrant spaces – critical reflections on this novel overwhelmingly focus on Selvon's treatment of the woes of migration. The emphasis is primarily on how the challenges "the boys" face in the novel represent West Indians' remaking of themselves in a new, mostly hostile European city. What Forbes's revisionary treatment of gender attends to is Tanty's agency, her insistence that London too must change to accommodate the new "arrivants".[38] Tanty's introduction of a new credits system, the kind that is part of standard small business transactions in Jamaica, is an important moment in this novel and one that pre-empts later representations in which migrants engage in cultural imposition, such as that presented in Colin Channer's "How to Beat a Child the Right and Proper Way". I analyse Channer's story and explore these other representations of migrant subjectivity in greater detail in chapter 5 of this book. Thus, as in Reid's *New Day*, this aspect of Selvon's well-established contribution to contemporary migration discourses – efforts to change the social landscape of the migrant space – merges with his construction of a literary form grounded in Trinidadian vernacular. The result is a kind of fiction shaped stylistically by the oral forms of the folk, but which also offers a diverse representation of migrant interactions with the new environment. In such a representation, migrants are shown to be more agential in terms of how they choose to navigate their way in the new society.

It is also significant that Selvon's most assertive character in *The Lonely Londoners* is female. In this regard, too, Selvon's work anticipates later examples, such as those of Channer and James, in which the female character is central to the novel's overarching privileging of subaltern points of view. Although the central characters in this novel are men, the way Selvon presents woman, in terms of her voice and the force of her presence, is conceivably a pre-emptive representation of the woman-centred poetics that underpin the poetics of performance for which I argue. Selvon's Tanty anticipates Lovelace's Eva, Channer's Ciselyn and James's several representational female characters, who dominate their respective works in terms of voice and worldview. The intersections between Reid's and Selvon's novels and these later works underscore the formal and discursive shifts that *The Lonely Londoners* and *New Day* represent.

Taken together, *The Lonely Londoners* and *New Day* establish a Caribbean poetics of performance. They are shaped by locally generated creole performance modes, and they epitomize fiction that functions as a discursive space in which Caribbean ways of knowing and ways of seeing are foregrounded and elaborated. These two works are undoubtedly instantiations of the kind of performativity that has since become a defining aesthetic feature of post-1950s West Indian fiction.

(Re)membering

The Power of Stories in *The Colour of Forgetting* and *Unburnable*

"SLAVERY DAYS", ONE OF ten songs on Burning Spear's 1975 album *Marcus Garvey*, deliberately recalls and insists on a recollection of the slave experience. The chorus that opens this song – "Do you remember the days of slavery?" – is both a question and an entreaty to keep slavery in living memory. As it asks listeners to remember, the song also details specific atrocities – beatings, hard work, shackles – that characterized the experiences of enslaved Africans in the Americas, while at the same time celebrating via the song's persona, the survival of some victims. Underscoring the significance of memory, the listener is urged to "please remember, please remember". Read within the context of Rastafari protest music, "Slavery Days" may also be perceived as a call for the victims of slavery to take control of the stories of their past. Although "history can recall the days of slavery", as the song says, it is memory, it insists, that will keep these experiences of brutality and survival alive. Yet the tone of urgency in the calls to remember suggests that memory may not be automatic, nor can it always be relied upon to preserve the past; rather, it might need to be activated and constantly regenerated to keep the experience of slavery in the consciousness of its descendants. Further, by not only calling upon the audience to remember but also including details of the past, the song presents the oral tradition as a means of activating memory, and in this way performs the act of remembering itself.

This engagement with the past that preoccupies the persona of "Slavery Days" extends beyond the protest music of Rastafari and reverberates in postcolonial Caribbean literature, and specifically in performing fiction. Merle Collins's *The Colour of Forgetting* and Marie-Elena John's *Unburnable* employ rhetorical strategies similar to those used in "Slavery Days" and likewise insist on the importance of recollections, even as they contemplate and problematize how the past is remembered and represented. An examination of "Slavery Days" and these two works of fiction demonstrates how performing fiction shares with the Caribbean performance culture both formal features and concerns about representation, specifically how the past is remembered, reordered and disseminated. In this way, both novels and the song engage a conversation that has been central to postcolonial critics in general, and Caribbean studies in particular.

The Colour of Forgetting tells the story of a young man, nicknamed Thunder after the thing he fears most. In response to his excessive fear, Thunder's mother, Willive, takes him to see Carib, the community warner woman and seer, who prescribes storytelling (by his parents and grand-aunt) as the cure for the boy's psychological malady. The stories that Carib prescribes detail the real-life experiences of Thunder's ancestors, who include persons from all the major racial groups of Grenada and the Caribbean. The experiences that the novel reconstructs typify those recounted by Grenadians and others in Caribbean communities. Shaped by storytelling, this novel's self-directed gaze moves beyond critiques of colonial forms of historical representation to engage the local community's rejection of its indigenous stories and knowledge systems in favour of a written history that deliberately excludes and distorts Grenadian history. Through its exploration of one family's interconnected stories, *The Colour of Forgetting* demonstrates how a return to the oral tradition, specifically storytelling, not only validates oral modes of representation, but also recovers historical details previously omitted from the official records. Collins's turn towards stories debunks both the separation of the two knowledge systems – the official record and storytelling – and the inferior place ascribed to the latter. At the same time, this novel also acknowledges that oral stories, which, like official written history, seek to reconstruct the past, are likewise flawed and susceptible to both inadvertent and deliberate forgetting and selectivity. *The Colour of Forgetting* therefore advocates not for a privileging of oral stories (and, by extension, memory) over official historical writings nor a disavowal of history, but a reciprocal relationship between history as an academic field and storytelling as a living, vibrant and organic source of knowledge.

While it acknowledges the flaws inherent in oral stories, *The Colour of Forgetting* exemplifies the recuperative orientations of many postcolonial texts. I therefore locate this novel within the larger body of works – both creative and scholarly – that have sought to challenge the marginal place that orality has been assigned in the postcolonial Caribbean. This novel offers a compelling fictional representation of a conversation that has ensued over the years among Caribbean cultural theorists and critics, with an emphasis on how attitudes towards orality and writing have impacted representations of the past. Although scholars have for the most part been careful to avoid simplistic treatments of this subject, they have generally theorized the relationship between Caribbean orality and writing as one characterized by tension.[1] Édouard Glissant, for example, writes of the "tortured relationship between writing and orality" and also notes that "the song (the traditional oral culture) was impeded by Western education".[2] Similarly, Carolyn Cooper frames her collection of essays *Noises in the Blood* with an epigraph that sets up an oppositional relationship between "long head", representative of the oral tradition, and "book", the symbol of writing, which Cooper takes from the words of Old John in Henry G. Murray's *Manners and Customs of the Country a Generation Ago: Tom Kittle's Wake*.[3] Cooper further notes that *Noises in the Blood* "articulates a dialectical relationship between scribal and oral traditions".[4] In the book's introduction, Cooper is especially attentive to the nuances of the oral-scribal relationship in the Jamaican context; she ultimately establishes that not only are there identifiable differences, but that Caribbean scholars suggest that as a consequence of its marginalization and because it is a product of creole cultures, orality has emerged as a tool with which writers can contest hegemonies and recover distorted stories and suppressed narratives.[5] Among the most notable theorizations is Kamau Brathwaite's "nation language". Brathwaite defines this as a locally derived linguistic system that has developed from the region's oral traditions and broader sociocultural contexts, which is distinct from the colonially derived scribal culture. Brathwaite also explores how nation language functions in literature as a turn away from European scribal models as primary literary influences, and as a validation of Caribbean orality.[6] In this vein, Collins's novel, like the works of other writers who have challenged the ascribed superiority of the written word, is a celebration of Caribbean orature and, by extension, indigenous Caribbean cultures.

Published just over a decade after *The Colour of Forgetting*, Marie-Elena John's *Unburnable* takes up similar questions about representation and orality, but makes the critical engagement with oral stories that *The Colour of Forgetting* initiates as its central thematic concern. *Unburnable* treats the spoken word, more precisely stories and storytelling, as a central mode of representation and as its primary subject. John also breaks fresh ground, as her novel does not reflect a celebration of Caribbean oral traditions in which the power of written discourse is undermined by orality. And even more remarkable is this novel's almost exclusive attention to the ramifications of oral storytelling itself, a feature that distinguishes this work from the implicit celebrations and counter-hegemonic representations of orality. *Unburnable* therefore engages a metanarrative discourse in which Caribbean orality is, like colonial or colonially oriented writings, scrutinized and interrogated. The novel explores how orature that comes out of local Caribbean cultures also denigrates aspects of that culture. This examination lays bare the hierarchies, problems and ambiguities inherent in oral stories, even as it demonstrates their abundant and empowering possibilities. *Unburnable* therefore offers new possibilities for engaging the oral tradition in literature and, more broadly, for the nature of narrative representation.

Set in both the United States and the English-speaking Caribbean island of Dominica, *Unburnable* tells intersecting stories about the lives of Lillian, Iris and Matilda, three generations of women, over a roughly fifty-year time span. Lillian, the last surviving member of this line of women and the ostensible central character, is a successful international human rights professional in the Washington, DC, area, whose life is overshadowed by traumatic memories that she has carried since childhood. These memories centre on her grandmother Matilda's legendary life as an Obeah woman who was convicted and hanged for killing her daughter Iris's middle-aged lover, John Baptiste (also

Lillian's grandfather), and others. The killing of John Baptiste, legend has it, was revenge for the destruction of Iris's life, a punishment that resulted from Iris's affair with this married, middle-class man. Consumed by the memories, and convinced that her grandmother was innocent of the crimes of murder to which she had confessed, Lillian, at age thirty-seven, enlists the help of her longtime college friend (and, later, lover) Teddy in trying to uncover what she is certain is the truth about her grandmother's life and work. This journey back to Dominica, back in time and back to old stories and memories, takes Lillian, Teddy and their partners in recollective pursuits through the twists and turns of the stories. The recollections ultimately reveal that Matilda was a healer, a maroon (an African or person of African descent who escaped slavery) who lived in a community called "Up There" that was both physically and culturally separated from mainstream Dominica. In *Unburnable*, Up There is a place where a West African culture that was over two hundred years old had thrived until Matilda, the community's leader, was executed for the murders of Baptiste and others.

My attentiveness to the complex representation and critique of orality that underpins John's novel instantiates an interrogation of Caribbean critical orthodoxies in which a growing number of Caribbean scholars has been increasingly engaged. A number of studies, published mostly in the twenty-first century, explore new and previously neglected areas, and also ask new questions of some established discourses. Most notable among such works is Belinda Edmondson's *Caribbean Middlebrow: Leisure Culture and the Middle Class* (2009). In this work, Edmondson makes a case for the centrality of the middle class as producers of "authentic" Caribbean culture, which, she argues, "is assumed to be the preserve of the working class". The book aims to, in her words, "rectify that perception".[7] Another notable work in this category is Alison Donnell's *Twentieth-Century Caribbean Literature: Critical Moments in Anglophone Literary History* (2006), in which Donnell, using new lenses, examines key issues concerning "cultural politics, ethnicity, gender and sexuality" with a view to providing what she terms "new peepholes, supplementary histories and alternative moments" in the Caribbean literary archive.[8] Similarly, in her appropriately titled book *Out of Order! Anthony Winkler and White West Indian Writing* (2006), Kim Robinson-Walcott illustrates how one category within the West Indian literary canon, white West Indian writing, is destabilized in Anthony Winkler's oeuvre. Robinson-Walcott argues that Winkler's work – for example, his representation of black characters – is "out of order" and "out of synch"[9] with writings by other white West Indian authors. Here, I show how John's treatment of orality in *Unburnable* similarly stimulates new considerations about not only oral traditions but, more broadly, Caribbean folk cultures.The intervention that *Unburnable* has made into critical conversations about Caribbean orality resonates with Karin Barber's observation about Africanist literary criticism and postcolonial criticism in general: namely, that "orality remains the last unexamined, essentialist concept . . . it is a highly value-charged term which can be accorded almost talismanic authority".[10] Because it subjects orality to such extensive scrutiny, *Unburnable* insists on a departure from such criticism. By employing and focusing on multiple points of view, the novel explores the power of stories and shows how unreliability, one of the inherent elements of storytelling, expands conversations about how stories have historically functioned in Caribbean societies. It presents a hierarchy of stories in which some versions of the past are accorded more prominence than others, ultimately determining which narratives dominate and which ones are marginalized.

By going beyond the intersections and tensions between Caribbean orality and writing, *Unburnable* focuses more extensively on the diversity and range of oral modes within the larger oral culture.[11] Because one consequence of this treatment is that in this work, orality constitutes both dominant and marginal discourses, the focus on orality is the means by which John explores larger epistemological questions in a specifically postcolonial context. Oral tales, I contend, function as sources of both trauma and partial healing, and not simply as a cultural remedy for formerly colonized peoples who seek to recover a misrepresented past.

Formal Synergies: *The Colour of Forgetting* and *Unburnable*

Despite the variance in discourses on orality that these two novels offer, formally, the authors share a celebration of orature as the central structuring device for their stories, and deploy almost identical storytelling features throughout their respective works; as a result, these two novels are firmly grounded in a poetics of performance. A key strategy that the novelists share is a reworking of the narrative voice, primarily through their treatment of language, the inclusion of multiple narrators who approximate oral interlocutors and their recuperation of multiple storytelling strategies. Primarily because of the interplay among voices, *The Colour of Forgetting* and *Unburnable* are polyphonic novels that also recast the third-person narrators they ostensibly include as oral storytellers.

Collins's reshaping of the third-person narrative voice is achieved primarily through her creative exploitation of the range of possibilities presented by the language continuum. For example, one of her representations of Carib's disruption of a market scene is described as follows:

> But those who were trying to squeeze through the dark tunnel, on either side of the traffic, ignored both him and Carib, concerned only to get by. Other drivers sat in their cars leaning on the horns, not even bothering to go out to try and restrain him. *They knew, you see, that was just a big voose he making*, and that he, like them, would wait until Carib got whatever it was out of her system and moved on. (7; emphasis mine)[12]

In the following passage, the narrator discusses the family stories that occupy Willive's mind just before she relates the consultation with Carib:

> The story that came down to Willive through the generations and made her believe that Carib did in fact have this gift of prophecy that people seemed to accept mainly when it happened in the Bible, was the story of the village and more *particular the story of a family named* Malheureuse. It was Willive's family story, although now the Malheureuse family name was not there much *and Willive, for example, though Malheureuse blood, was a Mrs Janvier. . . . But even if the name gone, the story remain and the spirit remain.* (10–11; emphasis mine)

Here, Collins merges the voice of the narrator with that of the larger community's creole speech from which the quotation is taken, and ultimately diffuses the point of view. In the first passage, two standard English sentences are followed by "They knew you see, *that was just a big voose he making*". Not only does Collins inject a creole syntax, but she also includes a colloquial expression, "voose", which would normally be omitted or explained by a formal third-person narrator, or written in quotation marks to indicate that these are not the narrator's words. In the second passage, creole and standard English syntax overlap with each other in examples such as "Although now the Malheureuse family name was not there", followed by "Willive for example, though Malheureuse blood . . .". The second sentence is both creole and idiosyncratic. In the last sentence, Collins omits "was" before "gone" and omits the *s* at the end of "remain" both times the word is used, so that a paragraph that begins in standard English, ends in creole, and the overall effect is a narrator who uses creole speech.

Other passages omit quotation marks when another character's words are being included: "Generally, in response to the question about where the Caribs had jumped, people answered, around here so, indicating the expanse of green splendour" (4); "When you see that, said Mamag, the work they come to do finish" (12). In these examples, the narrator's words and the quoted voices are presented as both separate and joined – separate because there is direct reference to the quoted speaker, but conjoined by the omission of the quotation marks that usually set other speakers apart from the narrator. Taken as a whole, these relatively minor changes result in a creole rather than standard English passage, and a narrative voice shaped around oral discourse. The writer opts for the kind of movement along the language continuum that characterizes speech in the Caribbean, and in this way presents a narrator who more closely resembles oral storytellers from the community where the story is set.

Collins's use of language engenders a plurality of voices and points of view, rather than one in which the third-person narrative voice appears distinct. Her handling of dialogue enhances this effect because of the seamless movement and constant overlap between narration and conversation among characters. Collins's use of storytelling strategies that integrate different speakers facilitates a foregrounding of multiple perspectives, a characteristic of orality in contrast to historical discourse (as the novel presents it), which, in both form and content, is generally centred on singularity. The challenge that readers of *The Colour of Forgetting* are likely to encounter in marking different voices and isolating the "narrator's" voice from the others is an indication of the dissolution of a single, authoritative third-person narrator, and the consequent formation of an approach to writing history that takes into account the viewpoints of more than one group. This difficulty of isolating one authoritative voice is crucial to the novel's concern with the diffusion of authority in historical representation.

John's linguistic techniques, which are almost identical to those used in *The Colour of Forgetting*, similarly destabilize readers' perceptions of the narrative voice by creating unmarked shifts in that voice, as well as frequently overlaying different voices onto that of the primary narrator. Such stylistic choices also mark this novel as one whose discourse on orality centres on uncertainty as an inherent feature of narrative representation. The part of the story that relates Lillian's visit with her friend Teddy to persuade him to accompany her to Dominica illustrates the interplay of voices and narrative perspectives that are characteristic of this work. Lillian begins the story when she tells Teddy, "They say . . . that my grandmother was a murderer." She then reminds Teddy of his obsessive curiosity over twenty years earlier: "Once, you wanted to know me. My story."[13] The story and narrative point of view then appear to shift to the 1940s, and they detail as much as Lillian knows about her grandmother, up to the point when John Baptiste is "killed". Initially, it appears that the third-person narrator is relating this story, but as Teddy reappears alone, it becomes clear that the reader was eavesdropping on a story Lillian was relating to Teddy: "Lillian had told him that there was a lot more to the story . . . and he wondered . . . to what extent Lillian had internalized some things that were closer to myth than truth" (146). So while for the reader, the third-person narrator is the person who provides all the details about Matilda, for Teddy, Lillian is the narrator, one whom he finds unreliable because he does not trust her sources. The reader therefore leaves this part of the story hearing the narrator's voice, but knowing, based on what Teddy reveals, that Lillian was telling the story. This technique suggests and almost mirrors a cacophony of community voices, the performativity of the oral context it evokes, and multiple and competing versions that constitute the story about Matilda's life and work.

Consistent with the novel's thematic focus on uncertainty, John also unsettles the third-person narrative perspective through her use of techniques that call the authority of this omniscient third-person voice into question. The narrator of *Unburnable* simultaneously presents herself as the text's authority and undermines that authority by including the voices of multiple, competing narrators who approximate interlocutors in oral discourse. The novel's opening paragraph clearly illustrates one of *Unburnable*'s defining narrative strategies. The story begins with the authoritative claim one would expect from an omniscient narrator: "Lillian's mother, Iris, was known throughout the island for a number of distinct characteristics". However, instead of following this with a list of *known* characteristics, as set up by the writing conventions used here, the narrator slips into hearsay, presenting Iris's qualities as they have been described by various other sources: "the women would say . . . Others insisted . . . Men, though, [said] it was" (1). The narrator's inclusion of multiple perspectives and her explicit dependence on others for the stories she tells firmly establish the prominence of uncertainty as a central issue in this novel. Framed in this way, with the primary narrator explicitly conceding parts of the story to other narrators, thereby creating a cacophony of speakers in living oral discourse, this opening establishes a key feature of *Unburnable*: its emphasis on multiple and competing stories as characteristic of the construction and representation of the past. I return to some specific examples later when I show how John's formal innovations facilitate the problematized representation of orality.

Both *Unburnable* and *The Colour of Forgetting* are infused with a number of other oral forms, which they fold into the narrative and, in so doing, reinforce the dominance of orature as their primary aesthetic. In some ways, John returns the leitmotif to its musical origins in the manner in which she uses songs and repetition together. Her novel relies on repetition to underscore emphasis on the uncertainty that is at the heart of this work, as well as to show how songs keep stories alive through the community's repeated singing of them. The attention to doubt that recurs in this story is expressed in phrases such as "subject to much debate" (112), "they did not know" (130), "nobody knew for sure" (224) and "those who were skeptical" (105). Placed at strategic points in the story and recurring frequently, these references retain a focus on ambiguity and highlight the novel's interrogative orientation.

In *The Colour of Forgetting*, repetition functions as the primary means of keeping the novel's central preoccupation in sharp focus. The opening frame and Carib's riddle, "Blood in the north, blood to come in the south and the blue crying red in between", encapsulates the consequences of forgetting. Not only does this riddle open the text, but it also appears at various critical moments as the novel's primary leitmotif. Given this novel's preoccupation with forgetting, its extensive use of repetition as a performative and cognitive device is well warranted in the exploration of processes of remembering in which the book is engaged. Collins's use of repetition also augments the novel's emphasis on circularity and its challenge to linear representations of history. Overlapping and merging, which characterize both events and their recalling, are reinforced in the story's refrain of "yesterday is today is tomorrow". And perhaps most significantly, the importance of the oral tradition in the recuperative process is retained through the repetition of "walk back over the story".

The Colour of Forgetting and *Unburnable* showcase the dialectical relationship between text and audience, a key feature of orature that characterizes performing fictions. Akin to the storytelling traditions that Collins and John recuperate, the novels evince an interplay between performer and audience, or the performer's display of "responsibility to an audience".[14] The speakers in *The Colour of Forgetting* include such expressions as "let me tell you", "you see what I am telling you", "you know" and "I tell you" to maintain that link. Collins's use of these stock storytelling phrases not only maintains the performer-audience dialectic, but also evokes everyday Caribbean interactions, and therefore locates *The Colour of Forgetting* in a "situated" Caribbean storytelling tradition. In *Unburnable*, the tone is consistently intimate. With her reliance on gossip as one form of storytelling, John establishes an atmosphere of personal interaction between text and reader. Through a consistent use of "some say", "others say" and similar allusions to gossip and hearsay, the gap between reader and text that the solitary act of reading normally engenders is bridged; John's recourse to oral cues injects an intimate speakerly voice into the written story.

A Quarrel with the Community

By writing a text that departs from colonial writings of the past, Collins enters into a conversation that has preoccupied Caribbean critics for decades. For example, Edward Baugh, in "The West Indian Writer and His Quarrel with History", uses Derek Walcott's concern with history to examine a more general anxiety about history as a recurring theme, and animating idea, for generations of Caribbean writers. These writers' concern with history is not surprising, given its now well-established role in maintaining colonial hegemonies. For example, Dipesh Chakrabarty has argued that in "history as a discourse produced at the institutional site of the university, Europe remains the sovereign theoretical subject".[15] It is this tendency of history – its propensity towards sidelining the memories of subalterns – that *The Colour of Forgetting* confronts.

While the tendency of history to marginalize memory has been accentuated in and used to serve the purposes of colonialism, the tension between the two is longstanding. Pierre Nora's theorization of history and memory acknowledges these age-old tensions, as well as points of overlap. Referring to the difference between "real memory" and history as "brutal", Nora argues:

> Memory and history, far from being synonymous, appear now to be in fundamental opposition. Memory is life, borne by living societies founded in its name. It remains in permanent evolution, open to a dialectic of remembering and forgetting, unconscious of its subsequent deformations, vulnerable to manipulation and appropriation, susceptible to being dormant and periodically revived. History, on the other hand, is the reconstruction, always problematic and incomplete, of what is no longer. Memory is a perpetually actual phenomenon, a bond tying us to the eternal present; history is a representation of the past. . . . Memory accommodates only those facts that suit it.[16]

In Nora's formulation, both history and memory are "open to manipulation" and "problematic"; I find his argument that memory is "open to a dialectic of remembering and forgetting" especially germane to the concerns of this chapter. On the face of it, Nora appears to romanticize memory, making it seem the innocent victim of history. But a closer look at his own dissection of the two indicates that memory, like history, is vulnerable.

Nora's statement that history and memory *appear* to be in fundamental opposition is important, as this conflicts somewhat with the overall thrust of his argument, which shows more points of intersection between the two forms than might be apparent. Evidently, then, because memory is inherently unstable, Nora's treatment of history and memory cannot be read as oppositional. As Yosef Hayim Yerushalmi points out, "Memory is among the most fragile and capricious of our faculties."[17] That caprice is a consistent undercurrent in Nora's discourse on the flaws of history. Yet despite the similarities between history and memory that appear in Nora's theorization, it is arguable that the overt selectivity of historical discourse – more specifically, its proponents' refusal to acknowledge history's kinship with memory and its relationship to positivist inclinations – warrants the kind of scepticism about history that

Nora's discussion reveals. Thus, "official" historians' reconstructive impulses affect all those involved in recalling and recording the past.

In the society she depicts in *The Colour of Forgetting*, where book learning and an epistemological system informed by "objective" scientific methods are revered, Collins portrays Carib, the warner woman, as the single repository and articulator of the community's stories. While the novel's structure reinforces its preoccupation with the reciprocal relationship between history and memory, alongside the more demonstrable (stylistic) recuperative moves, character/narrators, particularly Carib, speak explicitly about the conflict between history and memory. In many ways, Carib embodies the concept of surrogacy that Joseph Roach proposes as part of performances of collective memory, what he describes as the "three-sided relationship of memory, performance and substitution". In Roach's conceptualization, surrogates are appointed to fill the "vacancies [that] occur in the network of relations that constitutes the social fabric".[18] Roach describes a more formal community's decision to fill the spaces created by loss. What I propose is an extension of Roach's idea: a less institutionalized, even self-appointed surrogacy in Collins's presentation of Carib as part of the social group that has forgotten its past. The Carib we meet in *The Colour of Forgetting* is the third or fourth in a line of seers and oral historians, and each Carib replaces the one before as guardian of the community's history and stories. Prior to the society's turn away from traditional ways of knowing, the community's reliance on such acts of surrogacy was more recognized and sanctioned, and most of its members understood and approved of Carib's role as a surrogate. As the community moved away from traditional knowledge systems, Carib became an object of ridicule and rejection; yet she persevered, and continues to do so. In a context in which the community no longer values or validates Carib's role, she not only replaces her ancestors but also "stands in", or, in Roach's terms, becomes the "effigy" for an entire older generation of storytellers.

Carib's statements about how history has deliberately and successfully tried to erase the community's memories are unequivocal. At the consultation during which she prescribes storytelling for Thunder's illness, she tells Willive: "Sometimes the children who should know the most is the ones that know the least. Walk back. Walk back over all of the story with him. Is the younger ones to stop the blue from crying red in between, but them self looking outside. They not listening inside here self. Is not that he don't know, but his head get twist with all kind of other things he *reading*" (emphasis mine).[19] Carib sets up a contrast between two systems of knowledge as she exhorts Mamag and Willive to tell Thunder the story. And against the story that family members tell, Carib places "things he reading in books". At this moment when the oral tradition is discussed in relation to reading and writing, the two modes are not presented as complements of each other (as they are in other places), but as competing forms. And Carib notes that though the boy knows the story, evidently, a mere recalling of the events is not sufficient, since there is another system of knowledge that overpowers the stories transmitted by his ancestors. The "walking back" that Carib encourages Willive to do, then, includes more than ensuring that Thunder knows; it involves creating a counter-discourse, storytelling as a way of counteracting both the distorted version of history that Thunder has received via formal schooling and the larger, more overpowering system of knowledge that informs his education. Carib presents storytelling as political action, and reiterates its significance when she urges Mamag, "You could only help . . . by telling him everything you know" (14). By including Mamag, Carib also stresses the importance of family and the community responsibility that these acts of telling involve. In a way, she encourages Mamag and Willive to join forces against a system of knowledge that threatens to erase their memories. The urgency to remember that speakers in *The Colour of Forgetting* insist upon resonates with the exhortations of the persona of Burning Spear's "Slavery Days", who similarly recognizes the necessity of active remembering.

In her public performances, Carib also calls the community's attention to its forgetting, and its rejection of ancestral stories in favour of another kind of history. In the passage below, she outlines specific examples of how history supersedes memory in the community:

> Carib walked back towards the cemetery, talking conversationally. "Look at them. Running and jumping. Jumping and screaming. You hear the voices coming up from the bush? Forgotten and consoled. Forgotten and drownded. And the blue crying red in between." . . .
>
> The informed observer . . . would guess she was talking about the Caribs. The Amerindian people, who, long ago, had escaped their French pursuers by jumping off the cliff into the sea. . . . A people who had given the island such a proud memory had on the spot no monument to their bravery. (3–4)

Carib's concern with the community's failure to remember the Caribs' bravery echoes the novel's concern with the community's refusal to remember its ancestors' achievements. The "forgetting" to which the passage refers speaks not only to the absence of the monument, but also to how traditional historians have represented Caribbean history. While the Caribs, one ethnic group native to the Caribbean, are mentioned in older Caribbean history books, they have been traditionally described as "savage" and "warlike" rather than brave. In her reconstruction of the story, Carib injects the bravery that the official discourse omits. Her intervention also presents an example of the overlap between history and memory – the tendency towards selectivity that I noted in Nora's discussion. The example shows how selectivity determines that the Caribs' culture and their resistance are framed in ways that render their contribution forgettable. Therefore, the issue here is not only what is remembered, but also how experiences and people are remembered by different groups. In referring to the Caribs as "brave", Carib demonstrates how one's choice of language can exemplify the ways in which a given group selects, represents and distorts the events of history. Carib's insistence on the need to remember the Caribs demonstrates that it is not just the selectivity of official historical discourse that preoccupies *The Colour of Forgetting*; Carib, too, selects a particular aspect of the Caribs' lives as crucial and warranting remembrance, which shows that her memory is just as susceptible to the selectivity to which, as Nora indicates, all memory is prone.

Yet as the passage later shows, despite history's disregard for their bravery, memory of the Caribs persists in the landscape and the oral tradition: "A people who had given the island such a proud memory had no monument to their bravery but the *voice* of the woman called Carib. . . . The Caribs were thus not quite forgotten, having as their shrine an entire hill, verdant with undergrowth" (4; emphasis mine). Carib's name is significant; while it is doubtful that she, her mother and her grandmother are Caribs by blood, they carry the name of this almost extinct group and are living reminders of their existence and bravery. And although the name itself is not enough to keep them connected to this group and command their respect, Carib's relentless performances keep some memories alive. Therefore, the conflict between history and memory does not result in a complete shattering of the latter; history's attempt to suppress memory is only partial because though the Caribs' bravery was never the subject of written historical discourse, it was always present in the people's memory, and transmitted through their stories. That Carib takes the responsibility to remind the community is evidence that while another perception of the Caribs (other than that of old history books) exists, Carib's version of the past is not the view that was once the dominant narrative in the larger community where the history from "the institutional site of the university" dominates;[20] hence, as repository and custodian of the community's stories, Carib's role is central.

Collins situates the absence of a sanctioned surrogacy as an important marker of the extent to which the community has departed from the oral tradition and its associated knowledge system. Her novel urges recognition of the critical place Carib continues to hold as well as the importance of tuning in to the messages she bears. Mamag is one of the few characters of Carib's generation who not only openly supports Carib's exhortations, but also ensures that Thunder hears and pays attention to his family's stories. She reiterates Carib's warnings about the dangers of either not knowing or failing to use the knowledge obtained through the oral tradition. Mamag's involvement is not surprising, given her understanding of how the suppression of the people's memories and stories has impacted the community. She exhorts Thunder:

> Study you book, but life sense is not book sense, so study you head. Watch up there how the sky so blue, but you hear what Carib saying only yesterday when she come up the hill here? The blue crying red. Blood gone and blood to come, and is people like you, that know the story of the life of the land, that have to stop the red from taking over. (96)

In Mamag's formulation, reading and writing surface as foils for the community's stories. "Book sense" is contrasted with "life sense", with the former being the formal education system and the latter, the oral tradition and folk ways of knowing. Mamag's inclusion of the skies not only indicates recognition of the spoken word as a single form that should shape Thunder's understanding of his community, but it also alludes to a more holistic, spiritual knowledge system that I discuss in greater detail later. Her suggestion that Thunder "study [his] head" also addresses the critical place of memory in the counter-discourse. The "head", as Mamag represents it, is the storehouse of latent memories. "Studying" his head would include activating these memories – walking back – and suggests equality between formal academic ways of representing the past and folkways. Mamag's use of the word "study" gestures towards the kinship between folk and academic ways of knowing and telling, which I explore later.

In *How Societies Remember*, Paul Connerton observes, "The oral history of subordinate groups will produce another type of history: one in which not only will most of the details be different, but in which the very construction of meaningful shapes will obey a different principle."[21] Similarly, Collins foregrounds a counter-memory whereby each of the storytellers revisits and reshapes specific events in the family's (and wider community's) history. They name specific examples of memories that have been superseded by official history and recall them according to their particular storytelling systems. When Thunder's father, Ned, finally accepts his responsibility to pass on the family stories, his performance provides missing details about relationships between enslaved ancestors and their masters. One specific story concerns Ned's grandfather, also named Ned:

> "Ned used to work in the corn, they say, planting, reaping, sorting.... But they say he always used to take the corn afterwards.... So he was kind of rebellious, like. Rebellious because he work for nothing and then have to hide to get a little bit....
>
> "They beat him merciful.... Beat him until the body and the spirit couldn't take no more and he go off and meet his Maker. And when the story of Ned get report in those official place like government and court and so, nobody speak up for him and explain what was what....
>
> "In those times ... only the white people that was in charge of estate that had voice to talk. Them and their friends in high society.... Ned couldn't talk for himself." (140–41)

Here Ned presents a critical history, and not simply a set of experiences, as he also outlines how his people have been cheated by history. In emphasizing that "nobody speak up for [Ned] and explain what was what", Ned provides an example of the omissions and silences for which storytelling is harnessed in Collins's form of recuperative narration. Thus, in telling Thunder about specific examples in which his ancestors were left out of official discourse, Ned names a central problem of written history that is the novel's concern: the omission of some details, not just through error, but as part of a larger system that deliberately marginalizes and silences some subjects of history.

The Word and the Spirit

Collins's attentiveness to suppression of the spoken word takes into account the disavowal of a more overarching epistemological system. In other chapters, I argue for an aesthetic of orality that draws on a creolized, primarily secular oral tradition heavily influenced by African cultures. Here, I am also concerned with Collins's evocation of a more holistic, if not spiritual, system, of which orality is a part: Collins presents the spoken word – informal conversations as well as personal and family narratives – as part of another way of knowing rooted in an Afro-Caribbean spirituality. The connection that I seek to make between the spoken word and a larger spiritual system is an already well-established one in African and African diaspora studies, which Catherine John has referred to as "a profoundly felt but deeply unspeakable aspect of African diaspora consciousness".[22] The spoken word, it is believed, possesses a power and force that transcend "rational" understanding of the limits and uses of orality.

By placing a "warner woman" at the centre of this text as main character, narrator, structural device and surrogate, Collins invokes a system of understanding in which the spoken word is imbued with the kind of power I describe above. As members of the Afro-Caribbean religious denomination referred to in different Caribbean territories as revivalist, Pocomania or spiritual Baptist, warner women usually prophesied based on dreams. Carib is therefore a symbol of a creolized, devalued past, a somewhat stand-alone figure who not only keeps the community's memories alive, but also insists on recognition of the disavowed spiritual system she represents. As the reactions of most characters in *The Colour of Forgetting* illustrate, the community no longer relies on warner women, nor does it recognize the way of knowing they represent as a primary or even complementary source of knowledge. Nevertheless, the use of Carib's voice as a structural device affirms her centrality to the novel's thematic thrust and its affirmation of (Afro) religious epistemological systems. Carib's riddle, and the novel's leitmotif – "Blood in the north, blood to come in the south and the blue crying red in between" – expresses her recognition of the threat to the knowledge system she represents, as well as the impending repercussions of years of ignoring the history of the ordinary people.

The way the novel treats Carib's prophecies affirms another way of knowing, more centrally than her prominent position in the text and the frequency of her appearances do. The community's general scepticism towards these prophecies is an indication of their overall rejection of knowledge outside of the (relatively new) academic system:

> One time Carib talk about a place called Leapers' Hill, where long ago some Carib people jump off a cliff rather than give themself up. Carib say how spirits always there moaning and weeping.... And Mamag watching and listening with her mouth open. And she watching, too, how some of the young men by the rum shop up the hill lean against the door and shout out. "We hearing them, Carib. ... They sounding just like you." ... People didn't take Carib seriously, really. (22)

The dismissal of those described in the passage above is not merely a rejection of Carib. "We hearing them, Carib. They sounding just like you" embeds a conflation of Carib and the Caribs, and a dismissal of the latter. Although many, particularly the young, reject Carib's messages and the system of knowledge she represents, the novel shows how, in all instances, the majority were wrong in their cynicism: "Not until after. Long after when time come and pass, after little people like Mamag ... become big people.... Long after. When people remember" (22) – and connect Carib's prophecy to events that unfold.

As a way of establishing Carib's continued relevance and that of the culture she represents, the novel includes several examples of her prophecies that come to pass in the lifetime of people who previously dismissed her as deranged. For example, the beating of Thunder's grandfather, Ti-Moun, by members of his own family demonstrates to the community the truthfulness of Carib's prophecies and their relevance to present-day events. "'Look at that, eh.... Grow up here hearing Carib talk about land confusion and about blood to come. Never thought I would see it in this Attaseat here'" (59) is the people's collective remark as they reflect on the family violence brought on by "land confusion" and the ongoing effects of the wrongs of the past that Carib had warned against.

The novel's claims for the sustaining relevance of the oral tradition and the larger spiritual system of knowledge it represents are emphasized through the links it makes between Carib's prophecies and events in Grenada's recent history. I refer specifically to the 1979 social and political upheavals and the subsequent killing of Maurice Bishop and others, followed by the US invasion of Grenada. Collins has written elsewhere about this experience.[23] But in *The Colour of Forgetting*, her inclusion of these events is related to the novel's overall epistemological concern: "That year, 1979, was the year that Paz City exploded in Revolution. After the years of demonstrations, of confusion, the government was overthrown. That is it, people said. This is the blood that Carib been preaching about all the time" (150).

In establishing connections between the fictional Carib's prophecies and the actual historical events of 1979, Collins affirms a relationship between contemporary historical experiences and an ancient and disappearing spiritual way of knowing. As the novel presents it, Carib knew about these events years before they occurred (because there are about three generations of Caribs) and warned the community. The novel shows how the community's dismissal of Carib impeded actions that would have prevented the death, destruction and foreign intervention that followed. The idea that an old folk figure – with little or no formal schooling, and no understanding of the means of historical inquiry or world events – saw these events before they occurred, defies the understanding of social and political forces propagated by Western academics and endorsed by Caribbean school systems. The community's recalcitrance persists; they erect a monument in honour of the United States soldiers, while none is built to mark the lives and contributions of Grenadian natives. This is one moment in which the novel calls attention to the continued, intense struggle between the different systems of knowledge.

The accounts recovered by Carib, Mamag, Ned and others show how the community has turned away from its own stories, and how in so doing, it has virtually invited some of its current difficulties. In Carib's words, its actions have allowed the "blue to cry red in between". In unearthing stories that this community has opted to suppress through erasure of its collective memories, Collins demonstrates an inwardly directed postcolonial critique that shifts the focus away from European historiography, instead turning its attention squarely to how the community's own complicity contributed to the exclusion of its voices, perspectives and ways of knowing and telling.

Discourse on Memory

The recuperation of suppressed memories that *The Colour of Forgetting* emphasizes can also have a profound psychological impact, such as the healing of trauma, allegorized here as a fear of thunder. Yet even as she calls attention to gaps in written records through an exploration of how various characters remember, forget and process the stories, Collins establishes incompleteness as an inevitable characteristic of memory. A substantial component of Mamag's performances is about the various accounts of family events that she passes on to Willive, and that Willive in turn passes on to her son Thunder. In a number of passages, Willive sorts through the information in her consciousness, trying to figure out which events she witnessed first-hand, and which ones she received from Mamag

> Strange. Willive could remember that day with Mamag on the hill and Granduncle Son-Son dancing like a person in a tac-tac nest. She could remember the room in Mamag's house and her mother and father sitting there, but her father's death, and details around the funeral, remained a blank. What she knew about that was what Mamag told her over the years.... As far as Willive remembers, one time he was there and all of a sudden he wasn't there. She doesn't remember an event that was his death. (81–82)

This account of Willive's father's death is part of an extended family story that includes the long-standing dispute over land that plagues Thunder's family, and that illustrates one aspect of the conflicts that history has misrepresented. This event is included as part of the family history that Thunder must learn and write into official history. Although Willive has to pass on the story to her son, she retains only sketches of it in her own memory. As the following example shows, Mamag's comment in another storytelling session rekindles Willive's memory and from its recesses, she later retrieves the rest of the story. Some events surface only when other related events, "associational loops", trigger them, and sometimes "the two things get mixed up in her mind".

> And while Mamag talked, a big bottle-fly got trapped in the curtain and stayed there buzzing.... Mamag said, "This one must be somebody visiting. Somebody visiting, when you see that."
>
> And it was then that Willive remembered, all of a sudden, her father Ti-Moun lying down on the bed with his eyes closed....

> And years afterwards the two things were mixed up in her mind. Mamag talking, the bottle-fly on the window, and Ti-Moun lying down with his eyes closed. And she Willive standing by the bed watching him. (87)

I have included these passages about Willive's reflections on the workings of her own memory, the uncertainty involved in trying to decipher where she gets the stories or their various strands, to address the novel's exploration of the nature of memory, and of how the intrinsic caprice of the latter determines which details enter stories and history. As Willive's example shows, memories are never complete and foolproof, nor are they usually coherent; hence, what one remembers, reconstructs and narrates is necessarily fractured and partial. It is worth reiterating that this is the family story that Willive has to synthesize and, in turn, pass on to her son. Evidently then, the story that gets passed down to Thunder, like the history being contested, is composed of the partial remnants of memory, and will be affected by its mutable nature. For Collins, the capricious tendency of memory, as demonstrated by Willive's reflections, does not make it (or its counterpart, forgetting) less valuable. Rather, her attention to this quality speaks to the importance of including different modes and methods in the recalling or representation of the past.

In the preface to his book *On Collective Memory*, Maurice Halbwachs argues that "memory depends on the social environment". Speaking of his own memory, Halbwachs writes, "Most of the time, when I remember, it is others who spur me on; their memory comes to the aid of mine and mine relies on theirs."[24] The reliance on the memories of others and the interdependence of individual memories that Halbwachs acknowledges find resonance in Willive's active engagement with the workings of her own memory. Willive's memories are shaped somewhat by her own perception of the events she recalls, but they are also shaped by Mamag's memories and the form that Mamag's representation takes. As the following passage shows, Willive's reflections on the uncertainties in her own recollections speak to the novel's treatment of memory as a social process:

> The family go through a lot, but Willive, people said, couldn't possibly remember. She was too young then. But she did remember. Perhaps what she recalled was partly what her mother recalled, but after the confusion her mother said little, although the child could hear her crying at night. So perhaps what she remembered was what she heard in her mother's sobbing and in her silences.

> Or it may have been what her father recalled, but Ti-Moun had been reduced to silence, so perhaps it was really what Mamag, her grand-aunt, painted for her, because Mamag remembered it all. And the thing is that later, many who weren't there remembered, too. (71–72)

The passage presents a web of memories – Willive's, her mother's, her father's, Mamag's and the community's. These memories converge in Willive's stories as she relates them to Thunder. Willive's memories are therefore presented as part of a "social framework of memor[ies]" rather than as an individual memory. This framework is not endorsed by the dominant culture as the official one, but is instead underground or peripheral, and it has to struggle to reemerge in a way similar to individual memory.

Halbwachs also suggests that the various groups in society frequently distort the past in the act of reconstructing it.[25] The uncertainty that Willive confesses in the passage above speaks to the inevitable incompleteness of the stories that will eventually get passed on to Thunder and, ultimately, the new historical record. It underscores the larger point that the novel makes about memory: there are no complete and untarnished individual or collective memories. Therefore, the memory that counteracts recorded history is also acknowledged as partial. However, Willive's open engagement with the gaps in her own memories still suggests that, as it is represented in this text, memory is reflexive and that the novel does not reject history because of its necessary incompleteness: rather, history is called into question for its refusal to acknowledge this incompleteness and accept different systems of knowledge and different ways of representing the past.

Towards a Revised History

Collins's main contribution to extant discourses on historical representation is her projection of fictive techniques that combine writing and orality and affirm the relevance of both memory, as the repository of stories and history, and academic discipline. Throughout the text, characters who call attention to the inadequacy of written history and writing in general also move beyond advocating for storytelling to an acknowledgement of the usefulness and necessity of writing and a diversity of ways of representing the past.

Alongside her awareness of the excluded aspects of the past, and the dangers of relying on written history and the school system for all of Thunder's knowledge of history, is Mamag's validation of writing. Therefore, when she instructs Thunder, she begins by telling him, "Study you book, but life sense is not book sense, so study you head." In distinguishing between "life sense" and "book sense", Mamag acknowledges the usefulness of each system and emphasizes the possibilities for the reciprocity inherent in these two modes. Thus, "book sense" and "life sense" are not merely foils for each other; they also complement each other in the world that Thunder and his contemporaries inhabit and, by suggestion, in the history that is to be written. Mamag also gives writing prominence by first telling Thunder to "study you book". In positioning books in this way, she presents the formal education system that writing represents not as a mere addition to Thunder's general education, but as a central part of it.

As Mamag's protégé, Willive follows her guardian's lead in telling Thunder the stories and insists that her husband Ned tell his side of the story as well. Willive also extols the importance of schooling and writing in Thunder's life. In my map of the text's structure, I noted Willive's persistence in ensuring that Thunder receives the best education available. That clear sense of the importance of education remains even when, as an adult, Thunder pursues higher education in England. Willive is therefore an example of the kind of mother figure that Collins presents in both *The Colour of Forgetting* and her first novel, *Angel*. The mothers in both novels are fully aware of the importance of formal education for social mobility in an emerging modern society, even as they try to keep their children and grandchildren connected to the traditional folk culture.

Undoubtedly, Ned tells Thunder the story about the older Ned's beating to show how written records exclude and often distort the truth. But in his contribution to the web of stories, Ned also stresses the relevance of writing and supports a history borne out of collaboration between orality and writing:

> Ned couldn't talk for himself.... And nobody of our people, the black people ... who they call slaves like Ned and so, couldn't do a thing to help him. So now is the generations to come, like you and everybody who getting a education, have to write Ned name in the ground, have to say all the things that Ned couldn't say. Have to write thing down, since writing is the fashion these days. (141)

Ned's repetition of "write" in the passage above is significant. Not only does it address the importance of writing, but it also reinforces Ned's claim that this act is a part of what will recover the voice of his ancestors. In Ned's representation, writing is what gets noticed, and it therefore stands in for the oral stories. He thus acknowledges the partnership between orality and writing that the new era necessitates. He implores Thunder and others like him to not only pay attention to the stories and keep the oral tradition relevant by telling them to their children, but also to write these stories.

By telling Thunder that he and others should write, Ned recognizes that the act of telling, the performance that brings these stories back to life, is (potentially) a part of written history. In other words, oral narratives should prompt *rewritings* of history that include these stories. In taking note of the fact that "writing is the fashion these days", Ned acknowledges that despite its necessity, telling by itself is not enough, partly because performance of these stories will not change existing records, nor will it impact the formal education process in which written historical records dominate. Ned's call for new writings therefore underscores Collins's use of orature and the novel's emphasis on telling as a way of balancing representations of history. Placing emphasis on storytelling does not translate into a disavowal of writing; rather, the focus is directed at what is written, whose voices are included, how writing gets done and, more importantly, the ideologies that inform it. Through a performance of the principle it advances, *The Colour of Forgetting* suggests a kind of writing that acknowledges its kinship with the oral, and that takes into account the diverse points of view and ways of talking about the past that reflect the range and vicissitudes of Caribbean experiences.

Through its emphasis on overlapping and merging, the novel also conveys the idea that orality and writing, history and memory should converge in explicit ways to fashion a new history that reflects different means of communication and knowledge systems. This is first evident in Carib's refrain, "Blood in the north, blood to come in the south and the blue crying red *in between*" (emphasis mine). The novel offers no clear explanation of this riddle, but one possibility is that "north" and "south" refer to the opposing ways of understanding and talking about the past that plague this community. Clearly, this is applicable to the tension that exists between orality and writing in the cultural context that the novel examines. The novel also states that "blue is the colour of forgetting"; forgetting is what causes the blood in both north and south, or separates seemingly divergent but complementary forces. Yet the "blue crying red *in between*" marks the in-between, the liminal, as the place of tension, eruption and possibility, the place where remembering might circumvent forgetting, and therefore stop the "blue from crying red".

While the novel ends on a note of ambivalence regarding the actualization of its vision for a different history, its internal structure and the content of the last three sections consolidate the emphasis on overlap and the fusion of different ways of seeing and states of being in ways that earlier sections anticipate. The blurring of narrative voices that defines this work intensifies as the narration moves ever more seamlessly back and forth between the two voices. Furthermore, Carib's internal monologues add what sounds like another narrator's voice to this amalgam of narrators, and a sense of uncertainty not emphasized in earlier sections becomes more pronounced through the representation of Carib's dreamlike or semi-sane musings. The emphasis on ambiguity is further accentuated in Carib's explicit questioning of different states: "Is dream or is wake? . . . Oh, God! I sleeping. No, I awake, yes. What I dreaming? . . . Sleeping and awake. Quiet and alive. Dead and screaming. . . . Forgotten and consoled" (178). That Carib begins by posing the question regarding sleep and wakefulness, opts for one, then the other, and finally accepts both, emphasizes even more the novel's investment in uncertainty, collaboration and plurality. The openness to different, sometimes opposing, states continues in the phrases "quiet and alive", "dead and screaming" and, significantly, "forgotten and consoled". Such an investment in "inbetween-ity" and crossings, particularly in how stories are told, emphasizes the novel's favourable disposition towards history and memory as well as writing and orality as complementary modes of recalling and representing the past. Carib's relevance is affirmed at the end of the section in the spirit of liminality: "Remembrance is coming. Is blue. Is red. And is the young ones, yes, to stop the blue from crying red in between. Can't see the sun. But it coming. Is night, but is not long before day" (194). Ending at dawn, with the promise of renewal suggested in the rising sun, presents a vision of hope made possible by the bridging of apparently divergent states such as night and day as well as of different states of being. Through its oscillation between and among forms, the novel therefore advocates for a reconstructing of the past in ways that combine written and oral modes. Thus, by tapping into both history and memory, *The Colour of Forgetting* places recovery and preservation of the past in a "twilight zone" where different modes of representation converge.

Interrogating Orality in *Unburnable*

My suggestion that Collins's evocation of twilight signals the space where oral and written forms converge underscores my contention that in her novel, the tension between orality and writing that animates postcolonial scholars remains a central focus. It is in this shared discursive space that John's *Unburnable* explores a related but distinct discourse on representation. Whereas Collins's explorations of history and memory, orality and writing evince a nuanced treatment of these modes through a focus on reciprocity, John's novel explores the problems inherent in oral representations and underlines how oral modes, like their scribal counterparts, are susceptible to elisions, distortions, omissions and deliberate suppression of some stories and narratives.

As part of its sustained attentiveness to orality in and of itself, *Unburnable* explores the general storyteller's awareness that the uncertainty intrinsic in storytelling often results in an impulse to control stories. In this regard, the narrators in *Unburnable* show an explicit awareness that the act of representation is always fundamentally problematic, that accepted claims are often questionable, and therefore the questioning of different stories and orthodoxies is warranted. Contributing to this impulse towards interrogation, other narrators, such as the character Reggie, reinforce the omniscient narrator's consistent references to uncertainty. Reggie is the Dominican from whom Teddy tries to extract parts of the story that he believes are missing from Lillian's version. This encounter presents Reggie very much like the omniscient narrator in the way he acknowledges the uncertainties surrounding the stories he tells: "a lot of it is hearsay anyway" (159); "I think of that [the Flying Masquerade story] more as folklore. I mean, oral tradition says *something* happened in the band" (160). At the same time, his reference to "the oral tradition" implies or feigns a distrust of the stories as well as their sources. Similarly, the narrator's intervention in Reggie's story uncovers the latter's deliberate suppression of parts of Lillian's account, foreshadows later acts of suppression and puts on notice the novel's explicit treatment of the problems inherent in representation within the oral tradition.

The novel's representation of Reggie as narrator, and as someone who is conscious of the ways oral stories have functioned in his experience in Dominica, contrasts with Nana Wilson-Tagoe's claims about the relationship between orality and writing in Caribbean societies. In her essay "Myth, Ritual and Song as 'Counter Text' in Three Plays of Derek Walcott", Wilson-Tagoe argues that the challenge to Western dominance apparent in writings from the Caribbean serves to "deflate the tyrannical hold of the written word" and that the "Oral Tradition . . . deflates the written word as a single totalizing mode of perception and signification".[26] Wilson-Tagoe's observation illustrates the kind of representations of orality that *Unburnable* disrupts. While the privileging of written over oral modes in some works is undeniable, *Unburnable* presents a much more complicated oral-scribal relationship than Wilson-Tagoe and others have espoused. In fact, far from being a "single totalizing mode", it is the written word that appears as the marginalized mode of representation in *Unburnable*. While I do not wish to suggest that one totalizing mode is replaced by another in this work, the prominence of orality shows more fluidity between these two modes.

As someone well aware of the ways in which the stories about her ancestors have been distorted, it is not surprising that Lillian turns to the official written records when she returns to Dominica to recover what she hopes to be an accurate version of the story about Matilda. Lillian has lost faith in the stories, and by extension the oral tradition, as sources of "truth" and healing. Therefore, one of the first places she visits in Dominica is the library where court records and other archival material are stored. Teddy and Lillian's inquiries reveal that "everything from forty-five to fifty-two" (235) was taken by Hurricane David, which struck Dominica in 1979. At this point, it becomes clear to Lillian that whatever she will learn about Matilda's trial, as well as the gaps in her own memory and stories, can be filled only by stories housed in other people's memories. This is a pivotal point in the novel: first, it marks the decisive exclusion of written and conventional official records from contention; second, it highlights the fact that the dominant narratives in this context are oral tales. Teddy and Lillian concede that the only official source to which they now have access are Mary-Alice's memories of her testimony in Matilda's trial.

What *Unburnable* presents here are instances in which oral modes displace written ones; therefore, the notion that writing is "a single totalizing mode of perception and signification" does not account for situations such as those represented in this novel.

Unburnable is thus distinguished by its presentation of official and folk beliefs as intersecting systems. What becomes the dominant view of Matilda is constructed from folk beliefs about the power of supernatural forces that the dominant culture openly denies, and this narrative is preserved in songs about Matilda and Iris and used strategically to influence the official system. The differences between the people and sources that come together to convict Matilda illustrate a repositioning of the official knowledge system and show the overpowering authority of the spoken word. Matilda is hanged because she confesses to a crime that is based on a narrative constructed by local community members from within the oral tradition: the story of John Baptiste's murder was "chronicled in a song" derived from local gossip and this is the story that the official legal system uses to convict Matilda. The formal legal apparatus had established a physical cause of death that, based on that same official framework, should have exonerated Matilda. Therefore, because an established system is in place, when the police go "Up There" to question Matilda, it is only out of respect for the middle-class Mrs Richard – who is desperate for revenge – since a cause of death had already been scientifically determined. Based on the official knowledge system, the police inspector tells Mrs Richard, "You know John died of natural causes", to which she responds, "Autopsy can't show no Obeah.... Is she kill him" (151). Here, the middle-class Dominican who generally aligns herself with the official system and devalues local culture chooses to believe the version of events chronicled in the songs about Matilda. The fact that Mrs Richard is able to use the power derived from her class privilege to invoke orality and get the official system to convict Matilda is indicative of the complex relationship between folk and official cultures. The official narrative, in the form of the coroner's written report, which the inspector had called "unequivocal", is trumped by the narrative preserved in the folk orature. Ultimately, it is the official system that had earlier exonerated Matilda that later convicts and executes her.

John uses the courtroom setting – an official space where the spoken word wields significant power – and the testimony presented there to even more firmly establish the interconnectedness between the formal legal system and the unofficial folk culture. Aside from the forensic and other physical evidence, word of mouth is the most powerful evidence used in court. And records such as those Lillian and Teddy seek are, as is well known, created largely from what people say. In recalling the events for Lillian and Teddy, Mary-Alice reveals that what she said about Matilda was important in the latter's conviction. Mary-Alice's character-witness testimony, which represents Matilda as "morally corrupt", highlights this intersection between the official legal system and the unofficial culture. At the time of her testimony, Mary-Alice is an outsider. She is a young, white, American nun who is unfamiliar with the creole culture and who represents, more than any other character, the neocolonial superstructure. Therefore, her word has particular force, authority and credibility because of who she is. At the same time, the narrative her testimony corroborates is the one based on folk beliefs, constructed within the local creole culture. As Mary-Alice tries to deflect the significance of her words, she inadvertently reinforces the importance of what is *said*, as well as underscores the interconnectedness of the creole and dominant cultures. In response to Teddy's query, "What you're saying . . . is that they convicted her on that one conversation you had with her?" Mary-Alice says, "They convicted Matilda because *she said* she did it" (218; emphasis mine). What Mary-Alice reveals here is emblematic of the dominant place of oral stories in this work. All that is "known" about Matilda is what is said, and often what is said is what is presumed and interpreted. "Moral corruption" becomes evidence for a crime that the official formal evidence (the autopsy and police report) disproves, but which hearsay has established as truth. This is especially crucial in the story of Matilda's conviction, since what Matilda confessed in court was that she was "responsible" for the deaths. In her conviction, then, the court system gives more credence to informal gossip and songs than it gives to scientific evidence, thereby blurring the lines between official and unofficial systems. But more importantly, this conviction establishes that the spoken word is the more powerful mode of representation in this context.

In *Unburnable*, the power of orality is underscored by an elaboration of its relationship to other sources of power, such as class positions and money. The stories about Matilda, Iris, John Baptiste and others remain in the public's collective memories through songs. Therefore, what is *known* about these people and others with whom they have had encounters rests in the oral tradition's self-sustaining capabilities. *Unburnable* presents the idea that historically powerful variables such as colour and class as well as modern capitalism are overpowered by a story's resiliency and inherent power. This understanding of the power of oral stories – in this case, to torture and traumatize – is apparent in the two mothers' meticulous efforts to protect their children from such stories. Iris's fight with Cecile Richard is, of course, rich material for *chanté mas* songs: "Mrs Richard [Cecile's mother] had gone personally to every single chantuelle and offered bribes in amounts that could not be resisted" (131) to ensure that the public brawl between her daughter Cecile and Iris was not chronicled in song. While this example calls attention to the awareness of the power of stories, it also points to the distinction between the official and folk systems, their influence on each other, as well as the power struggle in which they are engaged. The fact that Mrs Richard was able to bribe the chantuelles and effectively suppress the story she wanted to keep out of the history suggests that even in this context where stories are virtually irrepressible, the modern capitalist market holds some sway. Yet this is the song-story that Lillian's father, Winston, blames for bringing him to Iris's bed, which means that Mrs Richard was only able to buy temporary suppression of the story about her daughter. Thus, modern capitalism, often considered to be the ultimate source of power and often blamed for the demise of folk culture, has only temporary power because ultimately stories remain in the people's memories, both individually and as part of the community's collective repository.

The notion of stories as a dominant way of knowing rather than as a marginal mode of communication and knowledge is apparent in the novel's presentation of another mother's failure to protect her daughter from them. Icilma's concern that once Lillian hears the songs she will know her past, and that this knowledge will traumatize Lillian, prompts Icilma to shield Lillian from the songs. However, her pre-emptive protective efforts – placing Lillian in a private school and instructing the nuns to ensure that Lillian never hears the songs from other children – crumble under the resilience of orality. A field trip to the river takes the girls away from the strict discipline of the school setting and provides an opening for them to reveal what they know. It is here, when the teacher inadvertently allows a few girls to wander off, that Lillian hears enough of a song to feel compelled to probe for the full story:

> What drew Lillian that morning was the sound of the Big Girls' voices singing. . . . Lillian knew that something was off: there was the particular laughter. . . . Lillian began to inch away from the other girls, who were splashing water on their good-natured teacher. . . . She was listening hard to the snatches of song that were coming down-river, and she could catch enough of the melodies and bits of lyric to know which ones they were singing. . . . They were in the middle of "Matilda Swinging" when Lillian rounded the bend. . . . Lillian received understanding. (227–28)

Myrtle, one of the older girls, responds to Lillian's "Who is Matilda?" with "She is your murdering Obeahwoman grandmother" (229). This encounter with orature marks the end of Lillian's ignorance and precipitates her decades-long trauma. Lillian's knowledge of the song-stories leads to a confrontation with her godmother, Mary-Alice. She uses a song-like rhythm – in a way creating her own song – in telling Mary-Alice, "I know the songs. . . . I know 'Matilda Swinging'. I know 'Bottle of Coke'. I know 'Naked as They Born'" (186). This example further illustrates the futility of efforts to control or marginalize the informal oral tradition through modern institutions and mechanisms. The school system, which is well established as the main instrument that "exorcises and replaces" indigenous culture, is, like the capitalist system, unable to suppress the oral modes.[27]

It is by presenting a multiple and tiered system of stories that *Unburnable* demands a rethinking of what constitutes dominant discourses. As I have highlighted in the discussion of missing written court records, written accounts are not part of the problem of representation that this novel explores. Yet the conflict between dominant narratives and marginal ones remains at the forefront. The dominant narrative about Lillian's history, which consists of some true facts, some speculation, and some misunderstandings and distortions, essentially states that Matilda, Lillian's grandmother, was an evil Obeah woman who killed many people, used her magic powers to avenge her daughter's destruction and was eventually hanged for those crimes. Matilda, these oral sources indicate, confessed to these transgressions. Ultimately, however, through Teddy and Lillian's investigations, other oral narratives emerge; these accounts did not make it into the dominant oral version because the custodians of these other stories were in some ways marginal figures.

In this novel, both official and indigenous creole systems categorize Matilda's healing practices as evil and collude in getting the conviction that results in the death sentence. As is true for many court cases, the official written records (which the hurricane destroyed) are merely documentations of oral testimonies, such as that of Mary-Alice. Both systems share a belief that African-derived practices are simultaneously powerful and evil. Matilda's reputation as an Obeah woman and evildoer is a direct remnant of the disavowal of African religious practices that characterized plantation society, but it is also a view at least partially accepted by the informal creolized society in which these practices thrive. That a negative version of Matilda's story makes it into the songs that preserve events underscores the fact that dominant discourses are not always those constructed in the formal system, nor does this official system determine how events are remembered. The role of both frameworks in ensuring Matilda's conviction and execution illustrates *Unburnable*'s insistence on a more nuanced understanding of the representational roles that oral and written stories play in Caribbean cultural contexts.

The reversal of the modes in which Sylvie is able to provide missing pieces of Matilda's story underscores the prominence of oral tales over written ones. This version of the story comes from Sylvie's grandfather, a man who worked as a servant and whose perceived stupidity allowed him to eavesdrop on a private conversation among officials involved in Matilda's trial. This story, which remained in the family for over half a century, is only recovered after Teddy and Lillian try to find the official court documents that detail Matilda's trial. Ironically, although Sylvie is unable to assist Lillian and Teddy because the official written records for which she is custodian no longer include the records of Matilda's trial, she is able to provide parts of the story – those passed on by her grandfather, which were never part of the established oral and written records. From Sylvie's account, passed down through her family's private, marginalized oral tradition, Teddy, along with the reader, learns that "Up There" was officially known as Noir, a maroon community, and that the police had massacred hundreds of its inhabitants. The many skeletons found at the site were, according to Sylvie's grandfather's story, the remnants of human sacrifice. In the established version of the story that was preserved, Matilda was the one who killed all these people over time. The official oral tales present a one-sided view of African spirituality as evil and show insufficient understanding of that maroon community. As would be true of written colonial representations, the oral tradition's version of events does not acknowledge the African religious dimension as a legitimate or wholesome culture. Therefore, a shared belief system underpins both the official and unofficial modes of representation.

Sylvie's revelations to Teddy bring to the fore another important point that this novel makes about the division within the oral tradition and its intersection with official systems. The final piece of the story that Sylvie tells Teddy is that Simon, Matilda's former husband and Iris's father, was prevented from giving a testimony – one that could have exonerated Matilda. According to Sylvie, Simon "couldn't even get in [the trial]. In any case people didn't know it was him, because they had been saying for years that Matilda had killed him" (267). Simon's testimony, which conflicted with the official oral narrative, was not allowed in court, and there was no response to his cries of "Judge, judge, she didn't kill – she is not a murderer! . . . *Magistrat!*" (268). Simon's story is marginalized by the dominant narrative, which, albeit oral, is part of the ruling class's discourse. The ruling class, represented in this case by Mrs Richard and Mary-Alice, allows one oral version of events to flourish, while another, in this case Simon's, is silenced. *Unburnable*'s presentation of this intersection between traditional, official discourses and unofficial ones projects a more complex view onto issues of marginalization and power. In this representation, it is not a question of folk-oriented oral representations being marginalized by official written discourses, but rather of multiple layers of marginalization within the oral tradition.

In its representation of the sources of Lillian's trauma, *Unburnable* brings other perspectives to the notion that written, often colonially derived representations are those that have traditionally distorted history and traumatized formerly enslaved peoples. While the corrective capacities of orality are affirmed in this novel, the role of oral stories in inflicting trauma is given substantial prominence. Stories, the text suggests, do not guarantee healing from the trauma that initiates the search for other versions of events, a point made forcefully towards the end of the novel. The narrator, with the same kind of equivocation with which she started, reveals only that "justice had been served, the life of John Baptiste had been exchanged for the destroyed spirit of her child" (273). As in Matilda's confession over fifty years before, which only stated that she was "responsible for the dead in the forest" (272), there is still no certainty that Matilda killed John Baptiste. This "revelation" comes at a point in the novel when stories are being uncovered, and therefore reiterates uncertainty as a central subject: even in the disclosure of other, previously hidden versions of events, questions remain. The new stories are revelatory, but not fully so, because there is still uncertainty encoded in the ambiguous use of "responsible" and the equivocal representation of the way John Baptiste dies. Additionally, it is not clear that the parts of the story that have been recovered restore Matilda's decades-old tarnished reputation and bring Lillian healing. In fact, there is some doubt about whether or not these other versions of Matilda's story – those that would exonerate her – actually reach Lillian. In both instances in which the other versions are revealed (through Sylvie and Bird), Teddy is the one who hears the stories. *Unburnable* has what might be regarded as two endings: one that is told to Teddy, and which clears Matilda's name, and the other for Lillian, which is more like that of a conventional open-ended novel because it is not clear that Lillian hears the missing stories. Lillian and Teddy do not reconnect before the story ends, though at the end of the novel Teddy is on his way to tell Lillian all he has learned. Lillian, on the other hand, is contemplating what method she should use to commit suicide, join her ancestors and create another song.

The maroon community's separate oral culture further details how the management of stories and concomitant use of silence inflict and perpetuate trauma in *Unburnable*. To some extent, Matilda is convicted because of the maroon community's control of its own narrative and that group's related separation from the mainstream creole societies. The code of silence by which Matilda's maroon community lived allowed the official story told in the songs and housed in people's memories to persist. This code was also part of what distinguished the people of Noir from mainstream Dominica. In the end, it is Teddy who elicits this story from Bird, who, as a member of that maroon community, took a vow of silence. In the penultimate chapter, Bird presents other parts of Matilda's story that corroborate Sylvie's account and provide additional details. As he fills in the remaining gaps in Matilda's story, Bird also acknowledges the vow of silence that he and others in the maroon community took, which prevented any narrative that would counteract those established in the songs from being heard. Bird provides a history of Matilda as heir to a healing practice and the position of magistrate, or judge, among her people "Up There". The murders for which she had been accused were explained as "glorious deaths" of residents who had jumped when the village was burned down by outsiders. The bones left behind, which were used as proof of Matilda's numerous murders, were finally explained.

The facts of Matilda's case, which were completely hidden from mainstream Dominican society, not only call attention to the devastating impact of silence, but also challenge a core idea within academic discourse about maroon communities as revered cultural sites set apart from Caribbean creole societies. John's representation of the maroons' treatment of stories and silence showcases orality supporting a separation from the rest of society, not simply in a way that preserves threatened cultural practices but also in ways that negatively impact the maroon community itself. Matilda dies not only because other stories, such as Sylvie's grandfather's, were deliberately kept out of the dominant narrative. The maroons themselves, in their choice to remain apart from mainstream society, were co-architects of their own marginalization. Therefore, the genuine misunderstanding of maroon culture that this work portrays is attributed not just to the European-influenced creole society; the maroon community's custodial attitude to their stories makes them also culpable, and therefore similarly flawed.

By presenting orality in the complex ways that I have suggested, John moves the conversation about this central feature of Caribbean cultures in different directions. Her portrayal of orality as a larger, more complex phenomenon, rather than one that exists only in relationship to a written culture, allows for a more extensive probe into orality's multiple manifestations. As a result of the complicated picture that *Unburnable* presents, the oral culture, with its many forms of orature and its own hierarchical system, determines which stories emerge as the dominant discourse and which ones are marginalized. This portrayal of multiple stories, some of which are subsumed by the dominant narratives and others of which are deliberately excluded, draws attention to a pluralistic oral culture. Therefore, because orality is treated primarily "on its own terms" in *Unburnable*, and readers observe its varied forms and its internal dynamic, oral modes of representation are not seen as victims of colonial domination.[28] On the contrary, they are presented as vehicles through which multiple perspectives – some potentially damaging, others with the capacity to heal – can be perpetuated.

One consequence of the focus on orality in and of itself in *Unburnable* is a further complication of problems of representation as they manifest in a postcolonial context. Precisely because orality is not set against writing and, as a result, is not involved in a rescue mission of Caribbean cultural traditions, the lines between oral and scribal modes – in terms of which is the more reliable in providing accurate representations of the histories and cultures of postcolonial Caribbean peoples – are less clearly defined. John problematizes the notion that one might turn to the oral tales for a recovery of perspectives missing from official written representations, as occurs in *The Colour of Forgetting*. *Unburnable* does present instances in which the recovery of some memories, such as Sylvie's grandfather's, can fill in previously untold parts of a story. However, the fact that this formerly suppressed version of events emerges to counteract other oral tales marks a shift from earlier treatments of the problem of representation as one that tends to involve written versus oral modes. And because traditionally, the means of representation has also impacted what and how people know in the Caribbean, this novel also offers renewed perspectives on epistemological issues in postcolonial contexts. *Unburnable* shows that access to narratives embedded in oral modes does not necessarily foreclose epistemological questions. And in the same way that there is a tiered oral culture, there are multiple knowledge systems that determine what gets told, and what and how much is known, even when such knowledge is accessible from people's memories and through oral modes. The maroon community's management of its oral culture exemplifies such variation within the oral culture.

The dialogue between *The Colour of Forgetting* and *Unburnable* illustrates how Caribbean fiction is shaped by storytelling strategies while at the same time exploring age-old questions about problems of representation and the nature of storytelling itself. The novels' points of departure – Collins's attention to the value of recuperating distorted histories through a turn to oral stories and John's interrogation of orality – illuminate the shifts in critical debates in Caribbean literary and cultural studies. My reading of *Unburnable* illustrates the ongoing revisiting, rethinking and reframing of some key concerns that remain relevant as writers turn inward to examine Caribbean cultures, practices and orthodoxies in both scholarly and creative contemplations. John's revisionary treatment of orality and, by extension, maroon communities marks a shift in the representation of deeply cherished, almost sacred bastions of

Caribbean critical discourse. Fictional works by James, John and others that take up and re-examine the subjects treated by an earlier generation of writers such as Collins and Lovelace indicate a trend, in literary works, towards a more general rethinking of accepted notions. These recent writers build on earlier insightful contributions but ask new questions, and in so doing they offer fresh, more problematized accounts of Caribbean history and culture.

THREE

Inter-Performance and the Woman-Centred Poetics in *The Wine of Astonishment* and *The Book of Night Women*

Nuh bwoy cyan draw me 'roun nuh corner
Fi go show mi no Iguana
– Queen Ifrica, "Nuh Bwoy/Mek We Grow"

THE LINES ABOVE FROM Queen Ifrica's song "Nuh Bwoy" encapsulate my argument in this chapter. It articulates the assertive, sometimes confrontational, performance modes women deploy to claim agency and assert their vision of womanhood. A product of early-2000s Jamaican dancehall, "Nuh Bwoy" is an example of unabashed female resistance to sexual abuse and, more broadly, to male domination. This song also captures the spirit of active social and political engagement of formerly enslaved and indentured women in the Caribbean. More importantly in the context of this argument, the song illustrates the historical and ongoing turn to performance as a discursive space where hegemonies are contested, and where conceptions of womanhood are examined, interrogated and redefined.

In this chapter, I theorize Caribbean womanhood and its relationship with

75

and articulation through different modes of performance by analysing two novels, Earl Lovelace's *The Wine of Astonishment* (1983) and Marlon James's *The Book of Night Women* (2009), and two songs, Singing Sandra's "Die with My Dignity" and Queen Ifrica's "Nuh Bwoy". The songs are from Trinidadian calypso and Jamaican dancehall, respectively. I argue that together, these four works present complicated definitions of womanhood that simultaneously challenge and embrace some imposed models of acceptable femininity. Further, I suggest that one distinctive feature of Caribbean womanhood that these works project is that of the woman as an active participant and leader in freedom struggles. Such struggles span personal, female-specific social issues: community, national and diasporic quests for individual and collective agency. Ultimately, I contend that by defining womanhood along the lines of resistance and activism within the Caribbean anti-colonial and nationalist movements, these works recentre Caribbean liberation struggles, steering them away from their traditional masculinist associations. In that way, the "nation" is represented as a more feminized space, with the feminine aspect being more complicated, at once woman-centred and inclusive. All four of the works highlighted in this chapter bring into sharp focus the issue of citizenship in ways that contest any notion of gender blindness; instead, the role of women, their stake in nation-making and, importantly, their "sexual citizenship"[1] are brought into the open as part of broader conversations about nationhood, including who has the right and privilege to speak for and about the nation.

A discussion of womanhood – its diverse and multi-layered meanings, and its relationship to Caribbean freedom struggles and nationalism in particular – is by no means uncharted critical territory. However, my argument in this chapter intervenes in critical discourses on gender in a number of important ways. First, it examines gender through the lens of performance. While an examination of gender and performance also has precedence, for example in Forbes's *From Nation to Diaspora* (2005), this analysis centres on the inter-performative relationship between two specific live performance modes – calypso and reggae – and Caribbean performing fictions. This inter-performative analysis reveals intersections that transcend style to encompass historical, ideological and theoretical synergies between the novels and the songs. Secondly, this chapter focuses on an "inter-gender" poetics in which the feminine perspective is foregrounded in works by both male and female writers and artistes: I place in conversation two songs performed by women and two novels written by men, but all four of them deploy female speakers and narrative perspectives. This choice allows for a fresh set of theorizations about gender because of the cross-gender conversations that necessarily emerge from these works. In her editorial "Rethinking Caribbean Difference" in a special issue of *Feminist Review*, Patricia Mohammed notes that the inclusion of male scholars in the issue allows "feminism in the Caribbean to be a dialogue between men and women".[2] This somewhat revolutionary turn in feminist thought, which can be noted in feminist scholarship in the Caribbean more generally, is heightened in the works of contemporary Caribbean male writers who have chosen female narrators and gendered perspectives that foreground women's points of view; from this choice there emerges a feminist discourse that untangles itself from the man-versus-woman binary. Thus, by placing renowned nationalist writer Earl Lovelace's 1983 novel in dialogue with Marlon James's 2009 work, I argue for a revised and more overt expression of a Caribbean tradition of resistance – including Caribbean nationalism – that is rooted in female activism, as well as a more complex intersection of genders and gendered perspectives. My focus here is on nationalism as an ongoing set of discourses that engage questions of freedom and agency, and that include some of nationalism's staple concerns about the legitimacy of Caribbean cultural traditions. I also explore the engagement of Caribbean nationalist discourses with the rights of all citizens, including women, as I consider how such discourses have been represented in fiction.

The association between nationalist agendas and male dominance is an integral theme of extant revisionary feminist scholarship. For example, Hilary Beckles notes that "newly politically empowered men, described as 'founding fathers' of nation-states ... defined and declared what was the national interest and how it should be protected. ... There was no autonomous privileged place for feminist movements within the homogenized politics of nation-building."[3] This position, as Forbes points out, shaped nationalist literature in terms of its content and critical approaches.[4] As a result, one of the preoccupations of Caribbean gender critics and theorists, post-independence, is an interrogation of the masculinist representations of nationalist discourses. Such examinations address how the literature produced by Caribbean men appears to exclude women as central characters, as well as how female perspectives have been excluded, rendering Caribbean women as "voiceless".[5]

This necessity to steer nationalist writings away from their well-known maculinist associations is the stated goal of Belinda Edmondson's *Making Men: Gender, Literary Authority, and Women's Writing in Caribbean Narrative*. She writes, "If *authorship* is marked as a specifically masculine, specifically *gentlemanly*, enterprise, and national narratives are fundamental to nation formation, then in order to engage in an insurgent Caribbean nationalism the female writer must re-vision what constitutes literary authority by rewriting the paradigm of the gentleman author."[6] Forbes names Edmondson's work among a few that advance the discussion of gender and nationalism beyond a mere conversation about women's issues. However, Forbes also argues that scholars who have contributed to a more inclusive perspective of gender, including Edmondson, Paquet and Simoes, remain in the "deadlock of oppositional masculinist/feminist discourse".[7] Forbes's theorization breaks through this "oppositional deadlock" by transcending "overt textual ideologies" of gender, which in most nationalist literature evince a privileging of men and masculine perspectives. Forbes notes that the focus of *From Nation to Diaspora* is instead on "subtextual representations which may variously support, transgress, subvert, question or otherwise problematize the overt ideologies".[8] Forbes's theorization – grounded in subtextual subtleties – has certainly moved the conversation about gender beyond the binary of masculinist male writers and feminist female writers to unmask more complex discourses and a much more complicated cultural context.

Because women are the fictional performers in these novels, the subtleties that Forbes uncovers in her readings of Lamming's and Selvon's works are more explicit. They are, at least, paratextual; that is to say, the feminist discourses are less submerged and almost side by side with the masculinist representations. This is especially true in *The Wine of Astonishment*, where the story is about men but is told by a woman who intercepts the very masculinist apparatus that she is supposed to advocate. An exploration of performance, particularly the subversiveness inherent in it, allows for an arguable feminist perspective in this novel. The claim here is not that Lovelace is a feminist-womanist writer, nor that *The Wine of Astonishment* is a feminist-womanist novel. Rather, my argument is that a woman-centred poetics inevitably emerges from the choice of a particularly engaged and opinionated female performer as the narrative voice. In *The Book of Night Women*, a feminist-womanist poetics is more explicit, and therefore the dialogue between that novel and the songs performed by women is more apparent. Unpacking the performative elements of these novels and exploring their dialogue with the songs allow for an extrapolation of an interperformative relationship that highlights a shared womanist-feminist poetics. Thus the constructions of womanhood in these works are made more poignant and their nationalist import more vivid because of their grounding in (female-associated) folk expressive traditions.

Womanhood – its nature, its construction and especially notions about what constitutes good womanhood – has been at the forefront of Caribbean critical debates for decades, and has been contested terrain since slavery. As part of larger conversations about gender construction and ideology, definitions of womanhood and what constitutes proper or acceptable forms of the latter in the Caribbean context have been and remain central to feminist and larger sociocultural conversations. In fact, Patricia Mohammed identifies definitions of womanhood as one of the core concerns of Caribbean feminism. She notes that "feminism within Caribbean society has . . . been involved in an unrelenting dialogue about what constitutes manhood and masculinity and womanhood and femininity".[9] The argument I am making here is grounded in a consideration of the interactions between fiction and specific performances. In this discussion, I characterize "womanhood" as the characteristics, behaviours and experiences that define and determine how the female body is interpreted. In this conceptualization I am also referring to "woman" as the socially constructed category. However, I have opted for "womanhood" as the theoretical term which, for the purposes of this argument, I am suggesting is more dynamic, negotiable and encompassing and is constantly being redefined and re-conceptualized; womanhood is both the process of woman-making and the state of being woman.

There are multiple challenges to arriving at any coherent definition of womanhood in a Caribbean context. Beckles locates this problem of definition within the colonial history of Caribbean societies. Referring to the term "woman" as a politically "challenged one", Beckles notes that "the very notion of 'woman' was consistently challenged by women within the highly politicized gender order of colonialism, and for them it was a deeply problematic category".[10]

What Beckles addresses here is the way in which the diverse collection of women who populated slave society under colonialism destabilized the fixed category of "woman" that the dominant European order took for granted. On the one hand, there is the iconic femininity, the European-derived models of good womanhood, which in the English-speaking Caribbean have been based mainly on Victorian ideals of decency. On the other hand, because of the slave experience, black women have been, in the context of idealized femininity, defeminized, since they worked alongside men, were similarly punished and fought alongside men in freedom struggles.[11] This uncertain sense of what constitutes "woman" and by extension "womanhood" has been further complicated by the entry of other racial and ethnic groups into the Caribbean after emancipation and formal colonialism. Rawwida Baksh-Soodeen's observation that "there has been no multicultural framework . . . within which the specific experiences and interests of non-African women could be viewed and contextualized"[12] speaks to the more general problem of definition that has challenged women's and gender studies in the Caribbean. This problem arises from the fact that in the post-emancipation era, the category "woman" has been challenged to include not just black/"coloured" versus white females; East Indian, Chinese, Middle Eastern and many other groups of women and cultures with different conceptions of woman and womanhood have entered the fray.[13] With this complex set of traditions and histories, each with its own ideologies, but with some traditions overlapping with others, the notion of a coherent and cohesive conception of Caribbean womanhood has become even less likely, and the need for inclusiveness more urgent.[14] Added to the mix of races, ethnicities and cultures are issues of social class and other culture-specific markers of difference, which Caribbean feminists have consistently included in their analyses and theorizations. This complex gender landscape therefore informs the ensuing discussion, which is especially attentive to the need for more inclusive theorizing. Thus, while some of the textual examples presented here, particularly those from *The Book of Night Women* and *The Wine of Astonishment*, are specific to the experiences of black Caribbean women, others, along with the theorization that emerges around them, present more inclusive conceptions of womanhood.

Despite women's long history of involvement and leadership, "woman" has largely been viewed as a distant supporter in freedom struggles; or, where there is acknowledgement of leadership, female leaders are most frequently portrayed as outliers in movements led and dominated by men.[15] Therefore, definitions of Caribbean womanhood have generally not included activism or freedom struggles, especially at the level of leadership. Recent scholarship, particularly in the fields of history and literary analysis, has challenged the ideologically masculinist orientations and representations of freedom struggles – particularly related to nationalism – in the Caribbean. Beckles traces female activism as far back as indigenous women's involvements in anti-colonial resistance to Columbus and early colonists. He writes, "Though there are no detailed accounts of women who emerged as heroic leaders ... scattered references document aspects of their daily social and military offensive against Europeans."[16] In her revisionary work on women in Jamaican history, Lucille Mathurin Mair situates the undervaluing of female agency and activism within the context of a "monolithic plantation structure" and "masculine and white" historiography.[17] Among the areas she recovers is women's central role in destabilizing the plantation economy and structure, which eventually contributed to emancipation. She notes:

> [The enslaved woman's capacity] for action, reaction and aggression held firm in the face of determined white domination. She was among the most articulate in the slave community, and used to great effect what an exasperated West Indian official described as "that powerful instrument of attack and defence [her] tongue, which is exerted in insufferable insult". It was the noise and quarrelsomeness of the female slave virago that provided the rationalization for those who insisted that without the threat of the whip, field women were uncontrollable.[18]

It is clear that enslaved women were key participants and leaders in the "black mass communication media of word, drum, chant and dance" that Mair argues maintained "the viability of the enslaved community".[19] The inclusion of the oral culture, women's tongue and an Afro-centred vernacular culture is of particular significance to the constructions of womanhood that emerge from the performances included in this chapter. In each of the texts analysed here, the women's assertions of agency and proclamations of self-defined womanhood and, ultimately, female-centred nationalism are articulated in their performances. While scholarly attention to women's historical role in freedom struggles has increased since the 1970s, attention to the performative element – that is, the central place of orature as a vehicle for articulating women's positions on liberation movements – remains a fertile site for critical explorations.[20] More recent work on women's involvement in freedom struggles shows women actively engaged in important groups such as Marcus Garvey's Universal Negro Improvement Association and Trinidad's Negro Welfare Association, the latter of which had women in critical roles as founding members in the 1930s. This political consciousness and activism that defined black West Indian womanhood in the Caribbean also characterized the experiences of Indian women.[21]

The works under consideration construct womanhood as primarily self-determined. By this I mean that in these works – the two male-authored novels and the two songs performed by women – it is the woman who sets the parameters for how woman is constructed, and it is through performance that the state of womanhood emerges as complex, dynamic and responsive to particular socio-historical exigencies. Performance, then, is a central mode through which this complicated womanhood is revealed, thereby making woman and woman-centred performances epistemic sites; that is to say, these performances are sources of knowledge about how womanhood is constructed. Furthermore, although "woman" is defined as a category distinct from "man", womanhood is not simply defined against manhood, nor do the texts simply reject all imposed versions of womanhood. They include performances of womanhood and performances against certain ideas and expectations of the latter, even as they embrace some conventional conceptions of it.[22] The more stereotypically female performance mode used in *The Wine of Astonishment* – as well as in other forms, specifically reggae and calypso – are as much a part of the negotiation of womanhood as the bold, even aggressive, assertions that emerge from *The Book of Night Women* and the two songs.

The analysis undertaken here is especially attentive to the texts' constructions of woman as a central figure in the struggles for freedom and justice, not only for herself and for women as a group, but also for the larger colonized and formerly colonized West Indian communities. My explorations of Lovelace's representation of Eva as a central participant in postcolonial nationalist struggles, James's construction of woman as leader in emancipation movements, and both novels' intersection with the private female experiences expressed in "Die with My Dignity" and "Nuh Bwoy" highlight the diverse ways in which female activism is defined. That Caribbean literature challenges constructions of womanhood is well documented. Therefore, aside from their groundedness in performance and inter-performance, what is remarkable about these texts is the way in which they facilitate a change in the conversation of existing scholarship, which tends to focus on how women writers contest traditional constructions and reconstruct womanhood. Here, I argue for an inter-gender poetics in which woman's centrality is recovered by male writers and female performers.

Texts, Performance and Inter-Performance

Set at the time of the Shouters Prohibition Ordinance of 1917 in Trinidad (which placed a ban on the worship style of the Spiritual Baptist congregation), *The Wine of Astonishment* explores the challenges confronting the people of Bonasse, a rural community in Trinidad, as they seek recognition of their religion and worship style as well as protection of their rights in a society hostile to any cultural practice that does not adhere to an obvious European model.[23] Consistent with nationalist ideals, *The Wine of Astonishment* offers an explicit critique of the community, calling attention to the complicity of local leaders whose support of the 1917 ban shows a rejection of local cultural traditions similar to that of their former colonial leaders. This quest for recognition also includes the community's search for political representation and leaders who will recognize their indigenous African-derived religion as legitimate. The leaders presented in this novel, Bee, Ivan Morton and Bolo, are all men. But Eva, Bee's wife and apparent supporter in the fight for religious freedom, tells the story. Therefore, at face value, *The Wine of Astonishment* pursues the male-centred inflections of nationalist discourses that critics such as Edmondson address. However, this novel has also been lauded for the way in which it uses the personal narrative and a creole-speaking narrator to extol the value of what Thorpe refers to as "the creative and regenerative impulses inherent in the black creole cultural tradition"[24] that the Spiritual Baptist church represents. It is here – in Lovelace's use of a narrator cast in the tradition of female storytelling – that I locate this discussion of a more transgressive and women-centred poetics.

Earl Lovelace's attention to womanhood is often overshadowed by critical focus on his treatment of the status and role of men. The nominal consideration given to the engagement with female subjectivity in Lovelace's fiction is not surprising, given his reputation as a nationalist writer. But as Forbes argues, the critical oversight of the gender discourses in novels by nationalist authors such as Lovelace may be part of a more widespread critical inattentiveness to gender in the works of those who dominated the literary scene at the time.[25] In addition to Lovelace's well-known nationalist concerns, there are his own elisions, which are apparent in his non-fiction works such as his essay on reparations. Lovelace often omits gender as a variable in the issues of personhood that anchor much of his writing.[26] Yet analysis of his oeuvre reveals not only a strong presence of female characters but also attention to female subjectivity and, in the case of *The Wine of Astonishment*, a subversive representation of a woman as critical participant and leader in the specific nationalist struggle fictionalized in the book. Therefore, embedded within the story about religious freedom, the recognition of Afro-Caribbean cultures and the search for leadership is Lovelace's engagement with gender ideologies and a construction of womanhood that departs from his more overt commitment to male-centred nationalist struggles. Eva's performance unmasks moments of gender overlap and female dominance that are often overshadowed by nationalism and the rhetoric about gender distinctions and roles within the official culture.

The Book of Night Women is Marlon James's second novel.[27] Set mostly on Montpelier Estate in the latter part of the 1700s and early 1800s, and through a recuperation of oral storytelling strategies, the book details in graphic and compelling ways the day-to-day lives of enslaved women. Its central characters are women, and the narrative point of view is that of the performative female speaker. The action takes place mostly in the Great House or other domestic spaces where enslaved women are in relative control. The protagonist, Lilith, is the child of the plantation overseer, Jack Wilson, and an enslaved adolescent girl who dies in childbirth. Lilith is from birth set apart from other enslaved people: she is brought up by Circe, who is virtually a free person, and Circe's ostensible husband Tantalus. Lilith is also, because of her "spirited" nature and special gifts, chosen by Homer, arguably another protagonist, to be one of seven (later six) women who plan and execute the burning and destruction of Montpelier Estate. This fictionalized rebellion, like many of its real-life counterparts, is only partially successful. Most of the enslaved die as a result of the uprising, a few escape to the hills and the plantation is completely destroyed, leaving only its owner, who flees to England, and his fiancée as sole white survivors. Lilith, the only remaining Night Woman and one of the few surviving enslaved persons, tells the story to her daughter, who writes it down.

Because it centres women as primary performers and builds a story on well-developed female characters, *The Book of Night Women*'s engagement with constructions of womanhood is apparent even from a cursory reading. Here, I want to demonstrate how this work expands Lovelace's more tentative, covert female-centred discourse and argue for a kind of male-authored performing fiction that debunks the myth of the centrality of men as leaders of revolutionary movements. Furthermore, in both novels considered in this chapter, especially *The Book of Night Women*, the emphasis is less on a gender-neutral or gender-equal discourse and more on one in which the role of women is presented as the dominant one.

Singing Sandra's song "Die with My Dignity" is an artistic rendition of one woman's rant over the frustrating, unwritten law that her job prospects depend on her willingness to grant sexual favours to potential male employers. The speaker vehemently expresses her opposition to this practice and vows to abide by her own principles about sexual behaviours, even if such a defence of her principles requires violence or results in her own death. Similar to its counterpart, *The Wine of Astonishment*, "Die with My Dignity" taps into the Trinidadian performance tradition. This time the chantwell, a precursor to the calypsonian, is fully unmasked. In the song, the speaker is not veiled by a traditionally female storytelling form. Singing Sandra exploits a performance space that, as Denise Hughes-Tafen notes, has been dominated by men for most of the twentieth century.[28] Singing Sandra explicitly claims this male-dominated performance space, and in contrast to Eva in her ostensibly "female" storytelling tradition, Sandra uses calypso to launch a more explicit critique of power relations between men and women. In so doing, she projects a picture of womanhood that explicitly challenges men's imposition of a debased version of the latter. Significantly, too, Singing Sandra has chosen a performance genre that has served as a platform to mock and denigrate women, to instead claim and define womanhood, as well as to challenge male power. Furthermore, by using explicit language in this calypso, she pushes the limits of the genre, dispensing with much of the disguise of the calypsonian achieved mainly through wordplay and suggestion; instead, in this work, the woman's "grumble", as it is referred to in the Jamaican folk song, is brought to the fore and claimed as a means of protest as the speaker explicitly complains about sexual exploitation as the means of social mobility for females.[29] Indeed, the notion of the "voiceless" woman is summarily dismissed, and the female calypsonian emerges as an example of how women have engaged in critical debates through performance.

The woman-specific poetics infiltrates the calypso form to address the concerns of the female citizen in the conversation about "nation", thus insisting that this homogenizing category attends not just to the diversity but also to the fissures within the nation. The specific context of struggle that "Die with My Dignity" details is that of the presumably uneducated, working-class woman for whom work is essential not just for self-sustenance, but also for support of the larger familial community: "You want to help to mind your family, you want to help your man financially / But nowadays it really very hard to get a job as a girl in Trinidad." Here, Singing Sandra evokes an experience of black womanhood in which women work side by side with or in place of men as breadwinners. Thus, the persona speaks of a struggle that is shared by the working-class community. However, as a woman, she faces a specific form of social inequity, and she therefore frames this particular experience as a woman's problem. Although she encounters a challenge in her efforts to address the family's economic needs, it is her status as a woman that becomes the basis of her socio-economic vulnerability. Therefore, the centring of the female self in which the persona is engaged in this song is essential for the well-being of the community or the "nation".

"Nuh Bwoy" is also about sexual exploitation, with the performer assuming the persona of an underaged female who confronts and speaks directly to grown men guilty of pedophilia. As in "Die with My Dignity", the female performer in "Nuh Bwoy" openly rejects sexual exploitation and engages in a verbal battle akin to that which enslaved women used against men involved in pedophilia in the days of slavery. "Nuh Bwoy" also addresses dancehall performance culture, which the song's persona identifies as a source for promoting what she considers unacceptable or indecent expressions of sexuality. Like

"Die with My Dignity", it presents a woman in a traditionally male-dominated performance space, in this case the Jamaican dancehall. Since the 1980s, when dancehall music emerged as a prominent subgenre of reggae music, this form has come under severe criticism for its debasement of women. Although such characterizations do not fully account for the gamut of themes in the genre, nor its treatment of women, a preoccupation with women and female sexuality is a stock feature of dancehall music. A number of female artistes have sought to gain their performance credentials by following in the path laid by men. Some, such as Tanya Stephens, have used this performance genre to treat "conscious" or social issues. However, when womanhood, or sexuality, is the main theme, men continue to control the terms of the discourse on gender because female performers tend to behave similarly to their male counterparts; while they may swap the genders, they still remain within the same paradigm. The most notable of such female performers is Lady Saw, whose oeuvre includes responses to songs by men, in which she seeks to contest men on the grounds that male artistes have laid.[30] Much of Queen Ifrica's work, including the piece I have selected for analysis, changes the terms of the conversation and opens new possibilities for the ways in which the genre is used as a discursive space.

Both songs under consideration here – one calypso, the other belonging to dancehall, two modes of performance that have come to be associated with men and gender discourses different from those engaged in these works – also situate themselves in other conversations, such as Donette Francis's exploration of sexual citizenship. Francis argues that "attention to sexual citizenship . . . opens a window into sexuality as a crucial yet underexamined aspect of female subjectivity and citizenship both inside and outside the nation".[31] The performers' explicit and confrontational engagement with female sexuality, as a site for engaging power relationships and contesting abuse of power, centres women's sexed bodies and sexual relationships as a crucial battleground for laying claim to Caribbean citizenship in the post-independence era. These works also demonstrate how attention to performance extends the discursive range in conversations about vexed issues such as female sexuality, while calling attention to other forms (outside of the literary) where illegitimate claims to the female body have been ceaselessly contested.

Performance and Inter-Performance

Aside from their shared thematic and ideological inclinations, *The Wine of Astonishment* and *The Book of Night Women* are marked by their performative synergies, specifically the ways in which they tap into some inherent features of the novel to fashion a Caribbean adaptation of the form. Consistent with the novel's intrinsic tendencies towards improvisation, these examples of performing fiction engage directly with the local performance culture. Both novels emanate performativity through their engagement in a constant appropriation, rewriting and re-appropriation of another's words and another expressive system.[32] *The Wine of Astonishment* and *The Book of Night Women* therefore signify upon (to use the term popularized by Henry Louis Gates) what Bakhtin and Kristeva refer to as broader structure and an anterior context that includes history, society and the entire social and cultural framework.[33] Lovelace and James use personal narratives, specifically informal storytelling, as their primary narrative strategies, and they mine these oral forms by including an array of other types of Caribbean orature. In her performance, Eva includes quotations from written texts and impersonations of other characters, and incorporates many oral and written forms such as sermons, songs, proverbs and anecdotes in her general narration. The intersection between formal (performative) choices and meaning in each of these texts effectively portrays the poetics of performance in the way I use the term throughout this book. James's narrator includes the anterior culture in similar ways with her use of proverbs, tracing and Jamaican expletives. The battles over ideology that *The Wine of Astonishment* presents are expressed through an evocation of this array of performance modes. *The Book of Night Women* recreates a brutal plantation society, which makes the use of confrontational and aggressive oral forms in this work particularly judicious. A "performative style" or an "aesthetic of orality" is not simply a stylistic choice; performance modes are essential to meaning in the sense that meaning – at both the thematic and ideological levels – emanates from the performance modes themselves.

Funso Aiyejina has argued that Eva "is an aggregate of the multiple voices in her community and . . . evolves into a chantwell/griot figure".[34] Cast in a male-dominated oral form, Eva enjoys the latitude that a chantwell traditionally has in the public performance space. Noting that Eva is "not a chantwell by normal definition", Aiyejina acknowledges that "she affirms the notion of women as the active carriers and . . . vocalizers of tradition". An examination of the implications of the term "carrier" is useful here: implicit in Aiyejina's reading of Eva is the idea that she straddles different performance traditions, each of which is gender specific. If we read Eva's performance as one that recovers elements of the chantwell narrator, then we can also understand her as more than "an active carrier of tradition", since chantwells were inherently subversive and creative.[35] She not only carries and "vocalizes" existing traditions; she also critiques and reshapes these traditions through her performance. As a reinvented chantwell, Eva's performance is quintessentially carnivalesque: she is operating in a traditionally female genre and domestic space, but as Aiyejina's title suggests, when a female performer is 'unmasked", the audience sees or hears a chantwell – a traditionally male performer in a public space. Aiyejina's characterization of Eva as chantwell narrator therefore speaks to the ways in which performances can reveal the elusiveness and variability of gender constructions.

Both novels open with a framing device, a stock feature of both formal and informal storytelling practices in the cultures whose orature shapes these works. *The Wine of Astonishment* is framed with "God don't give you more than you can bear",[36] while James begins, "People think blood red, but blood don't got no colour."[37] In *The Wine of Astonishment*, Eva uses a creole version of a Bible verse that has become part of the oral tradition of her speech community as a frame for the story about her struggles for religious freedom. The opening frame in *The Book of Night Women*, "People think . . .", is drawn directly from Jamaican informal speech culture. The choice of framing device here performs the novel's confrontational posture and immediately reveals its emphasis on counter-discourse. "People think blood red" signals scepticism, which is immediately confirmed by the counteractive statement "but blood don't got no colour". This early turn away from conventional beliefs sets up the context of struggle that preoccupies this work. In both instances, the framing device locates the novel's narrative strategy within a situated performance tradition.[38] Richard Bauman refers to such an opening as "an interpretive frame within which the messages being communicated are to be understood"; these words "are to be interpreted as the words of someone other than the speaker".[39] These framing devices belong to the Caribbean communities in which the novels are set, and therefore establish their narrative strategy and overall poetics as community-based oral-performance modes and nationalist literature because of their rootedness in the indigenous expressive forms. Performance therefore functions as the central interpretive mode, since the cultural location of the texts and the performances they evoke are integral to the meanings they convey.

The Wine of Astonishment and *The Book of Night Women* also epitomize performing fiction in the way they set up a dialectical relationship between speaker and audience. In other words, the interlocutory features of storytelling are inscribed on the page through each writer's use of culturally coded performance cues or novelistic techniques that show a clear speaker-audience dynamic. In *The Wine of Astonishment*, this dialogic relationship is achieved through the inclusion of specific terms such as "You will hear it when I come to it" (23) and "Let me tell you" (31). The use of such explicitly conversational phrases as the novel's structuring device illustrates more than the overall oral-performative quality of the text. It also evinces one important element of the particular storytelling tradition that Lovelace recovers here: the implied presence of an audience. This is evident in the way Lovelace crafts Eva as a narrator, which impels the reader to imagine actual conversation.

This performer-audience interaction also infuses *The Book of Night Women*; it is apparent in the conversational relationship that James sets up between the primary narrator and her multiple interlocutors. As the following example illustrates, James also achieves such an interactive relationship through the omniscient narrator's direct address to an immediate audience: "I goin' call her Lilith. You can call her what they call her" (3). However, the novel is characterized by a unique conversational quality in which the gap between omniscient narration and characters' dialogue is substantially narrowed. Because quotation marks are excluded from the novel and James uses identical linguistic registers for both narrator and characters, it is difficult to differentiate speech that is directed at the reader/audience from that which takes place among characters:

> Anyway, things me have to say can wait till tonight, Pallas say and leave. Lilith and Homer in the kitchen, one eating and one drinking soup, neither saying nothing. (27)

Montpelier done have a mistress, Lilith say.
—And lo and behold, she not you. Second time me telling you that, Homer say and look straight at Lilith until Lilith look away. Lilith go down to the cellar. (100)

Although dashes are used to mark dialogue, such markings are only partial, since there are no clear breaks between the end of a character's speech and the beginning of the narrator's. The absence of quotation marks creates in the reader the feeling that he or she is being directly addressed or, at other times, listening on a conversation among different speakers. This sense of a conversation among multiple interlocutors also problematizes the notion of narrator, making narration in this text more like a conversation. Through this technique, then, the reader becomes part of an internal audience, which in turn changes what we would refer to as a reading experience to a reader-text *interaction* that more closely resembles an audience listening in on an actual conversation. These interventions also give *The Book of Night Women* its polyphonic texture.

Language choice, which has always been central to discussions about the presence of Caribbean speaking voices and speech culture in literature from the region, is also germane to the discussion about the performative orientations of *The Wine of Astonishment* and *The Book of Night Women*.[40] The novels are written in Trinidadian and Jamaican vernacular respectively, and while my focus is not on language per se, language usage is important because the performance mode of informal storytelling that is being appropriated here is defined by the creole languages that performers use. In *The Wine of Astonishment*, the narrator, Eva, is a working-class creole speaker, and the informality of the setting in which she tells the story, as well as that of the narrative form she uses, makes the choice of Trinidadian Creole logical, if not essential. For *The Book of Night Women*, language – more precisely, linguistic performance – is of special significance because it is largely through the choice of culturally specific aggressive and, at times, profane language that the characters' militancy and their vociferous defence of womanhood are articulated. Expletives are a core feature of the storytelling strategies James employs, and these signal a forceful performance of womanhood that is central to the dominance of women in the especially oppressive setting of a slave plantation.

The formal similarities between these two novels and the songs "Die with

My Dignity" and "Nuh Bwoy" are also crucial, and manifest most vividly in their shared interactive quality, use of creole language, and bold and aggressive tone that explicitly expresses the performers' militancy and activism. Stylistically, the songs are more closely aligned to *The Book of Night Women*, which takes the feminist turns anticipated in Lovelace's *The Wine of Astonishment* in more radical directions. Singing Sandra's tone is confrontational, clearly registering her strong aversion to the system of female oppression that keeps women in economic dependency and undermines their place as legitimate citizens of the "nation". Similarly, Queen Ifrica's irate tone expresses her infuriation with a kind of sexual exploitation that has been accepted as an inarguable part of gender relationships in her society.

As examples of calypso and dancehall reggae, the songs are also firmly located in call-and-response tradition, which aligns them closely with the interactive quality that defines the two novels. While Singing Sandra's interaction with her audience is more apparent in her live performances of this song, both songs tell an audience or interlocutor about the men they deem decadent. While they do not directly address their male targets, the women appropriate other oral forms such as tracing and gossip, bordering on a kind of public brawl or "cuss-out".[41] Thus, the songs insert more stereotypical female forms into these established male-associated genres of dancehall and calypso.

Because their constructions of womanhood and the fresh theorizations they facilitate are located in performance, all four of these works also provide fertile ground for meta-performative discourses. By this, I mean that in addition to allowing for fresh theorizations about gender, the four texts offer scope for contemplations about the nature of Caribbean performances themselves. Furthermore, these texts engage genres that interrogate the boundaries of gendered performance. Lovelace's Eva is ostensibly cast as a traditional female storyteller, but as Aiyejina shows, Eva may also be read as a masked chantwell narrator.[42] In *The Book of Night Women*, the female narrators and characters adopt performance styles traditionally associated with a kind of warrior (male) griot. Similarly, Singing Sandra and Queen Ifrica inhabit two male-dominated forms to claim and define woman. In all of these representations, despite the cross-gender performances, the women assert and embrace the category of woman; these works therefore project a self-determined womanhood that embraces existing societal expectations and straddles multiple (gendered) performance modes to demand the primary role in demarcating their place in society and in shaping conversations about women, particularly in their role as activists.

Debunking the Myth of the Male Leader

Beckles and Shepherd delineate how the inherent masculinist orientations of historical discourse have elided women's contributions to anti-slavery movements. Beckles notes that this tendency to exclude women also appears in nationalist movements as direct suppression of women's contribution, skills and leadership.[43] In this section, I examine how recent performing fictions, including Lovelace's hardcore, nationalist novel, have aligned themselves with popular culture to topple what Beckles refers to as the "boys-only club" of Caribbean nationalism (and, more broadly, freedom struggles). The move away from male-centred representations of liberation work that dominates *The Book of Night Women* appears as a consequence of the performance culture that James creatively exploits to tell this story of leadership struggles. Both novels – explicitly or tacitly – address women's historical centrality in such work. *The Book of Night Women* not only (re)presents women, but also potentially changes the terms on which conversations about anti-slavery and anti-colonial activities are engaged.

All four works displace male leaders, or more precisely male authority, primarily by controlling the modes of representation. *The Wine of Astonishment* appears to reflect Lovelace's reputed preoccupation with male leadership in its depiction of the mechanisms of public, political and religious control over the fictional creole community. Bee, the religious and community leader; Ivan Morton, the homegrown elected leader (and his political opponents); and Bolo, the would-be community leader, are *The Wine of Astonishment*'s ostensible subjects. But the narrative control Eva wields eclipses the perceived central position of the men in this text. Her narrative performance blurs the lines of demarcation between male and female roles, thus laying bare the façade of male dominance and further destabilizing one assumption about gender roles – that men are the ones who take charge in public affairs and women follow their lead – on which this story rests.

The disjuncture between the idea of male leadership and the prominence of woman that Eva's role as narrator represents resonates with Forbes's theorization of a hermaphroditic gender construct for Caribbean societies. Forbes argues that "gender is one of the primary constructs by which nations are represented" and notes that "West Indian societies, like the Western societies which shaped their beginnings, have represented themselves at the level of nation in masculinist terms, a mode of representation which was particularly visible and focused in the era of West Indian nationalism".[44] But Forbes also acknowledges the contrast to this ideological construct in the lived experience of Caribbean peoples, noting that women often play roles ideologically assigned to men. She argues that the resistance to iconic masculinity is rooted in plantation experience:

> In seeking a way to describe/understand the self-(re)presentation of the slave, I propose the concept of the slave collective as hermaphrodite, which is diametrically opposed to the concept of iconic masculinity. . . . This hermaphroditic presence, essentially a manifestation of the carnivalesque, opened the way for a gender-equal concept of social organization which has been constantly circumvented since emancipation, however, by the society's attraction to patriarchy.[45]

In Forbes's conceptualization, West Indian societies have always been at once masculinist and gender-equal. She sees the hermaphroditic gender construction of the enslaved community as a response of both enslaved men and women to "a man [the slave master] who had the freedom, privilege and power",[46] and whom they fought as one gender-neutral "guerilla army".

Despite its apparent focus on male leaders, *The Wine of Astonishment* shows, through Eva's performance, the people of Bonasse – men and women – confronting a common enemy: neocolonial leaders who refuse to grant them the religious rights afforded to members of established churches. Ideologically, and to some extent in reality, the men take the lead in finding ways of tackling the challenges that the community faces, but women are also at the forefront of the fight for religious freedom. It is the less obvious involvement of women that Eva's performance allows the audience to see. Lovelace engages with both the ideological and experiential facets of gender relationships in the Caribbean, wrestling with a simultaneous rhetoric and practice of male privilege alongside the more inter-gender and cross-gender realities of this creole society.

Lovelace's choice of a narrator cast in a "female" storytelling tradition offers a viable alternative view of women's involvement and contribution to liberation struggles. Against the backdrop of the failure of male leaders and the dominant presence of a female voice and body in this novel, there is interpretative room for at least a reconfiguration of what constitutes leadership in postcolonial nationalist movements. Eva's role as storyteller provides her with the latitude to inhabit several other spaces and bodies. Her representation of her active role in the church and community reveals a much more complicated picture of gender interactions than the novel's explicit attention to men initially suggests. Thus the heretofore easy conflation of male and nationalist leader is dismantled in the hands of one of the Caribbean's foremost nationalist writers. Despite the novel's overt attention to men as central characters in the story and the implication of their virtual dominance as leaders in these movements, it is arguable that Eva at least shares with Bee the lead role in this performance because of the recourse to woman-associated storytelling. As first-person narrators tend to do, Eva provides the lens through which the narrative and, by extension, all the characters are represented and read; in this regard, her power is unmatched by any other character's, including the men who are the apparent leaders in the story. Yet this argument is counterbalanced by attentiveness to how that same transgressive performance retains traces of male dominance.

One explicit goal of nationalism is to eclipse differences such as ethnicity, race, social class and gender under the convenient and avowedly progressive rubric of "nation". As Caribbean scholars have repeatedly noted, rather than offering proclaimed neutrality, the "nation" is often framed as masculine. By foregrounding the agency of the collective, Eva emasculates the nationalist project in this novel, replacing it with a more gender-neutral struggle. Her use of repetition as a central rhetorical strategy, along with the communal ethos that underlines her representation of events, keeps the battle over culture within the context of a collective struggle, thereby undermining the prominence of men. Eva's use of the collective "we" throughout the novel – even as she discusses male leaders – expresses her investment in a less male-centred freedom struggle, in terms of both the impact of oppression and the means of contestation. In the chapter titled "We Church", Eva presents the central conflict as a problem that involves not just the men who are supposed to lead, but the entire group: "Now everything *we* do is something wrong. *They* complain that *we* sing too loud, *we* disturbing the peace. *They* send six police with a paper to make us move the church from off the main street. *We* build new church. *They* decide it ain't build strong enough; *they* make us break it down; and when *we* try to build another one, *they* wouldn't okay the plans" (33; emphasis mine). Although Bee is the leader of the church, the emphasis here is on the congregation. Here, the challenges confronting the church are not framed as problems that Bee, the (male) leader of the church, must address by himself. The juxtaposition of "we" and "they" sets the community against the ruling class, while it erases gender differences by placing emphasis on a class or group struggle: the working-class blacks against the ruling class. What Lovelace offers here is a reenactment of the gender-neutral conflicts that enslaved people faced – what Forbes references in her theorization of a hermaphroditic Caribbean gender landscape. Similarly, when Eva comforts Bee, her repetition of "we" shifts the burden of leadership and the disappointment that accompanies failure from Bee the leader to Bee and Eva, the two leaders: "I tell him: 'Bee, boy, *we* still have the children, and *we* have some years left and health and strength. If God give *us* this is because *we* could bear it'" (13; emphasis mine). This example places emphasis on a couple, co-workers, not on a man who is strong enough to withstand the challenges to free expression of culture. When Eva encourages Bee to be patient, although freedom to worship is not forthcoming, the collective "we" resurfaces to define the community through erasure of gender distinctions. Eva opportunistically exploits rhetorical strategies and the space she is granted to tell – to shape, even – how the struggle to reconfigure the discourse about freedom might look, and in this way she helps to move conversations concerning nationalist struggles away from their "boys only" inclinations.

Nationalist writers have consistently insisted that Caribbean indigenous cultures should constitute the expressive tools used in representation of the "nation". Edmondson characterizes such efforts as explicitly masculinist and cites the way nationalist writers such as Brathwaite and Lamming framed their deliberations about the significance and necessity of folk culture in Caribbean literature as prominent examples of men's apparent control of that aspect of nationalism. Paradoxically, while rhetoric about the significance of folk culture in the construction of nationalist identities may well be male dominated, when read as performing fiction, a somewhat more complicated picture emerges. Performance-driven literary works in which the promotion of folk culture manifests as a fictive tool potentially undermines explicit and perhaps intentional privileging of men as the dominant voices and workers in nationalist endeavours. Through this recourse to performance, Lovelace's nationalist novel exemplifies a movement away from the masculinization that Edmondson suggests and a shift towards acknowledging the nationalist discursive space as two-gender terrain.

Not surprisingly, a claim such as this one – that Lovelace opts for a female-associated form of orature-performance – raises other questions, such as those that emerge in Sandhya Shetty's claim that *The Wine of Astonishment* "feminizes the colonized or politically weak".[47] Shetty's insightful essay "Masculinity, National Identity and the Feminine Voice in *The Wine of Astonishment*" makes a compelling argument that potentially challenges any notion that this choice of a female narrator might be read as a sign that the male-centred focus of nationalism is about to abate. Arguing that the feminine voice is "recruited" to serve the phallocentric nationalist agency, Shetty summarizes her argument about the tension between nationalism and gender in *The Wine of Astonishment* in the following way: "From this told and apparently unimpeachable story, we may be able to unravel the other story – of male political and cultural hegemony – of ventriloquism – the manipulations of gendered voices – in this anti-colonial narrative of gendered voice I hope to demonstrate a relationship between male nationalist hegemony and narrativity."[48] That *The Wine of Astonishment* continues the well-known male-centred outlook of Caribbean nationalism is quite defensible. However, to read this text as a total manipulation of the female voice and the choice of a female narrator as serving to only to reinforce a male agenda and rhetorical tradition is to miss some of the complications of the *lived* Caribbean gender experience that are drawn out in the novel, as well as those of the nationalist movement itself that are creatively represented in this work. Importantly, too, such a claim ignores the subversive potential of performance.

Lovelace's turn to the performance tradition is itself an important move away from male domination because that choice changes, or at least alters, the conversation about nationalism by putting gender on notice as a vital component of the latter, instead of serving only to "reinforce rigid gender ideologies", as Shetty suggests; because Lovelace uses a female voice and performance mode to tell the story, gender appears as an area of contestation. In other words, the presence of a female voice in a text about men introduces gender constructions as one of the novel's subjects, and also compels critics to recognize gender as a problem in nationalist discourses. Furthermore, as has been noted, women were never truly absent from the nationalist struggle, nor were they missing from nationalist fiction.[49] In those regards, too, Lovelace (inadvertently, perhaps) recovers women's important roles, even if his aim is to "recruit women in the service of a male agenda". Thus, Lovelace's choice of narrator constitutes an inevitable representation of things as they have been. Whether or not this representation of the reality of women's place in nationalism aligns with Lovelace's reputed and self-proclaimed preoccupation with men as the key, if not exclusive, players in nationalist endeavours, Lovelace's use of Eva puts gender in nationalist fiction on notice in unprecedented ways. That is to say, *The Wine of Astonishment* includes woman in a way that is analogous to her active participation in actual nationalist struggles. Therefore, while the tradition of male hegemony in which *The Wine of Astonishment* can be placed cannot be ignored – even in a revisionary reading of Lovelace's treatment of gender – analysis that is attentive to the intersection of gender and performance allows us other interpretive possibilities.

Any notion that women rely on men's leadership and actions to ensure cultural legitimacy is dispelled in Eva's open expressions of her frustrations over Bee's reluctance to go ahead and "break the law":

> I could understand how Bee, tired of waiting for this war to end, feeling he must give a answer to Bolo, wanting in a *man-way* to rise to the *man-challenge* in front of him, not to mention wanting a hold on the congregation . . . I could understand how Bee would want to break the law . . . but talking ain't making it break, and we have children. The children hearing him . . . they waiting to see him break the law. (51; emphasis mine)

Aside from Eva's backslide into an implied reliance on male leaders, her explicit critique of Bee, and by extension nationalist male leadership, is noteworthy. Of particular significance is her expressed desire to see Bee rise to the challenge to defend his culture in "a man-way". The open engagement with gender as a factor in this struggle goes beyond the obvious observation that men have dominated, or are perceived to have dominated, nationalist endeavours. Eva's reliance on rhetorical devices in her repetition of "man", "man-challenge" and "man-way" underlines her struggles and therefore the text's engagement with gender as a problem within the nationalist movement. Furthermore, Eva's brazen inclusion of "man-challenge" not only claims the "boys only" ethos of nationalism; it also places the gap between rhetoric and action in clear view. Subtextually, there is the insertion of a question as to whether the challenge being addressed here is a gendered challenge at all. Eva's agitation arises mainly from the fact that Bee says he would break the law, but "the law don't break yet". When we consider that Lovelace, the man and the masculinist, is the writer, it becomes plausible that this novel also represents an awareness of the incomplete, gender-biased rhetoric of nationalism.

Eva's performance further destabilizes perceptions about male power and leadership in the way she calls attention to Bee's failure to create a path for male succession: "Reggie is a boy-child, eight years old, just at a time in his life when he looking for a father in his father, and what he seeing is this man mumbling how he going to break the law and the law still there" (52). Eva's annoyance with Bee is evident in her shift in tone, as well as in her outright criticism of Bee's failure to take charge as she considers her options as a kind of alternative to his inaction: "What to do? I could talk to the child, tell him about the histories . . . and how the law strong and the police wicked and we few, and how is not every time that a man could do the things that he say he going to do. But how to do that? How to let a boy-child know as soon as his eyes open to the world that we ain't have no power. No. I can't do that to my own child. . . . I have to let him see his father as warrior" (52). Even as she acknowledges Bee's powerlessness, the weight of an entrenched preference for men as leaders continues to bear heavily even on a woman who performs society's challenge to patterns of male dominance. Eva is still willing to indulge the idea that men are the exclusive leaders, even as she openly acknowledges her role as not just storyteller, but also as the one who has to take the lead, the woman who must train the next generation of male leaders. The fact that Reggie is a "boy-child" makes her feel more responsible for providing him with a "warrior" role model, even though she knows Bee really is not a warrior and that the larger structure, as well as Bee's personal inadequacies, render him virtually incapable of making any substantial impact. This tension complicates the claim to a challenged masculine ideal even further. It is arguable that Eva's willingness to defer to the gender ideology of her society, even as she openly critiques the "man's" lack of leadership, indicates that women are in some ways among the most ardent upholders of nationalism in which men exclusively are accorded power. However, if we take into account the fact that Lovelace – the "arch nationalist" who actively promotes male leaders – is the author of this work, then what Eva's oscillating perspective reveals is a deeper investment in the kind of male-centred nationalism on which scholars such as Edmondson have insisted.[50]

Even as Eva paints a picture of Bee as a compromised leader, she positions herself as the one the family now turns to for the leadership that Bee should be providing, according to their society's expectations. Eva presents herself as someone who has the answers that Bee lacks and the tenacity to persevere when Bee does not seem to be able to cope. She represents herself as a leader through her inclusion of scenes in which Bee's vulnerability is apparent: "Bee there . . . standing up by the kitchen door, with his two hands stretch out across the door like how Jesus Christ had his hands when they crucify him on the cross, and his face half turned to me, listening, as if what I have to tell the children is for him too" (1). According to Eva's representation, Bee also sees her as his source of strength. Like the children, he looks to her for explanations, words that provide guidance and leadership. The contrast between Bee and Eva is therefore quite stark, made visible to the reader through Lovelace's presentation of Eva's representational power as narrator and her skilful use of storytelling strategies that allow her to characterize Bee and the other men in the ways I have described.

The multiple performances Eva inhabits suggest that she is stepping out of the role of a woman telling a tale and into the role assigned to more public, traditionally male performers. For example, she opens the worship scene in which they break the law with "Like a strong wind, like a mighty water, like a river of fire, like a thousand doves with wind" (62). The tone of these opening sentences, the rhetorical devices and the paralinguistic features that the audience is prompted to imagine are those of a preacher who, within the context of the story, is most likely male. As Eva continues in this passage, her voice and performance slip back into the traditional "woman" voice that the audience has become accustomed to hearing from her. Similarly, when she relates Ivan Morton's speech, Eva adopts the voice, tone and other performance strategies of the political orator, and at times her performative voice is virtually intertwined with Ivan's, which highlights the inter-gender performance of which I speak. This slippage in and out of different (gendered) performative modes is crucial, as it represents Eva's refusal to fully accept the "iconic masculinity" that the society offers and instead challenges perceptions of a stable, uniquely male freedom struggle. Indeed, such oscillations imply Lovelace's problematization, whether inadvertent or deliberate, of the presumedly stable-gendered categories and roles within the nationalist movement and the larger Caribbean society.

"What Can a Niggerwoman Do . . . ?"

While it is clear from the performance mode that Lovelace deploys in *The Wine of Astonishment*, as well as from the choice of a female speaker, that there is some disruption of the perceived dominance of men as leaders in this fictionalized freedom struggle, Lovelace's representation is equivocal. Although Eva is by no means a self-effacing storyteller, there are several moments in which she accords men privilege in leadership and educational advancement. The differential and preferential treatment of men that seeps into Eva's performance finds no place in *The Book of Night Women*, in which James unequivocally places women at the centre as leaders in emancipation quests. By making women and womanhood the primary subjects of his novel, James amplifies the shift in male-authored performing fiction to a womanist-feminist poetics.

In the penultimate page of *The Book of Night Women*, the novel's narrator asks, "What can a niggerwoman do but endure? What can me do but tell the story? Who is there when we recall great womens?" (416) These questions euphemistically call attention to women's critical roles in the freedom struggles that *The Book of Night Women* details, as well as the place of orature in such struggles. Because these questions are placed near the end of the novel, the reader already knows that endurance for these enslaved women has taken on new meanings. For the "nigger" Night Women, to "endure" is to "fight and bear it". Therefore, in this context, "telling" (or retelling) moves beyond a necessity to recover stories about women's active roles; it constitutes a larger counter-discourse whereby these inclusions of female roles change the conversation about the history of liberation struggles. James's contribution is especially significant in this regard because of its unwavering recuperation of women as leaders at the forefront of the renowned, destabilized Jamaican plantation system and of the enslaved people's ultimate emancipation. The storyteller in *The Book of Night Women* presents a picture of plantation life in which women dominate the enslaved community on a day-to-day basis, undermine the official white male power structure and successfully plan and execute a rebellion that significantly disrupts life on the Montpelier plantation, creating notable financial loss to the plantation owner. Thus, *The Book of Night Women* makes a bolder intervention into the gender discourse by moving the conversation beyond gender-equal freedom struggles. The female characters in this novel are victims of sexual abuse, as well as of torture similar to that meted out to men, and like men, they live under the constant fear of (or hope for) death; yet this novel presents women as the ones with the grit, fortitude and extraordinary organizational skills to destabilize and completely disrupt the plantation structure.

The woman-centred poetics revealed by an inter-performative analysis of *The Book of Night Women*, as well as of "Die with my Dignity" and "Nuh Bwoy", displays a level of engagement with female activism and womanhood that reaches beyond Lovelace's initial shift from a male-centred nationalist account of postcolonial liberation struggles. The logical corollary of this treatment is an explicit exposure of different strains of the masculinist power structure in colonial and modern-day Caribbean societies. The section that follows explores how female performers claim and redefine womanhood by presenting themselves as vocal and courageous revolutionaries. The militant postures and aggressive performance modes that the personas in each of these works adopt centre women as power brokers in contestations over control of the female body, socio-economic advancement and freedoms for the wider colonized or otherwise oppressed community. At the same time, the representation of Lilith's self-fashioning in *The Book of Night Women* highlights the subversive potential of performance. Thus, by accentuating the woman-centred poetics initiated in *The Wine of Astonishment*, these later works signal new directions: first, in breaking the female writer/male writer binary in Caribbean feminist conversations, and second, in the possibilities they open for inter-performative dialogues between performing fictions and texts from popular culture.

One important ideological shift that emerges from these works is their explicit disavowal of the accepted male-centred power structure. In *The Wine of Astonishment*, although Eva is critical of Bee and calls his "man-ways" into question, for the most part she leaves the constructed "iconic masculinity" of nationalism and Caribbean societies intact or, at best, leaves it moderately ruffled. *The Book of Night Women* sets the reality of powerful womanhood that it presents squarely against the notions and practices of male hegemony, and therefore tackles head-on the disjuncture between the ideological sense of gender and the lived experiences that is endemic to Caribbean societies. In one of her early appearances in the novel, Lilith initiates the novel's sustained attack on this established gender hierarchy:

> [Lilith] swing the club, clap the ball clear 'cross the field and make one run to all four base and beat the boys but couldn't understand when the wet nurse slap her and say that a good girl was supposed to make manchild win. Lilith cuss and ask if manchild can't win if girl don't lose and she get another slap.... Lilith tell them same boys that is 'cause they have worm between them legs why they can't run fast like she and the girl get a swift kick from a passing niggerwoman who tell her there be a grave already dug for the uppity. Lilith cuss under her tongue and say, Is you must go to grave since you already stink like dead puppy. (4)

This early glimpse of the "spirited" Lilith sets the tone for the novel's articulation of a kind of womanhood that projects its strength from within – and even in spite of – the hierarchical plantation system in which gender is one of the bases of stratification. That the person who attempts to put Lilith back in "her place" is a woman reveals the extraordinary entrenchment of this system of stratification. Here, "uppity", a term usually used to describe the self-assertion of blacks, is extended to women, thus underscoring the centrality of gender demarcation in the formative Caribbean society being represented. In the same way that there is a *place* designated for blacks, there is also one designated for women. Lilith's confrontation with the power structure is direct; she questions the notion that men's agency must come at the expense of women's, as shown in the last line of the above passage. Lilith's defence is also remarkable because of the rhetorical tools she chooses and the performance posture she adopts. Her recourse to tracing or cussing at this point in the novel foreshadows the centrality of aggressive performances in projecting the kind of womanhood that vehemently departs from and challenges the established power structure.

The battle against an established gender-based order in this early example anticipates *The Book of Night Women's* more extensive treatment of women's leadership in the Montpelier rebellion. The novel presents the destruction of Montpelier Estate as an exclusive triumph of womanhood and women's work, and its virtual erasure of men from the freedom struggles is explicit. Motivated by the example of the Haitian revolution, the women in this novel determine for themselves what will make them successful: "All it take is some smart thinking. That be why womens do the thinking and plotting, just like woman do in the Africa" (337). While the women are credited for "smart thinking", men are presented as hindrances to the rebellion: "Yes", Homer says, "[men] strong in arm and strong in leg, but they head weak. They don't have the bearing for planning and thinking and waiting, 'specially waiting. That be woman work" (352). Of note here is Homer's tone, which is less oppositional than it is matter of fact or dismissive, an interesting way of overturning what has been taken for granted – that men have been at the helm of any emancipation efforts. The men whom Pallas dismisses for seeing the rebellion as an opportunity to sexually exploit a white woman (294) or to punish black women who refused their sexual advances in the past (390) support Homer's view of men as lacking the focus and capacity to participate in a sustained struggle for freedom. The examples of men's inadequacies in *The Book of Night Women* expand Eva's critique of Bee, who, according to Eva, did not have the courage to "break the law" and prove his manhood and warriorhood to his son and heir.

James's presentation of ineffective, obstructive and frivolous men is contrasted with his presentation of the women, whose brave acts during the Montpelier rebellion confound the population: "The redcoats scratching them head 'cause they can't explain how so much nigger manage to plan something so big and still keep it quiet. . . . Rumour start to spread that is woman who plan the whole thing, which make white man and niggerman, slave and free man perplex, cause such devious and nefarious thinking was beyond the capabilities of the fairer sex, much less a bunch of goat-rutting savage womens" (402). Strikingly, both black and white men are perplexed by the women's feat, which underscores the fact of the enslaved women's double (or multiple) marginalization. But by successfully disrupting the status quo of the plantation, these female characters also unsettle the racist-patriarchal structure in which women are placed on the lowest rung of the colour- and gender-based hierarchy.

In response to the question of what differentiates black men's writing from that of black women, Audre Lorde suggests that women use the personal as a basis for exploring more general social and political issues.[51] In "Die with My Dignity" and "Nuh Bwoy", the personas foreground their personal struggles as a platform from which to expose and challenge the more general hierarchical system of their societies, which favour male leadership. Interestingly, although *The Book of Night Women* was authored by a man, in this work, too, the intersection between public and private realms is central, as the quests for freedom from slavery are explored through the women's domestic and private experiences. This is a key point of intersection among the four works under consideration here. Whereas *The Wine of Astonishment* exclusively focuses on a stock nationalist theme – the defence of the indigenous culture – which it treats as a public concern, "Nuh Bwoy", "Die with My Dignity" and *The Book of Night Women* explore the larger concept of liberation through a focus on women's private, domestic experiences. In all three of these works, female sexuality is a central basis of women's oppression and a staging ground for the claim to a liberated womanhood.

The persona in "Die with My Dignity" is presented with a set of unwritten rules in which the masculinist power structure has laid out the terms by which a working-class woman can achieve socio-economic mobility. But she dispenses with those standards and claims the right to her body and how it gets used:

> Using the power of the kazan position, waiting to abuse and exploit any woman
>   To get to work you have to go to bed with he, become a slave second wife and deputy
>   And as a next woman get on the line, he start to tell you you ain't good you can't wine.

Men's power to determine a woman's livelihood, how and when she may be disposed of and replaced by another, and what place each woman takes in the male-dictated line-up initially sets up a context in which women are rendered powerless. However, in "Die with My Dignity", that power is weakened by the persona's resolve: "So before I have to lick down somebody and cuss them so the police come for me / I tell them they can keep their money, I go keep my honey and die with my dignity!" Thus, any notion of helpless surrender on the part of the woman is overturned in her firm resolve to resort to violence, if that is the only option that allows her to claim the vision of womanhood that she has accepted as honourable. Singing Sandra's persona refers to the men she denounces as "scamps", "vagabonds" and "blinking Sunja". Through name-calling, the female persona's bravado further emphasizes her confrontation with systemic oppression. Thus, from this persona's declarations, a complex picture of woman emerges: she retains the stereotype of the strong black woman who is capable of fighting, yet she uses that aggression to defend a version of womanhood traditionally reserved for more genteel white or upper-class women.[52] And she rejects the stereotype of the loose black woman that feminist scholars have repeatedly addressed.[53]

The schoolgirl persona in Queen Ifrica's "Nuh Bwoy" similarly establishes her confrontational stance in the launch of the song: "Nuh bwoy cyan draw me 'roun nuh corner / Fi show mi no Iguana". The defiant tone and the demystification of male power inherent in the use of "bwoy" in reference to grown men further restructure the power relations between males and females.[54] Variations of this line constitute the song's refrain, which asserts that this denial of access to the schoolgirl/woman's body results from the latter's refusal, rather than from any kind of negotiation or plea for the man to exercise his power in more morally acceptable ways. "Yu cyan tek mi virginity" makes a similar assertion. In all these examples, "cyan" is used in its creole sense, and means not that he is unable to do it, but rather that he will not be allowed.

An important feature of the performance of this song is the variation in communication modes and tones presented. In all instances, the particular form that the performer assumes is an emphatic confrontation with, or dismissal of, the men she interpellates. The song opens with a short conversation between two girls, one inviting the other to go with her to a bus where men, presumably older men, will be waiting to meet them. The girl who turns out to be the persona in the song asserts, "My girl mi a go home to my mother go *do* my schoolwork 'cause *my* education come *first*" (emphasis in original).

From the outset, the young woman presents herself as an agent who takes ownership of her body and her future. The speaker's emphasis on *"my"*, *"do"* and *"first"* makes it clear that power is located within her; it is not a power that has been bestowed upon her but rather one that she has claimed. The girl's choice of emphasis underscores her agency in determining what counts as important and marks her rejection of the kind of attention given to her body, a way of thinking imposed on her primarily by men.

The shift from dialogue to singing highlights a resolute, though at this point not aggressive, speaker. Her tone is even and reflects control and certainty. However, when she moves from singing to direct address to scold the men, the song enters the realm of the confrontational. The forms used here have resonances of deejaying, rapping, singing, preaching and exhortation. At times, the persona assumes what might be perceived as the masculine tone of dancehall, thereby emanating a kind of bravado and power that vociferously challenges and dispels the notion of the subservient young girl who is vulnerable to pressures exerted on her by older men. Her refrain "low me mek me grow" asserts and demands a right as citizen. Donette Francis's idea that the women in the novels she analyses in *Feminine Citizenship* are denied the right to "to dwell comfortably and safely in any domicile"[55] resonates in "Nuh Bwoy". The immediate community outside of the home of the young woman being defended in this song is an unsafe space, a hostile environment where her body is under constant attack. The persona, who sometimes wears the mask of the schoolgirl, has chosen orature-performance as a strategy of defence of her citizenship.

In both songs, the critique of male supremacy diminishes male domination on moral grounds. Ironically, the moral standards to which women are held by all in the society – including by men who often refuse to marry women deemed unchaste – are the very standards that women are sometimes expected to compromise. The female personas in both songs do not claim womanhood through a rejection of society's religio-moral standards; rather, they embrace and co-opt them as the basis of their rejection of one element of the male power structure. Queen Ifrica's persona consistently evokes religious principles and social respectability: "Mi body is the temple of the Most High / plus mi nah go mek you disrespect mi school tie"; "Yu cyan tek mi virginity / cauz dat a God precious gift to me". Furthermore, the persona evokes God, a male God from whom she expects to receive protection. In so doing, she presents herself as the one upholding the moral standards, decrying the men's undermining of the very principles espoused by the patriarchal structure they uphold: "Mi trust inna de fada / A dat yuh haffi know". Similarly, Singing Sandra's persona invokes that patriarchal society's moral values as the basis of her refusal to trade sex for a job: "But if you value yuself as woman, you will be demanding respect from the vagabond / Stand up and let them know the truth, it [sic] you want you are no blinking prostitute".

In both songs, the female personas take on "slackness" in a space where a culture of slackness is a prevailing element. I want to focus specifically on the Jamaican dancehall space within which Queen Ifrica engages slackness and extend that theorization to the calypso tradition, which has its own, more subtle, "slack" lyrical content. In this regard, Carolyn Cooper offers a very useful theorization of slackness in the introduction to her book *Sound Clash*. She writes:

> Slackness, though often conceived and critiqued as exclusively sexual in politically conservative discourse, can be much more permissively theorized as a radical, underground confrontation with the patriarchal gender ideology and the duplicitous morality of fundamentalist Jamaican society. Slackness is not mere sexual looseness, though it certainly is that. Slackness is a contestation of conventional definitions of law and order; an undermining of consensual standards of decency. At large, slackness is the antithesis of restrictive uppercase Culture. It thus challenges the rigid status quo of sexual exclusivity and one-sided moral authority valorized by the Jamaican elite. Slackness demarcates a space for alternative definitions of culture.[56]

Cooper's theorization here is characteristically provocative – for its radical shift as well as for its capacity to accommodate how these female performers embrace and exploit the culture of slackness in both dancehall and calypso. They simultaneously concur with and challenge Cooper's suggestion that "slackness is a contestation of conventional definitions of law and order ... [and] the antithesis of restrictive uppercase Culture". Cooper is exactly right that slackness challenges law and order at the level of the superstructure, that of "uppercase" patriarchy. And there is another set of laws and another kind of order that these women overturn, and this further challenge allows for an expansion of Cooper's theorization. The female performers contest a subset of the order that allows men to impose their version of slackness – sexual looseness – on women who are supposed to be defenceless against these impositions. It is the kind of "duplicitous", "one-sided moral authority" that Cooper refers to here – a system that determines when a young woman can consent to sexual activity even though the "uppercase" structure has a legal consent age, and under what circumstances prostitution is admissible, even though prostitution is officially illegal. Paradoxically, both female performers use superstructure moral standards as the basis of their recourse to slackness. By this, I mean that they use dancehall and calypso as the tools to reject that male-imposed subset of law and order, and in that way they demarcate for themselves a set of moral standards within both the "uppercase" convention and the (slack) discursive spaces of dancehall and calypso.

Dancehall music is renowned for its explicit and fearless treatment of taboo subjects, making this form a judicious choice for exploring pedophilia, a phenomenon that has been insufficiently challenged in Jamaican culture. To some extent, male-female pedophilia has been met with either indifference or tacit endorsement.[57] Queen Ifrica's choice of performance space, therefore, facilitates an explicit treatment of the subject, and the performer thoroughly exploits the ribald language characteristic of dancehall. The song's opening, "Nuh bwoy cyan draw me 'roun nuh corner / Fi go show mi no Iguana", projects the bold rejection of accepted norms, but in a calypsoesque manner; sex is couched in "show mi no Iguana" or, later in the song, "show mi no banana". However, by the end of the second stanza, the explicit tendencies of dancehall music emerge – "Since yu love sex so much / Dweet wid yuself" – and as the song progresses, all mention of sex is verbalized in the more explicit dancehall style, with phrases such as "Yuh cyan tek mi virginity". Thus, in some ways, Queen Ifrica stays within the genre. However, while she remains faithful to the genre within that performance culture, some of these quintessential features of dancehall music – sexual explicitness, for example – are redirected towards a liberation of women.

In "Nuh Bwoy", the challenge to male hegemony extends to contesting the way in which men have shaped dancehall by being the dominant performers who have made particular representations of sexuality – slackness defined as sexual looseness – standard fare in that performance culture. As she chides men for reneging on the stipulation that there is a legal consent age, Queen Ifrica's persona also holds the performance culture of dancehall music accountable for its negative portrayals of women:

> Wheh di big bredda dem deh
>   Fi di likkle sista dem
>   Why every song weh unno sing haffi deh bout unda dem
>   Why yu [nuh] teach dem fi build song more like Etana dem?
> ("Where are the men who are singing about female anatomy? Why don't you teach them to sing songs like Etana and others?")

The contrast between male performers and the more positive female performers like Etana (Jamaican reggae singer Shauna McKenzie) resonates with James's representation of women in *The Book of Night Women* in that they are focused on building a stronger society and not on the male characters' preoccupation with illicit sex. Queen Ifrica's persona further challenges the dancehall culture in her reference to a recent song, "Ramping Shop" by Vybz Kartel and Spice: "If it mek yu feel good / to sleep wid children in yu rampin' shop". While "Ramping Shop" does not promote pedophilia, Queen Ifrica's reference to this song, which has become the iconic anthem for lewdness in the dancehall, invites a critique of dancehall while simultaneously showing the range of discursive possibilities that the genre allows.[58] Therefore, contrary to what some segments of the Jamaican public would claim, the way that explicit language is used in "Nuh Bwoy/Mek We Grow" in the defence of "decency" debunks widely accepted notions of dancehall as a one-dimensional site of slackness where men control the discourse on female sexuality.[59] Here, dancehall, as Cooper has written, can serve as a liberating space for women, but in ways that include but also extend beyond the "assert[ion] of freedom to play out eroticized roles". In "Nuh Bwoy" and other songs, liberation also manifests in the way the female singers have explicitly redrawn the discursive parameters of the dancehall performance space.[60]

Similarly, the eponymous chorus line of "Die with My Dignity" affirms some agreed-upon standards of respectability, and the performer exploits and reshapes calypso towards that end. Calypso has a long and distinguished tradition of being a space where social ills are overtly and covertly contested. In this regard, Singing Sandra taps into one of the form's best-known features; her words remain within the tradition of protest and social critique for which calypso is well known. However, she alters the form in terms of what she brings into the public conversation about social ills, how she redraws the boundaries of citizenship and the way she expresses these ideas. As addressed in the chapter that follows, calypso is known more for its mockery and deprecation of women. In "Die with My Dignity", Singing Sandra makes men's conduct and their attempts to control women's bodies and their livelihoods a social problem.

> You want to help to mind your family, you want to help your man financially
> But nowadays it really very hard to get a job as a girl in Trinidad
> You looking out to find something to do, you meet a boss man who promise to help you But when the man let down the condition, nothing else but humiliation,
> They want to see you whole anatomy, they want to see what you doctor never see,
> They want to do what you husband never do, still you ain't know if these scamps will hire you.

In this first verse of the song, the narrative tendencies of calypso remain, but this time it is a woman's story of oppression, thus bringing to the fore the fissures in the nation. Like "Nuh Bwoy", this song, in keeping with the calypso tradition, begins the complaint with fairly mild, even suggestive, language. However, later, the persona dispenses with the subtleties of the genre and states in unambiguous terms how women are being bullied by powerful men:

> And as a next woman get on the line, he start to tell you you ain't good you can't wine.
> They want to see you in a fancy fancy pose, they want to see *how you look without you clothes*
> They want you *cock up like a bloody acrobat*, the wife at home they can't ask she to do that. (emphasis mine)

In this second passage, nothing is left to the proverbial imagination; therefore, the men are fully exposed. Dispensing with the disguise characteristic of calypso, Singing Sandra reconfigures the form to expose and ruffle some unwritten law that permits a full expression of female citizenship. For the persona in "Die with My Dignity", social mobility and economic survival could have been made more accessible by judicious use of her sexuality. Her conclusion is:

> Well if is all this humiliation to get a job these days as a woman
> Brudda, dey go keep dey money
> I go keep my honey and die with my dignity!

A further challenge that is mounted against the tendencies of the calypso genre is worth noting here. The notion that women often use their bodies for economic gain is one of the stock themes of calypso and the basis of the denigration of women in several songs.[61] Therefore, by using this genre to project a different vision of womanhood, Singing Sandra not only contests the perceptions of women perpetuated in the larger society but, as Queen Ifrica does in her dancehall piece, also extends the genre's potential for social commentary.

In *The Book of Night Women*, the otherwise private world of female sexuality is inextricably bound up with more public concerns about slavery and freedom.[62] Lilith's initiation into womanhood and the fact that her female body marks her for a certain set of experiences that I am defining as womanhood are directly linked to her sexuality. As Lilith enters puberty, her guardian Circe makes clear to her the loss of freedom she faces on two fronts: "Sake o' you, man start hitch up round here like pee-pee cluck-cluck" (6); "Lilith did think that turning woman was going to make her smile but instead things was pushing out of her skin without permission. Things growing and won't stop. ... Lilith seeing how pickney is the only thing that not be a slave and start to wrap osnaburg cloth tight round her titty so they won't grow" (7). *The Book of Night Women* therefore links the awakening of womanhood with awareness of the differences between black and white, and between free and enslaved (6). The novel suggests that the body that signals readiness for enslavement and sexual abuse launches womanhood, an awareness of the female's new identity as an enslaved person. At the same time, these physical markings of womanhood also awaken a desire for freedom and claims to the rights to such freedoms. Although Lilith manages to delay her entry into slavery, it is her newly developed body, with its obvious secondary sexual characteristics, that takes her to the Great House, where she witnesses the imbalance of power. Her decision to kill the Jonny Jumper who comes to rape her gives her the first taste of "true womanness that make a man scream" (16). Her actions to defend her womanhood give Homer the cue that she is the kind of enslaved person who has the fortitude to mount a defence of collective freedom, that she could become one of the Night Women.

Despite the allowance it makes for a strategic use of sexuality towards the greater goal of freedom, in *The Book of Night Women*, sex – particularly interracial, interclass sex – is represented as mostly a hindrance to this objective and a place of potential compromise of "true womanness", that which makes a woman claim freedom. That idea is elaborated in the novel's representation of Lilith's relationship with Robert Quinn, the overseer with whom she cohabits. Homer's frank conversation with Lilith about the potential pitfalls that her sexual relationship with Robert Quinn poses encapsulates the novel's more general cautionary impulse. Once Lilith has settled into her relationship with Quinn, Homer confronts what she considers to be a threat to the freedom mission that drives and sustains her: "Me think me like you more before you mouth and you pussy turn friend. . . . Things change, but man don't. You good to remember that now that you have Robert Quinn right where you want him. . . . Mayhaps is time you learn how to have power over that kind of man. We meeting tonight" (266). This restoration of profanity here keeps in focus the way the orature of "you mouth and you pussy turn friend" recalls the posture of aggression and the combative performance modes that this novel recuperates. And the metaphor of a friendship between body parts that should be kept apart for the greater good poetically reinforces the potential danger that sex poses in the fight for freedom. Yet even as Homer warns Lilith that being in a sexual relationship with the overseer can make her forget the struggle, she reminds her that it is also in this relationship, through a strategic use of her sexuality, that her power rests: "You goin' own him after that, ... He goin' hate you for taking the power, but he goin' love you too 'cause giving up power never sweet a man so" (268). The double-edged potential of female sexuality is underscored here, but even more prominent in Homer's remark is how judicious use of sexuality can reconfigure the power structure. Homer's recourse to expletives and crude language removes the veil of shame from sex and revisions women's relationship with sexuality by directing Lilith's attention to its liberating power, sexuality being one aspect of womanhood that makes enslaved women especially vulnerable.

However, if there is any sense that under the duress of slavery, the only thing that women have at their disposal is the strategic use of their sexuality, this is dispelled by Homer's more sustained attention to women's organizational skills, which can undermine the plantation system even as the women are being whipped, raped and tortured. The abovementioned discussion between Homer and Lilith is aimed at educating Lilith about the importance of keeping her eyes on the ultimate prize of freedom from slavery. Homer emphasizes that the power that sexuality makes possible should serve that greater end, reminding Lilith: "Well since you been thinking woman, you think you not goin' get whip again? ... How long you think you goin' go till they hang you for some foolishness? ... Don't be a fool.... No black woman safe as long as white man alive" (272). As a way to underscore the distinction for Lilith, Homer resorts to orature: "If white man want to fuck you, there nothin' you can do 'bout that, but don't make him fool you, that be your business" (353). Through her declarative, even aggressive tone, as well as the use of the expletive, Homer lays out for Lilith the limits and location of her power: the power embedded in womanhood is of the mind ("don't make him *fool* you"), and not the body.

In seeking to establish connections between womanhood, freedom and performance in *The Book of Night Women*, I have attended to the adoption of aggressive performance modes, primarily through analysis of the language that the female characters and the narrator deploy throughout the novel. Performativity in this work also manifests in the way in which it represents performance itself. For example, Homer's insistence that Lilith walk a tightrope between being Quinn's ostensibly loving partner and also being a loyal member of the Night Women draws attention to how enslaved women must feign loyalty to the plantation power structure in the path towards freedom, whether this is the limited freedom they experience within the context of a slave society or a more systemic emancipation. Lilith's example illustrates the larger performative context of the plantation: she must have multiple selves in order to survive all the challenges, encounters and expectations she needs in order to survive. With Robert Quinn alone, she needs more than one self. If she steps out of line or makes an error, she has to retreat to her slave woman's position to make sure that she retains the relative protection she gets from being Quinn's woman:

> —Lilith, what's this?
> —Me never mean to do it on purpose, sah, me never mean to do it on purpose.
> Lilith still stepping back, Robert Quinn still stepping forward.

—Don't . . Out with it at once. At once!
—Lawd o' massy, sah. I broke a plate, sah.
—You did what? Lilith jump. Robert Quinn back her into a wall.
—You . . . fuckin' . . have ye got butter sticks fer fingers!
—No, massa, mi sorry, massa. Don't kill me now, massa! Don't kill me and go buy new me in Spanish Town. (297–98)

This performance of fear and submission is counteracted by Lilith acting in her role as common-law wife:

> She know that her mouth can say what her heart can't swear. . . . The same heart that should want to give all to Robert Quinn say no, or mayhaps it can never say yes. So she cry. . . . She wanted to give everything to him, she could say that to herself now. But she can't do this again for he white and he be the overseer and he control the whip . . . and a nigger girl must be sensible 'bout white man behaviour, for it set like the sun and sunset always different on any given day . . . she bawling and Quinn think it be tears of joy. (309)

This depiction of Lilith's performance during her times of intimacy with Quinn clearly lays out how essential performances are for negotiating her relationship with the overseer. Lilith has other selves, too – for example, the one she performs when she is alone in the kitchen with Homer, or the one she assumes when she meets the Night Women to plan the rebellion. Lilith's performance of these multiple personas exemplifies the negotiations that Homer and all enslaved women, especially those working in close proximity to the white ruling class, have to make to stave off torture and afford themselves time to execute rebellion. The performances are presented almost like a playwright's script, with visual representation and a performativity so palpable that such moments appear to be plays within the novel. In these and other passages, James uses dialogue, a standard element of fiction, in ways that accentuate the performances being inscribed on the page and the overall performativity of this novel.

The representation of performance that is apparent in examples of Lilith's encounters with Quinn is also part of the novel's discourse of performances in general. In other words, the different selves that Lilith and other women fashion call attention to the usefulness of performance in self-preservation and, more specifically, the preservation and achievement of womanhood.

Womanhood, *The Book of Night Women* suggests, is attained through performance – both in the actual fashioning of the women as warriors and in the way performing equips individuals to project multiple selves. Therefore, because of the potential inherent in performance, womanhood is undermined only partially in the plantation system that the novel recreates. Furthermore, it is through performance that the women experience some modicum of freedom and that the plantation system, with its racism and rank sexism, is undermined, even when the women are legally in bondage.

On the Question of Womanhood

While I do not wish to argue for a linear trajectory in the construction of womanhood in male-authored fictions, an argument for a shift in representation is warranted given the differences between Lovelace's and James's representations of female performers. In *The Wine of Astonishment*, "woman" is constructed as an essential figure in nationalist struggles, but her interventions are subversive and transgressive because her insertion is made from within the ostensible "female" performance space. In this framework, "womanhood" is constructed as a constrained, though insurgent, subjectivity whose expression is contingent upon the extent to which the woman can exploit her proximity to men and the male power structure. Because Eva is the wife of a leader, she has the privilege of working alongside Bee; Lovelace casts her in an obvious female performance tradition and through this disguise, she (re)presents herself as an activist whose work matches and sometimes surpasses Bee's.

In *The Book of Night Women*, that kind of contingency on partnership with a male leader is completely undermined, and "woman" is therefore constructed as a more self-defined subject who claims womanhood, with her resemblance to traditional conceptions of the latter virtually erased. Homer's body bears marks of excruciating punishment: "Homer back look like a washboard with big thick scars running across. . . . The scars continue from her back to her front, so much that she don't have no titty no more" (25). The torture Homer has experienced has literally defeminized her because she lives in a body that, in conventional terms, has been stripped of womanness. Yet her use of aggressive performance modes, and those which the novel's narrator uses to describe her, explicitly project a superior personhood: "Homer carry herself so tall and proud that one would think she be the only unblemished nigger in Montpelier", and "Homer whiter than any white man" (25, 26). The comparison to "white man", the established location of power, is significant here. But even more notable is the suggestion that Homer is "whiter than any white man". In other words, she is more powerful than white men, a claim that is affirmed in the Redcoats' response to the scale of the rebellion that she spearheaded. Interestingly, too, it is the loss of her children, a key determinant of womanhood in this context, that motivates Homer to bring down Montpelier plantation. Thus, it could be argued that it is Homer's dogged claim to and fierce defence of womanhood that has shaped her as a powerful revolutionary and defender of freedom, the true expression of womanhood.

By calling Lilith "a nigger who not going to be a woman till she take womanhood for herself" (354), Homer makes explicit the novel's definition of womanhood as freedom. Homer's pronouncement that "freedom comin' before next Easter" is challenged by other Night Women: "Massa not 'bout to give no nigger free paper." Homer's response encapsulates the novel's vision of womanhood: "Who say nothing 'bout the massa, chile? We not getting free, we taking free" (70). Homer's terse turn of phrase and the juxtaposition of "getting" and "taking" keep in the forefront the relationship between these women's claims to freedom and their location in a combative oral culture. And the visual representation of "massa" in lowercase letters in Homer's response calls attention to the repositioning of power, even as the women are subjected to the "massa's" formal control.

A similar picture of strong and complex womanhood emerges from the female performers in "Die with My Dignity" and "Nuh Bwoy", who explicitly claim and defend themselves as women based on established models of decency and chastity. Yet like Homer, these women's adoption of an aggressive posture and their location in a male-dominated performance tradition depart from the models of womanhood that are defined along the lines of decorous, "clean" speech. By tapping into male-dominated performance modes, they not only make their claim of "respectable" womanhood, but they also reframe how womanhood is viewed.

One of the most important contributions that Caribbean feminist scholars have made to this area of study is a resistance to uni-dimensional definitions of "woman" and "womanhood" and a concomitant attentiveness to pointing out more complicated definitions and representations of these two terms. Therefore, what I have sought to address in the foregoing discussion is how attention to inter-performance can expand those theorizations. By this, I mean that the dialogue between male writers of performing fiction and its female performers builds on the conversations that have so far mostly attributed such complex representations only to female writers.

FOUR

Affirming the Female "Subject Person"

Rereading Gender Discourses in *The Dragon Can't Dance*

> I am offering a warning to men to take care
> Of modern women beware
> Even the flappers we cannot trust
> For they're taking our jobs from us
> And if you men don't assert control
> Women will rule the world
> – Atilla the Hun, "Women Will Rule the World"[1]

ATILLA THE HUN'S 1935 calypso "Women Will Rule the World" contains several misogynistic and anxiety-driven lines in addition to those quoted above, including "Long ago their one ambition in life / Was to be mother and wife"; "We shall next hear of them as lecturers, / Authors and engineers"; "We will next hear of them as candidates / For the President of the United States"; and "If women ever get the ascendency / They will show us no sympathy". "Women Will Rule the World" and other songs such as "Jean and Dinah", which epitomize what Gordon Rohlehr describes as "fiercely anti-feminist calypsos [that were especially popular in] the 1940s and 1950s", have come to represent the dominant gender narrative of calypsos.[2] Yet despite the prominence of these songs, the deprecating and deeply insecure mindset reflected in their lyrics does not fully account for calypsonians' perspectives on women and gender relationships. Take, for example, Roaring Lion's "Mary Ann", which, though suggestive of questionable activities "by the seaside", includes verses in which the persona expresses love and desire for Mary Ann: "In her heart there's love, but I'm the only man / Who's allowed to kiss my, oh Mary Ann". And the persona's desire for Mary Ann extends beyond kissing: "Oh, when we marry we will have the time we ever thought / I would be so happy I'd kiss my mother-in-law". In this representation, Mary Ann is not an object, but a highly desirable full-time partner. In a later calypso, "No Woman No" by Black Stalin (1986), the persona entreats a woman to stay with him so they can continue building a family: "A little a your sweat and my sweat / as we rub up together". Here, intimacy with a woman and female sexuality are not feared, nor are they scoffed at. Remarkably, too, the man presents himself as the more vulnerable party in this relationship.

The examples above illustrate the range and variety of gender discourses that emanate from calypsos.[3] However, despite this range, in the overwhelming majority of calypsos in which female subjectivity is explored, the representations are, by and large, unfavourable. As a result, this performance genre has come to be associated with negative characterizations of women. One may even question the use of "subject" or "subjectivity" as a way of characterizing the treatment of women in a genre reputed to objectify and disparage women. It is this limited view of calypso and Earl Lovelace's creative exploitation of the form and its range of discursive possibilities that I seek to complicate in this revisionary reading of *The Dragon Can't Dance*.

In chapter 3, I argued that *The Wine of Astonishment* is underpinned by a female-centred poetics. Because Lovelace restores the voice of a female storyteller and a performance tradition associated with women to tell the men's stories, it would seem reasonable to most for there to be some room for a conversation about female agency in that work. However, given the use of calypso as the structuring device in *The Dragon Can't Dance*, and that genre's reputation as a form hostile to women, it appears that any gendered reading of this novel that departs from the accepted and well-founded claims that *The Dragon Can't Dance* is overwhelmingly masculinist and anti-feminist would be unsustainable. Yet precisely because of Lovelace's recourse to calypso and carnival as structural and narrative devices in this novel, I argue that alongside the engagement with the roles and failures of men in this work, there is a comparably complex treatment of female subjectivity. Beyond the representation of women that I extrapolate from my textual analysis I consider how Lovelace mediates his concerns about personhood and related issues through gender. That is to say that attentiveness to the extensive range of possibilities that the genre of calypso offers, and my location of this work within the larger context of Lovelace's concerns with and representations of personhood, allow for an argument that there is a more favourable and complex treatment of female subjectivity than has heretofore been suggested.

Given the explicit arguments he makes in his non-fiction works and the themes he explores in his fiction, Lovelace's ideological orientations, notably his concern for the personhood of Caribbean peoples, are well known. Lovelace uses the term "personhood" in reference to the humanity of all Caribbean people, which was called into question, violated and virtually wrenched from them during and after the slave experience. In Lovelace's conceptualization, this personhood has been threatened not only by European racism, but also by the prejudices of Caribbean people (blacks, East Indians, people of mixed race, Chinese people and others) who continue to violate the personhood of others like themselves. Funso Aiyejina notes that Lovelace's discussion of reparation shows how that restorative impulse makes demands on both "victims and victimizers", since descendants of both groups make up present-day Caribbean communities. For Lovelace, the recovery of personhood requires "a new valuing of the human person, a new respect for life, a new appreciation for the need to trust, that affirms for us the need for fair play and respect that goes beyond colour, class, race, and creed".[4] The conspicuous absence of gender from this list has no doubt supported arguments that Lovelace is concerned primarily with men's lives, the way they have been marginalized by colonialism and how they in turn participate in their own marginalization. Yet I contend that the nature of the forms that Lovelace recuperates as the means of telling his stories allows for a gender inclusiveness that may not be explicit in his non-fiction works nor in his proclamations.[5]

The general nationalist vision within which *The Dragon Can't Dance* is located does indeed reflect the "nationalist norm",[6] in which the male protagonist is given the gender inclusiveness that attentiveness to the performativity of the novel allows. Because Lovelace draws on the performance culture for his expressive tools, he paradoxically undercuts the nationalist (and therefore his own) predilections towards a singular focus on the myth of man as leader and saviour. This paradox results from his choice of the calypso genre – the same form that ostensibly supports his attention to men in this novel – and from a thorough exploitation of the possibilities of the form.

As I have already noted in chapter 3, critical attention to Lovelace's oeuvre has centred on his nationalist vision, which construes the actualization of Caribbean personhood through renewed and improved masculinity. This is particularly true of the criticism of *The Dragon Can't Dance*. For example, Linden Lewis's assertion that "while [Lovelace] is clearly able to read into the mind of the male in society, his renditions of the female are not so incisive" reflects the dominant critical perspective on Lovelace's treatment of gender in this novel. Even more significant, Lewis further suggests that the novel's female characters, "though not as well-rounded" as its male characters, "play key roles in the definition and shaping of masculinity".[7] While I concur with Lewis's suggestion that the preoccupation with male subjectivity in this novel is glaring, and agree that female characters do play a role in advancing Lovelace's discourses on masculinity, I would argue that at least two female characters are well developed, and that the novel attends to female subjectivity beyond using women to develop men. Furthermore, male characters also play a role in the development of female characters. By focusing on the general concern with questions of identity in calypso traditions as well as the historical and contemporary attitudes towards women that characterize that form, I maintain that Lovelace's use of calypso demonstrates the complex attitudes towards women inherent in the genre, and by extension the entire Caribbean oral tradition. Specifically, Lovelace's "bacchanal aesthetic"[8] is part of his overall nationalist thrust, and his nuanced depiction of Cleothilda and Sylvia – the two most extensively developed female characters – allows for gender inclusiveness in Lovelace's larger nationalist vision.

Even Lovelace's choice of nomenclature – "personhood" – leaves room for gender inclusiveness. At the most basic level, Lovelace's choice of the word "personhood" over the more exclusive term "manhood" allows for a more expansive reading of his representation of women, one that unsettles assumptions about what kinds of gender ideologies are reinforced in *The Dragon Can't Dance*. Each of the characters presented in this novel, male and female alike, represents some aspect of the larger quest for personhood that the narrative addresses, and each is in some way a victim of historical exploitation in a society based on the subjugation of formerly enslaved and indentured people. The women in this novel are part of that greater struggle to defy the implicit ordinances of a society that continues to marginalize them. Consequently, any discussion of Lovelace's portrayal of women must be located within the larger frame of his preoccupation with personhood.

My rereading of Lovelace's engagement with gender ideologies does not ignore or contest the arguments in favour of his overt masculinist discourses, nor do I dismiss the representations of women that bear obvious traces of the calypsonian's penchant towards mockery, derision of women and preoccupation with sexuality. Instead, I am suggesting that within such representations, Lovelace's portrayal of Sylvia and Cleothilda, as well as of other women in this novel, expands the reach of the kinds of nationalist conversations within which Lovelace's work is located because of the range of possibilities that calypso allows. Attentiveness to Lovelace's aesthetic choices therefore reveals that his interrogation of the local postcolonial leaders' failure to fashion a society that fosters the optimal development of all persons also includes a concern for the systemic marginalization of women.

The Calypso Tradition

While they retain some of the more universal features of carnival – including "festive laughter" and the reversal of the social hierarchies of their West African and medieval European roots – carnival celebrations in Trinidad (out of which calypso emerged) reflect the region's particular social and historical contexts. Whether they are performed inside or outside of carnival celebrations, calypsos embody the creolization process and the socio-historical exigencies of their production. Rohlehr notes that calypsos evolved out of "a complex of African song-forms and via the absorption of varieties of European, West Indian, Latin American, North American and later Indian music".[9] Aside from their inclusion of a variety of aesthetic resources resulting from the meeting of cultures, carnival celebrations also reflect conflicts arising from racial, ethnic, class, gender and other distinctions rooted in the history of the region. From their earliest days, these celebrations offered space for the construction, recuperation and assertion of identities that were otherwise threatened. As Gordon Rohlehr notes, "Festive space was freedom to celebrate identities that were separate and different from the powerfully imposed, but by no means absolute, plantation identity as chattel, slave, functioning and expendable tool. . . . If the dance assemblies were the contexts of performed 'freedom' before Emancipation, Carnival evolved as the grand stage upon which identities were asserted, contested and performed in the post-Emancipation period."[10] As the most significant verbal component of carnival celebrations, calypso has historically served as the discursive space in which identities were claimed and contested. Along with their inherent wit, humour and sometimes-deceptive innocence, calypsos have consistently retained commentary on social and political issues as one of their core features. As central vehicles for social discourse, calypsos serve such functions as celebration, censure, praise, ridicule, verbal warfare, affirmation, social control, satire and the generation of laughter.[11] Rohlehr argues that calypsos have also served as a primary expressive site for working out the tensions of postcolonial Trinidad. Further, he lists "sexual conflicts" among those conflicts that he posits calypsos have historically "mirrored".[12] Therefore, Lovelace's recuperation of the formal features of calypso as aesthetic material for *The Dragon Can't Dance* allows for an engagement with gender relationships and tensions in ways that transcend mere celebration of, and preoccupation with, Caribbean masculinity.

Laughter is one of the enduring hallmarks of carnival and calypso in the Trinidadian context, and one characteristic that facilitates the discourses that Lovelace engages in the *The Dragon Can't Dance*. Significantly, Rohlehr notes that there are differences between the carnival laughter of medieval Europe and that of Trinidadian carnival. In contrast to the scenario that Bakhtin describes, where "carnival laughter is the laughter of all the people",[13] Rohlehr suggests that in societies such as Trinidad, "it is a mistake to think of Carnival laughter or any other kind of laughter as 'the laughter of *all the people*'" (emphasis in original).[14] Instead, the laughter in Trinidadian carnival, heard mainly in calypsos, "is more often than not a weapon to reduce and cut down the 'enemy'".[15] While Lovelace's use of laughter seems to uphold the calypsonian's tendency to use the latter as a weapon, I hope to demonstrate in my reading of Lovelace's representation of Cleothilda that the laughter generated from the representation of that character, although used to mock her, is a veneer for a broader critique of the society that produces such a person. Thus, Cleothilda could also be read as a victim of the society at which this critique is directed. Laughter, then, transcends its uses for the creation of festive spirit and as a tool for mockery to function as a means of social critique as well.

While Caribbean men and women share a history of enslavement and oppression, their experiences of and responses to that history have not been identical. Writing about the gendered nature of responses to the slave experience, Merle Hodge notes that while the roles of black men were limited to fieldwork and procreation, black women had authority over their children (or their charges). Hodge further suggests that this situation has given the Caribbean woman "moral authority" that her male counterparts never had, and therefore men's acts of violence are meant to "put her in her place, to safeguard his manhood threatened by the authority of the female upstart".[16] Enslaved men received mixed messages: on the one hand, the European patriarchal leadership fostered male dominance, but on the other, the social position of enslaved men prevented them from exercising the authority associated with masculine privilege. In the absence of formally sanctioned authority, enslaved men and their descendants had to create other means of asserting their humanity and authority. The "festive space" of carnival offered opportunities for reclamation of that aspect of their personhood. As a traditionally male-dominated genre, calypso provided for the male performer a means through which his masculinity, which was threatened on and beyond the plantation, could be reconstructed and affirmed through performance.

The specific historical relationship between calypso and gender discourses has no doubt shaped the prevailing readings of Lovelace's work and *The Dragon Can't Dance* in particular as explicitly and overtly masculinist.[17] Calypsos, like multiple other forms of orature, played a significant role in the construction of masculinity, particularly the demarcation of the male self from women in ways that sought to configure the male as superior. Calypsos drew their inspiration from the stickfighting face-offs that preceded and influenced them. The chantwell who accompanied stickfighting bands offered another site for showcasing male physical prowess and warriorhood, and provided a battleground for self-assertion and male dominance. Rohlehr argues that "confrontation and mastery, violent self-assertiveness and rhetorical force" were among the essential features of the chantwell.[18] It is also significant that since women were often the prize for the stickfighter's display of valiance, the objectification of women that was a natural part of early calypsos continued to shape the genre.[19]

Caribbean theorists and critics such as Hodge, whose characterizations I included earlier, have argued that verbal aggression towards women, staged in calypsos, portrays the insecurities that Caribbean men have carried over from the slavery and colonial experiences – thus, the desire to "put [the woman] in her place", as Merle Hodge suggests, has been articulated in the lyrics of many calypsos. Carole Boyce Davies's discussion of the Mighty Sparrow details how post-independence calypsonians extended the misogynistic tendencies of earlier performers. Within a nationalist framework, Forbes offers a similar reading, focusing on the role of calypsos in recuperating male selves "under threats of national change".[20] Logically, then, as one of the most prominent literary voices of nationalism and, even further, one who draws heavily on this historically misogynistic form, Lovelace's appropriation of the calypso shows traces of the genre's historical association with the confrontational, aggressive style of the chantwell, particularly when this use is examined within the larger context of Lovelace's focus on resistance and personhood.

As the few critical reflections that I have cited illustrate, overwhelmingly, discussions about the relationship between calypso and gender evince a preoccupation with how this form has been historically used as a means of asserting aggressive brands of masculinity and simultaneously disparaging women. Yet such accurate depictions are only part – even if a large part – of a more complex and nuanced treatment of gender in calypsos. Consistent with the realities of the Caribbean, Boyce Davies notes that some women, usually mothers, are accorded deference both in calypsos and in the larger oral tradition. And even in calypsos where hostility seems obvious, as Forbes observes, "the representation is ambivalent". In many instances, she argues, calypsonians recognize women's "man-like" behaviour and recognize them as "equal opponents". Forbes also calls attention to the inclusion of the female voice in calypsos that "used the dramatic dialogue or call-and-response form to inscribe the woman's voice in direct speech, partly as an indication of her aggravating refusal to shut up". Perhaps most relevant to this discussion is the observation that the woman's presence in calypsos shows significant ambivalence because "what made the calypsonian's . . . task impossible was a basic contradiction: that linguistic power in the mode of picong, subversion and hybridization was an aspect of West Indian cultural sensibility in general, non-gender-specific and produced out of hermaphroditism of the slave collective, yet it was the basis on which manhood was to be defined."[21] It is this conundrum inherent in the calypso form itself – based on its gender-inclusive aesthetic features such as picong, as well as its historical context – that makes the representation of women at the very least ambivalent and, as I will argue, also affirmative in its reincarnation in *The Dragon Can't Dance*.

Lovelace's "Novelypso"

The Dragon Can't Dance (1979) is Earl Lovelace's third published novel and one of his most celebrated works. Set in an urban area – Calvary Hill, or "the Hill" – during carnival season, it tells the stories of multiple characters, each of whom, in his or her own way, struggles to survive economically and to claim personhood in a socio-economic context designed to marginalize formerly enslaved and indentured people. It is obvious from even a cursory reading of *The Dragon Can't Dance* that the characters who live on the Hill – Cleothilda, Sylvia, Philo, Aldrick, Fisheye and others – are victims of the larger Trinidadian and Caribbean communities' failure to forge a society that is able to move past its history of exploitation. Each of Lovelace's chapter titles bears the assumed carnival name of one of the main characters, and each begins with a description of that character's involvement in carnival celebrations. This primary attention to each person's role in carnival stimulates further consideration of his or her specific experience of urban poverty and of the general hopelessness in postcolonial Trinidad. The majority of these characters are men and Lovelace includes a scathing critique of his male characters' self-destructive ways of responding to their marginalization. Despite his attentiveness to male subjectivity, Lovelace's representation of men is more damning than his representation of women. Of course, it can be argued that men are harshly criticized because they are the ones to whom

Lovelace entrusts leadership of the nation. Even so, although *The Dragon Can't Dance* engages closely with men, it is not particularly celebratory of them. A similar point can be made about Lovelace's treatment of race relations, even though his central characters are black men. His portrayal of Pariag, the East Indian resident on the Hill, facilitates Lovelace's confrontation with the predominantly black community's internal racism. Through his depiction of the community's ostracism of Pariag, Lovelace indicts the black characters in the story for contributing to Trinidad's pervasive Afro–East Indian divide. *The Dragon Can't Dance* also makes visible the specific challenges of women – those whose names are used as chapter titles and many others – as part of his preoccupation with the failings of his compatriots.

The novel centres largely on Aldrick, the unemployed bachelor of the Hill who is best known for the elaborate dragon costumes that he remakes and wears annually during the carnival parade. The story also explores the disillusionment of Aldrick and other black men with their societies, their social paralysis and their eventual rebellion – led by the "Bad John" Fisheye – which lands the group of rebels in prison.[22] *The Dragon Can't Dance* also details the experiences of female characters, particularly Sylvia and Cleothilda, who are engaged in their own quests for personhood.

In all respects, this novel embodies a located postcolonial Caribbean ethos. Its characters carry the yoke of slavery, and the setting reflects the decay that characterizes urban poverty, an especially conspicuous and worrisome symbol of an agonizing past. At the same time, the context of carnival, which resonates throughout the novel, as well as Aldrick's renewed costume, exude vibrancy, hope and promise. Therefore, paradoxically, the novel presents the characters' poverty as being, as Peter Nazareth suggests, "resistant to slavery of over a hundred years".[23] In this way, the novel's reliance on calypso, the resilient music form that served as a virtual opiate for the people on Calvary Hill, whose particular postcolonial condition is defined by their struggle to break from the socio-economic conditions brought on by slavery and neocolonialism, tempers the harshness of the people's circumstances. As the first extended work of fiction in which style and texture are shaped by calypso, *The Dragon Can't Dance* is a monumental example of performing fiction: only a few works before it, such as Samuel Selvon's fictions, deployed calypso in the comprehensive way in which Lovelace recuperates the form in this work.[24]

Aiyejina's suggestion that this novel is "executed in a style that acknowledges the calypsonian as . . . a documenter and articulator of events and sensibilities"[25] is therefore a useful point of departure for my exploration of Lovelace's treatment of female subjectivity in *The Dragon Can't Dance*. Vividly displayed in the novel are Lovelace's strategic use of a range of stock calypso features (laughter, mockery, picong, double entendre); the way in which he uses diction, rhythm and other formal features of calypso as the constitutive elements of the novel; and how the text presents woman, a stock concern of the calypso form. In casting a narrator who "restores the behaviour" of the calypsonian, Lovelace recuperates features of the form that are often overshadowed by its more prevalent hostile tendencies.

Aiyejina contends that Lovelace's utilization of a calypso aesthetic in *The Dragon Can't Dance* should be read in the context of his deployment of indigenous Caribbean artistic creations and as part of his preoccupation with resistance to the dominant Euro-Caribbean culture. My consideration of his representation of women in this text is likewise predicated on the notion that there is congruence between the form Lovelace appropriates and the complex representation of women he undertakes in this example of performing fiction. As I have suggested earlier, while calypso's hostility towards women is well documented, the inherent characteristics of the genre also allow for a more nuanced engagement with the gender ideologies that it confronts. Rohlehr expresses a similar point when he notes that "as products of the carnivalesque frame of mind, [calypsos] are concerned with ceaseless masking and unmasking, in which stereotypes may be simultaneously celebrated and demolished".[26] The carnivalesque orientations inherent in calypsos allow Lovelace to creatively appropriate the form as part of a larger thrust towards resistance, in ways that engender representations of women in complicated ways.

In the prologue to *The Dragon Can't Dance*, Lovelace anticipates this nuanced portrayal of women as well as some of the aesthetic features of calypso he uses throughout the text:

> Up on the hill with Carnival coming and calypso tunes swimming . . . everybody catches the spirit and these women with baskets and with their heads tied, these women winding daily down this hill on which no buses run, tramping down this asphalt lane . . . on their way, to Port of Spain city, to market, to work as a domestic, or to any other menial task they inherit because of their beauty; these women

in this season, bounce with that tall delicious softness of bosom and hip, their movements a dance, as if they were earth priestesses heralding a new spring.[27]

Lovelace titles this section of the prologue "Calypso", suggesting a conscious linking of calypso to the women he portrays here. At the same time, he infuses the prologue with the cadences of calypso, so that the repetition of the phrase "these women" inscribes the rhythm and timbre of the form. The specific way in which Lovelace uses calypso in this passage – retrieving its vitality through rhythm – is especially noteworthy within the context of this argument. In this linkage between character and rhythm, women are presented in lighthearted, ways; they are also represented as embodying the spirit of resiliency and fortitude that persists despite the burdensome repercussions of colonialism.

Lovelace also creatively exploits the double entendre, another stock device of calypso, signifying upon the established features of the genre as one of the key devices by which he explores questions about personhood. The women are described as "winding . . . down" the hill, and this play on the word "winding" suggests both their literal movement down a meandering road and "wining", the word used to describe dancing to a calypso beat. The double entendre allows the audience to see women who are at once industrious and playful. "These women . . . with that tall delicious softness of bosom and hip" conveys the sensuality that pervades the language of calypso, yet the narrator moves beyond a focus on sexual suggestiveness to present the daily struggles for survival that these women face, and to affirm their contribution to the region's economy. In lines such as "these women with baskets and with their heads tied . . . tramping down this asphalt lane . . . to Port of Spain city, to market", there is an intertextual relationship between Lovelace's novel and Daisy Myrie's poem "Market Women", which catalogues and celebrates the fortitude of Caribbean women in their role as breadwinners. Lovelace reinforces that idea by referring to the women as "earth priestesses", a sentiment we do not typically associate with calypsos. A connection such as the one I am making here between Lovelace's and Myrie's representations of women is conceivable only when readers attend to the multiple interpretive possibilities that the calypso form allows. In a novel in which the majority of the men are depicted as failures, this affirming portrayal of industrious women is noteworthy. Additionally, the suggestion that these women "herald a new spring" not only acknowledges the role women traditionally play but also places them at the centre of Lovelace's nationalist vision for a new postcolonial community.

Cleothilda is one of the female characters whom the novel treats extensively, and whose representation yields rich complexity when examined within the context of the wide range of stylistic and discursive possibilities of calypsos. The body on which Cleothilda depends for self-actualization also serves as a fertile site for ridicule and critique in this narrative, and for this treatment of Cleothilda, Lovelace recuperates the mockery through the picong tradition that informs this novel. The narrator juxtaposes Cleothilda's "rouged cheeks and padded hips" with the "wrinkled knees that show her years more truthfully than her face". The tone in which he describes her "husbanding her fading beauty" and showing a "delightful flourish of middle-aged sexiness" is imbued with mockery (9–11). The calypsonian/narrator ridicules Cleothilda for hanging on to a fading beauty bolstered by props from the beauty industry. These examples also illustrate the backhanded compliments for which calypsonians are renowned. The mention of Cleothilda's "wrinkled knees" neutralizes any compliment that may be suggested in the description of her face as still bearing "traces of youth". And sexiness, which is a favourite topic for the calypsonian, is qualified by the insertion of "middle-aged". A victim of the calypsonian's quick wit and sharp tongue, Cleothilda's body is held up for ridicule; thus, Lovelace's representation of her epitomizes calypsonians' fascination with the female body, which runs the gamut of attitudes, viewing it as a source of sexual gratification, men's territory, ugly and repulsive, or a potential trap for men.

However, Lovelace's portrayal of Cleothilda also skilfully combines the calypsonian's tendency to ridicule women with a critique of the impact that the colonially derived class structure has on women. Cleothilda understands very clearly where she stands as a woman of colour in a postcolonial – and still racist and sexist – society. But she is also fully aware of the tools that society has given her to assert her personhood. As we are told in the first sentence of the story, Cleothilda is a "mulatto woman" and former carnival queen runner-up. As one whose proximity to white standards of beauty has been formally acknowledged by society, Cleothilda's body demarcates her from the group of poor black women who inhabit the tenement yard. Lovelace's critical turn to the community and its endorsement of a colour-driven class system is made visible in his extensive description of this character's body, which conflates critiques of Cleothilda's attitude and those of the Hill's inhabitants: "her nose lifted above the city, her long hair plaited in two plaits, like a schoolgirl, choking with that importance and beauty which she maintained as a queenship, that not only she, but the people who shared the yard with her, had the duty to recognize and responsibility to uphold" (9). Cleothilda is also depicted as "carrying on hostile and superior and unaccommodating [because of] her presumed gentility" (10); the queenship she enjoys is described as being "impossible without her mulattohood" (11). Here, the calypsonian's attention to the body moves beyond a fascination with its relationship to sexuality to explore how both Cleothilda and the community become victims of an ideological construct that makes the racialized (and gendered) body the basis of her claim to personhood. This representation of Cleothilda epitomizes Lovelace's exploitation of calypso to not only deride women as the genre historically does, but also to expand that critique to engage broader socio-historical concerns.

Thus, by tapping into a wide array of calypso features in this text, Lovelace moves his representation of Cleothilda beyond a preoccupation with the end of her queenship on the Hill. His attention to her body is conceivably a mere pretext for an exploration of other concerns related to Cleothilda's quest for personhood, her negotiation of her environment and the ways in which she exploits the values of her society to maintain a sense of self-worth. For example, though initially she makes it clear to others on the Hill that she is their social superior, Cleothilda also understands the importance of being part of this community during carnival time. In some instances, rather than being the object of ridicule by the calypsonian, she too wears the calypsonian's mask. With Miss Olive and others as her audience, Cleothilda uses calypso to underscore her subject position as well as her oneness with the rest of the community in this narrative: "Bachanal! Trinidad! All o' we is one . . . Miss Olive, we is all one people. No matter what they say, all o' we is one" (11). And later, when she is fully displaced as queen, Cleothilda uses calypso again to establish her camaraderie with the community: "We could all live very nice here, if it wasn't for one or two hooligan. Look at the weather how it nice. Look at the steelband boys how they getting civilize" (141).

To some degree, Cleothilda's recourse to calypso, which is evident in the rhythmic patterns of her outbursts, makes her an informal practitioner of the form that the narrator uses to ridicule her. Thus, the woman uses calypso to advance her quest for personhood, as a way of defining herself as part of a community. And, in fact, the passage's seamless enfolding of calypso into Cleothilda's prose illustrates her understanding of the diverse uses of this situated form. While the typical male calypsonian often uses the form as a weapon against the woman, in this case the woman uses it in her own service – a useful example of the complex relationship between woman and calypso in this text. Cleothilda's co-opting of calypso presents other subversive possibilities that the carnivalesque orientations of the genre facilitate, since she overturns the form that is used against her and uses it to retrieve her personhood and even temporarily connect herself with the community.

Lovelace's critique of Cleothilda also shows a turn to the community in ways that address the more general attitudes towards indigenous culture that, within the larger context of Lovelace's ideological inclinations, are critical to resistance and the retrieval of personhood. Throughout the year, Cleothilda "carries on hostile and superior", showing little regard for her neighbours and the local culture that she embraces during carnival time. She is still shackled by the society's colonially generated ideas about race, colour and class. Therefore, Cleothilda exemplifies what Lovelace refers to as the "bacchanal elite": "people, especially the middle class, whose identification with the folk is seasonal and superficial".[28] Lovelace presents Cleothilda as falling into this category for most of the year. And while Cleothilda's use of calypso indicates that individuals like her are fully aware of the value of these traditions, their willingness to embrace them seasonally and only for their personal aggrandizement prevents a fuller realization of their liberating potential.

Sylvia, Cleothilda's successor as queen of the Hill, is also the subject of complex representation: Lovelace presents her as sexual goddess, victim and symbol of promise in this calypso novel. There is a fascinating intertextual relationship between Sylvia in *The Dragon Can't Dance* and the song "Who is Sylvia?" in William Shakespeare's comedy *The Two Gentlemen of Verona*. This song seems particularly relevant given its representation of Sylvia as an extraordinarily desirable woman.[29] Lovelace's introduction of Sylvia exemplifies the preoccupation with female sexuality that characterizes calypso and, by extension, the novel. The chapter entitled "The Princess" opens with the line "Sylvia ain't have no man", a phrase that not only frames the chapter but is also used as a refrain throughout, helping to create a sense that the chapter is a calypso written for Sylvia. By beginning his introduction of her with these words, Lovelace appears to objectify Sylvia, presenting her as many calypsonians would: as another pawn in the hands of a man with means, a potential object of exploitation. But by framing the text with "Sylvia ain't have no man", Lovelace also alerts the audience to the failure of society to offer viable, less exploitative options through which a young woman may pursue her quest for personhood. These words call attention to much more than an obsession with sexuality. When the lecherous, middle-aged landlord enters into a tacit agreement with Sylvia's mother that he will "keep" Sylvia in exchange for rent, we are told: "She was the gift arranged even before she knew it, even without the encouragement or connivance of her mother. She was the sacrifice. She would let him pat her on the head, feel his hand sliding down her back" (18). The pace of this passage is slower, the tone more sombre than that of other moments in the text, and these qualities connect its message to different kinds of calypsos, such as those of the Mighty Shadow, that offer scathing critiques of society's social ills. And while the explicit sexuality remains, the mocking tone gives way to seriousness and contemplation, which indicates sensitivity to the historical and social conditions that lure young women and their mothers towards any semblance of escape from a life of deprivation.

The language of *The Dragon Can't Dance* reinforces the idea that Sylvia is being groomed by her environment to pursue a life of prostitution and to define herself through her body. That notion of the female body as a site for sexual exploitation and commodification is characteristic of many calypsos. The ideas that Sylvia and her male peers are "growing up in [a] tight space", that "she move too fast for things to penetrate her" and that she is "getting close to the danger coiled in the crotches of this slum" (18) focus on Sylvia's vulnerability to sexual exploitation, the most likely challenge for a young female dweller of the Hill. The sexual overtones in the language, characteristic of calypsos, simultaneously sexualize and empower Sylvia. In this world, sexuality envelops her for better or worse, and Lovelace's rendering of her predicament recasts this well-established characteristic of calypsos as the source of both innuendo and social critique.

Even in his evocation of calypso's characteristically sexual innuendos, Lovelace still represents Sylvia as a complex human being, and in some passages he presents her as superior to her male counterparts. Despite the sexually suggestive language and the objectification of Sylvia by both the narrator/calypsonian and her male peers, she is also presented as much more than a body to be exploited:

> A few of them had delved fumbling hands beneath her dress, a few of them, growing up in this tight space, this hot yard; but even so she was always too quick for them, too much the humming-bird blur; and her mind was never in it, and she had watched the whole act, felt the trembling knees, the groping hands.... She had watched, felt the whole performance as if she wasn't there, from a distance. (17)

Although Sylvia is portrayed as prey, she is also able to build a fortress around herself that fosters a detachment from the realities that she seems doomed to face. Using the language of calypso, Lovelace restores the performance of adolescent petting and uses this scene as an entry point into an uncovering of Sylvia's personhood, emphasizing her resilience and instinctive rejection of the future to which the culture of the Hill is determined to relegate her. Lovelace portrays Sylvia as an agential human being fully cognizant of her circumstances, opening herself up somewhat, but finding a way to protect and keep part of herself intact. Thus, although there is the distinct glare of the proverbial male gaze, Sylvia is somewhat removed from it, and she is treated as a person in and of herself. And while Lovelace's representation of her serves to advance his discourse on masculinity, readers have an access to Sylvia that suggests an interest in her as a character who opens up more varied discourses, as well as a view of personhood as a broader, more inclusive category.

The variety of points of view that this novel's narrative strategy allows also represents the tendency of the calypsonian to speak with the voices of a range of individuals in the community, and Lovelace skilfully uses this technique to facilitate a more nuanced representation of Sylvia. For example, his inclusion of the perspective of the older women on the Hill helps to create an even more sympathetic and varied picture of her:

> So the women, the older women, who had eyes, who had felt the burnings of this living, would watch her sweeping along with the sunshine, dancing on her head, moving with that careless inviting speed and slowness, that bold swinging openness that narrowed men's eyes ... [they] would want to wish a magic guard

> over her so she would not be trampled by this Hill . . . but with all these young men coming into the yard and asking for Sylvia, with so many eyes pressing down on her, they felt she was doomed: the miracle they dared to wish was too staggering for their faith. (18)

Although some of the language associated with male desire betrays the traditional ribaldry of the calypsonian, the injection of the older women's point of view, the expression of their understanding of the danger awaiting Sylvia, and both a glimmer of hope and a sense of hopelessness are all conveyed in this passage. In this instance, too, the focus on Sylvia as a sexual object ready to be plundered – so typical of certain brands of calypso – is balanced, if not eclipsed, by a deeper probing into the social victimhood and tenuous promise that Sylvia represents.

Lovelace maintains the link between calypso and carnival in the novel through his depiction of the body on display at carnival time. But here as well, his focus on the female body is also a veneer for other fundamental concerns in *The Dragon Can't Dance*:

> Then he saw Sylvia, dancing still with all her dizzying aliveness, dancing wildly; frantically twisting her body, flinging it round her waist, jumping and moving, refusing to let go of that visibility, that self the Carnival gave her; holding it balanced on her swaying hips, going down and coming up in a tall, undulating rhythm, lifting up her arms and leaping as if she wanted to leap out of herself into herself, a self in which she could stay forever, in which she could *be* forever. (119)

The narrator moves beyond the characteristic male gaze that calypsonians often vocalize, and uses this description of the body in performance as the basis for an exploration of a deeper need for personhood. So when Aldrick, through whose consciousness we get this description, watches Sylvia and is captivated by her body, his response transcends the lust typically conveyed by the calypsonian; he understands the profound message that Sylvia's gyrating conveys: "He wanted to join her in the tall, rejoicing dance, cry; to swirl with her in the cyclone of affirming tears, and lose and gain himself in her . . . until together they disappeared into the self that she was calling back. . . . He wanted to give her life; her self" (119). While maintaining the double entendre typical of the calypsonian – sexual desire is still being suggested here –

the latter part of this passage moves the desire to another level. Aldrick is not simply a man captivated by physical beauty, but one who connects with a pursuit of self-actualization that he shares with Sylvia. Through his diction, Lovelace transforms a typical moment of objectification into an affirmation of Sylvia's humanity, using the focus on the female body as a starting point. Sylvia is portrayed not just as a sensual dancer, but as a strong, visible and self-aware person who is fully conscious of the opportunity to claim the self she desires – and which she holds within her *self* – through her carnival dance.

Sylvia's dance is a staging of the restorative possibilities of performance that Lovelace's use of a carnival aesthetic highlights. Through this dance, Sylvia moves, albeit temporarily, out of the Hill existence that threatens to lock her in a cycle of poverty and despair and reduce her to sexual prey. Like all participants of carnival parades, Sylvia assumes another persona. Accordingly, her performance announces the existence of another Sylvia, the defiant one that Lovelace hints at in an earlier depiction of her response to her peers' sexual overtures. Sylvia uses the visibility and performance space that carnival provides to perform not "the self that Carnival gave her" as Lovelace suggests, but rather a self that she herself imagines and constructs. Her dance is therefore emblematic of the possibilities that carnival performance can facilitate.

This dramatic moment is also important for the ways in which it positions men and women as equals in the struggle for visibility and in their understanding of the importance of this particular performance space. The passage's diction, which includes a number of first-person masculine and feminine pronouns, as well as the collective pronoun "they" affirms this equality. Aldrick reads the codes of Sylvia's dance accurately and experiences a spiritual oneness with her. This moment harks back to Rohlehr's discussion of the importance of carnival in colonial and early postcolonial societies in providing a space within which identities were assumed, reclaimed and validated.

The idea that Sylvia's dance represents more than an erotic gyration or a presentation of the body as sexual bait is bolstered by Lovelace's use of dance as part of his overall aesthetic. Aiyejina notes that Lovelace refers to dance as "perhaps the most affirmative human expression of self, indicating as it does the exercise by the individual of power/control over *his* body" (emphasis mine). Lovelace's choice of pronoun focuses attention on the male, yet his portrayal of

Sylvia's performance suggests that his affirmative view of the expressive power of dance is more gender-inclusive than his diction would suggest. Aiyejina also writes that Lovelace "refines dance and dancing into signifiers of the complex colonial and postcolonial mentalities, postures and possibilities".[30] Lovelace's representation of Sylvia's body in the carnival parade suggests that she, too, is one of those "subject people" (to use Lovelace's coinage) for whom dancing becomes a symbol of possibility.

In its next turn, this scene appears to betray Lovelace's well-known nationalist tendencies by focusing on men as the ones who should ultimately lead society towards the achievement of collective personhood. Aldrick, watching Sylvia, acknowledges her humanity and connects with her desire for personhood, and yet for a moment he still imagines himself as her saviour. Aldrick's desire "to give her life, her self" may be read as a moment of authorial intrusion – that is, an example of Lovelace's male-centred nationalist voice spilling over into the narrator's. But Aldrick realizes his own limitations and retreats: "How could he . . . he had to learn how to live and how to give life. This flash came to his brain and humbled him" (119). Aldrick's recognition of his own inadequacies and, by extension, those of the men he represents allows Lovelace to gainsay his nationalist audience to reconsider their "man as saviour" outlook of the movement. But the phrase "he had to *learn how to give life*" suggests some hope that the man can eventually take charge, an idea that may reveal Lovelace's own struggle to let go of his male-centred nationalist worldview.

The calypsonian/narrator also presents woman as dangerous, as one whose sexuality potentially makes men vulnerable, as she might lead them to destruction.[31] This theme also informs the novel to some extent, but here, too, Lovelace takes advantage of the complexity that the calypso form allows and within that tradition explores another dimension of women. Aldrick is captivated by Sylvia's beauty and charm, but like many calypsonians, he sees the power to captivate as a threat to the carefree existence that he wants to pursue: "She was the most dangerous female on the Hill, for she possessed, he suspected, the ability not only to capture him in passion, but to enslave him in caring, to bring into his world those ideas of love and home and children that he had spent his whole life avoiding" (23). So while the generic calypsonian idea of the woman as danger is apparent, Lovelace turns in a new direction in which the man is not trying to exploit the body and avoid the person, but quite the opposite: Aldrick resists an encounter with Sylvia's body in the interest of her as a person.[32]

The Dragon Can't Dance ends with the voice and point of view of Philo, the character who becomes a calypsonian, as he contemplates his turn away from his community and his use of calypso to enrich himself. During a visit with Cleothilda, Philo also provides gossip about Sylvia: "That girl gone to look for Aldrick." With some encouragement from Aldrick, Sylvia rejects the life of luxury as Guy's kept woman, decides not to marry him, and goes in search of Aldrick instead. Yet although she goes in search of another man, Sylvia exercises agency by deciding (against the conventional wisdom that the women of the Hill might typically embrace) not to spend her life using her body as her means of livelihood, which is what marriage to Guy would amount to. While Lovelace ends the novel on an equivocal note, this last turn merges his two central concerns: a commitment to using indigenous forms and a validation of (women's) humanity. These examples demonstrate the potential value of indigenous orature to recover the personhood of both men and women.

The author's choice of calypso as the performance mode that shapes this novel is especially judicious given the history of this form, its presence across the Caribbean and the ways in which it incorporates numerous other locally derived forms. Calypso is, in many regards, the embodiment of creolization, and it is therefore among the best examples of what Antonio Benítez-Rojo refers to as the "supersyncretic [Caribbean] culture".[33] Because it is indigenous to the Caribbean and closely aligned to carnival celebrations, calypso encompasses a range of other performances, including storytelling, tracing, social and political reflections, and preaching.[34] Through its close links to carnival celebrations, calypso captures a particularly Caribbean version of the carnivalesque. The natural orientation of the form towards the carnivalesque is especially germane to my argument that through this traditionally misogynistic genre, Lovelace, unwittingly or not, engages a womanist-feminist discourse within his broader exploration of personhood. As Gordon Rohlehr has noted, calypso is historically a site of contestation and a central mode through which the kinds of social confrontations that have defined postcolonial Trinidad have been consistently worked out. Thus, its inherent discursive orientations allow for an incarnation of calypso in performing fiction that showcases the Caribbean poetics of performance.

The inter-performative relationship between Lovelace's fictionalized calypso and the examples from the songs quoted at the beginning of this chapter illustrates the wide-ranging treatments of gender in both genres. The inclusion of disparagement, sympathetic treatments, agential characterizations and a multitude of ways of portraying women illuminates the depth of possibility intrinsic to both Caribbean orature and performing fiction. This complexity derives from the immense stylistic and discursive range that calypso offers, especially through its inherent carnivalesque orientations. Therefore, it is because of his heavy reliance on this form, which is indisputably masculinist, that Lovelace – inadvertently or not – offers much more than a discourse on masculinity in this work, and presents instead a nuanced and gender-inclusive picture. As is the case in *The Wine of Astonishment*, which is shaped by storytelling, *The Dragon Can't Dance* offers a fictional representation of gender relationships that is consistent with the complex, lived gender realities of Caribbean societies.

FIVE

Globalizing Yard in "Joebell and America" and "How to Beat a Child the Right and Proper Way"

IN 1981, TINGA STEWART'S ' No Way No Better Than Yard", written by Sangie Davis, was the winning entry in Jamaica's National Festival Song Competition. This song – which was later covered by Admiral Bailey – as well as other songs such as Pluto Shervington's "I Man Born Ya" and, out of Trinidad, the Mighty Chalkdust's calypso "Brain Drain", illustrates the engagement of Caribbean performance culture with meanings of and attitudes toward migration. The title "No Way No Better Than Yard" asserts a sense of superiority by claiming "yard" (home) as the best place, better than even the materially prosperous North American and European migrant destinations. The title captures the song's central idea that despite its challenges, for Jamaicans, the home space or yard surpasses everywhere else in terms of its ability to sustain its citizens. Chalkdust's calypso, on the other hand, supports going away; in fact, the singer dispels the notion that "brain drain" results when professionals leave Trinidad in search of economic prosperity. Instead, he defines "brain drain" as a consequence of the failure to protect and preserve Trinidadian culture, and advocates making local culture part of school curricula as the best way to prevent cultural loss. In "Brain Drain", yard is also characterized in ways that transcend geographical conceptions; it is also a cultural, ideological and psychological space. In this way, Chalkdust highlights his interest in citizenship as something that moves beyond mere statehood.

As responses to particular national and regional events and concerns, these songs illustrate the discursive possibilities of orature-performance in the way they engage questions related to space and place. They set home and away, "here and elsewhere" (to borrow Edward Baugh's term), as competing zones, and construct the Caribbean home space as not merely valuable, but as what I term "a valuable" because of the purchasing power of yard culture.[1] That is to say, this culture is the bedrock of survival for Caribbean immigrants in Western societies. Such émigrés reach for yard culture in ways that extend beyond occasional "feel-good" practices or momentary reconnection; a groundedness in yard culture stands as the predominant way of being in what the characters of these songs construe as a hierarchy of cultures. Yard culture, then, determines the extent of one's success in migrant locations and simultaneously allows migrants to maintain cultural agency.

I place Earl Lovelace's story "Joebell and America" (1998) and Colin Channer's "How to Beat a Child the Right and Proper Way" (2006) with the aforementioned songs by Stewart and Chalkdust.The title of Lovelace's story (the significance of which I address later in this chapter), is provocative and ambiguous; it implies a close association between Joebell and America, and among other possibilities may even suggest Joebell was in the United States for at least a part of the time that the story covers. Yet except for a brief layover in Venezuela, Joebell remains in Trinidad for the duration of the story. A convict who has had several run-ins with the law, Joebell has not given up on material success, but he decides that Trinidad is not the place where this success will materialize. Therefore, he sets his aspirations on the United States. Because his previous convictions prevent him from going through legal channels to get a passport and visa, Joebell devises an elaborate scheme to orchestrate his illegal migration to the United States. He buys a passport with someone else's picture in it, with the intention of getting to the United States by passing as a US citizen and Vietnam War veteran. The immigration agents at the airport doubt Joebell's claims and interrogate him until, in reciting the alphabet, he uses "zed" instead of "zee", which confirms for them that he is not a US citizen.

In her book *Clear Word and Third Sight: Folk Groundings and Diasporic Consciousness in African Caribbean Writing* (2003), Catherine John accurately locates "Joebell and America" within "the oral storytelling tradition practice that is at the heart of African diaspora cultural expression" (101). Additionally, within the storytelling tradition to which John refers is Lovelace's inscription on the written page of elements of picong, which are integral to Trinidadian speech culture and to the aesthetics of calypso and other performance modes specific to Trinidad. An examination of the performative etymology of picong begins to illustrate how Lovelace's stylistic inward turn to a tradition of verbal duelling reaches back to a deep and established tradition of orature-performance.[2]

Writing about the origins of picong, Kemlin Laurence notes that originally, *picón*, or mocking, was particularly associated with singing contests: "Each singer must be able to reply to his opponent's questions and challenges, and the teasing, taunting, often bitingly satirical remarks and repartee that are directed by one singer to the other, are known as picón."[3] In contemporary Trinidadian usage, the term "picong" retains the general connotation of verbal dueling but also applies to everyday speech, primarily in the form of mocking and teasing. Picong has also evolved as part of the twentieth-century popular performance culture of calypso, where it retains one of its central features: verbal sparring in which two singers playfully trade insults. In these incisive exchanges, each singer seeks to outdo the other in the force and sharpness of the insults. This form of picong is performed for a live audience and therefore relies on audience participation, with supporters egging on each singer.[4]

Throughout, "Joebell and America" is a literary recuperation of the performance context of traditional picong. First, Lovelace uses the two-part structure of the cross wake ceremony, from which picong originates, as the overarching shape of the story: part one is told by an ostensible third-person narrator, the equivalent of the first singer in a picong exchange, and part two is Joebell's first-person point of view, representing the second singer. Second, Lovelace uses a number of stock stylistic features from picong, most notably irony, mockery and teasing. Additionally, the cadence of "Joebell and America" – the lighthearted (even deceptively humorous) tone – is grounded in traditional picong. The performativity of this written fiction is therefore accomplished by the way in which Lovelace captures both the structure and tenor of picong on the written page.

"How to Beat a Child the Right and Proper Way" is delivered as a performance by the main character, Ciselyn Thompson, an older college student living in the United States, having migrated there thirty years earlier. In this story, the monologue used in conventional short-story writing is recast as informal West Indian storytelling. Ciselyn's monologue, which turns out to be a very long, meandering story that recounts pivotal moments in her life, is her response to an assignment to write and deliver a five-minute "how to" speech. Ciselyn goes to class after a day of elation and agitation following a ceremony in honour of her daughter, Karen. She has also witnessed an antagonistic encounter between another mother and her teenaged daughter, and her dismay over the daughter's disrespectful treatment of the mother takes her back to a pivotal day in her life as a parent in Kingston, Jamaica, years before. Because of the intensity of the memories generated by Ciselyn's encounters with these strangers, she changes her original topic, "How to Make a Budget and Stick to It", to "How to Beat a Child the Right and Proper Way". Ciselyn is so overcome by the perceived importance of her new topic that she dispenses with her prepared speech and cue cards and tells the class that she will give her "how to" speech "on the fly".[5] She uses the occasion of the speech and the memories triggered by the mother-daughter interaction she witnessed not just to tell her story, but also to engage in a particular kind of self-fashioning and cultural construction whereby she extols the superiority of West Indian cultural valuables. In so doing, Ciselyn positions herself as an agent whose control is exercised mainly through performance. She also uses the performative in her attempts to "reshape the migrant space",[6] transforming the classroom space into her "yard", where she "spread out" to tell a story shaped by informal Jamaican orature.[7]

Drawing upon an array of interconnected forms of Caribbean oral storytelling, Channer recovers a particular brand of informal yard orature in which women in particular tend to engage. Although men and children may be storytellers at various times, such as in the Anancy, Duppy and Big Boy stories, it is the adult female performance that Channer creatively exploits here.

The yard performance that Channer recuperates is that of a woman telling a story in an informal domestic setting, such as the area outside a rural home, tenement yard or working-class urban roadside – the literal yard. Such yard-style performances may also take place in public spaces such as grocery shops, markets or vending areas where women tend to congregate to carry out business and engage in gossip or casual conversations. As represented in Channer's story, the speaker who tends to dominate such performances ostensibly sets out to make a brief point or relate a single incident, or maybe to respond to a specific question, but then uses the opportunity as an occasion to tell other stories, "throw words" on someone present, teach, admonish, self-aggrandize or offer philosophical insights. Thus, Ciselyn's multiple digressions are intrinsic to the particular form of storytelling on which "How to Beat a Child the Right and Proper Way" is modelled. By inscribing various performance cues, Channer also encodes the situated, situational and culturally coded gestures and range of bodily involvement that are intrinsic to yard performances, and in this way captures the physicality and the kinesthetic dimensions of these performances.

"Joebell and America" and "How to Beat a Child the Right and Proper Way", along with the two songs discussed earlier, "No Way No Better Than Yard" and "Brain Drain", form the basis of a reconsideration of cultural negotiation as the primary survival strategy and mode of adjustment that West Indian migrants employ in Euro-American migration locales. The two stories epitomize Caribbean migrant fictions that veer away from current critical discourses that espouse transnational, diasporic or border-crossing identities, as well as cultural negotiation as a standard characterization of migrant experiences.[8] The stories suggest a tenacious hold, and sometimes an insistence, on the idea of a superior West Indian culture as a primary mechanism for entry into and survival in Western societies. Ciselyn's firm conviction that Jamaican culture is the reason for her success as well as that of her children leads her to insist that this culture should shape child-rearing practices in the United States. Thus, West Indian culture is not only a mechanism for survival; it is also projected as an import with the power to significantly advance American cultural traditions – a perspective that marks a movement away from cultural negotiation (that is, cultural compromise or hybridization) as a survival strategy.

The choice of performance modes in Lovelace's and Channer's stories illustrates the nature and degree of investment in yard culture that these stories advocate. Because it is shaped by the disarming yet incisive tradition of Trinidadian picong, Lovelace's "Joebell and America" validates West Indian culture by playfully exposing the consequences of performing another's culture. Joebell misses the chance to access "foreign"[9] and the rewards therein because he chooses to adopt another cultural persona, reverting to being West Indian only after his performance of "American" fails. Channer appropriates a form of Caribbean storytelling that captures the assertiveness of Jamaican yard culture and projects a sense of female agency. Both writers advance a kind of model West Indian migrant as one who understands the purchasing powers of yard culture. As a cautionary tale, "Joebell and America" details the consequences of a turn away from West Indian culture, while "How to Beat a Child the Right and Proper Way" showcases the archetypal West Indian success story. Yet in neither case does the chief character unquestioningly adhere to yard values. Rather, both Joebell and Ciselyn break yard rules, but they differ in the choices they make about which laws and cultural codes to live by and which ones to challenge. Ciselyn defies Jamaica's colour and class barriers, while Joebell breaks the honour codes of honesty, industriousness and fair play.

Since the post-1950s era, anglophone Caribbean critical discourse on migration has focused on a number of recurring themes in the works of prominent migrant writers such as Austin Clarke, Samuel Selvon, Jamaica Kincaid, Edwidge Danticat, Dionne Brand, Andrea Levy and others. These themes include the difficulty of adjusting to Euro-American cultures, nostalgia for the homeland, identity challenges, language differences and managing memories of home as characters reshape migration locations. Beginning in the latter decades of the twentieth century and extending into the present, these concerns continue to animate critics, as do others, including the identities of first-generation citizens, the remaking of migrant locations as hybrid new "homes"[10] and the unique challenges facing migrant women.[11] Indeed, the plethora of critical writings on migrant West Indian experiences abroad has prompted a call for more attention to representations of Caribbean experiences situated "locally".[12]

Channer's and Lovelace's stories beckon critics towards other ways of characterizing responses to the demands of migration, even as they engage some generic concerns of contemporary discourses, particularly issues related to place, space and Caribbean identities. This is not to say that these fictions have set a completely new direction in migration discourse. Indeed, the presence of Caribbean culture in foreign spaces has been one of the enduring concerns of critical inquiry. What I am highlighting is the shift in these stories away from more mediatory responses to the migrant experience, away from what Page refers to as the creation of "hybrid homes" as an investment in indigenous cultural survival. These works, I am suggesting, project a more dogged attachment to Caribbean culture to the extent that, in Channer's story, yard culture is *the* superior culture. By exposing the cost of the misguided use of performance of the Other, Lovelace's story offers a tacit validation of yard culture, in contrast to Channer's more explicit assertion.

This discussion of Lovelace's and Channer's stories – which are set in the Caribbean and the United States, respectively – also addresses the recent critical attention paid to the nominal presence of Caribbean locations in conversations about migration, transnationalism and diasporic experiences.[13] However, in its engagement with questions about place, the analysis here moves beyond a concern with geographic location to focus more extensively on performance as the means of cultural trafficking. Here, performance is also the discursive nexus of these stories, the place where both spaces – the Caribbean and the North American diaspora – are brought together in critical conversations. Important, too, as narratives about belonging, the stories insist on engagement with the frequently posed question "Where is home?" and are the basis of a consideration of this question through the lens of performance. Home, theorized here as yard culture, is housed in the body and is retrieved, enacted or suspended through performance.

Consistent with Lovelace's sustained exploration of the roles and responsibilities of Caribbean men in nation-making, "Joebell and America" tells its story of the failure to embrace yard culture through the representation of a male anti-hero. In this way, it is reminiscent of Lovelace's depiction of men in others of his works. Correspondingly, the choice of picong for the narrative architecture recalls a male-associated performance mode and a performance context that showcases male bravado. Making a significant movement towards a woman-centred poetics, "How to Beat a Child the Right and Proper Way" also offers a revisionary representation of migrant female subjectivity in its depiction of an agential Caribbean woman who domesticizes the formal classroom and remembers home from a position of empowerment.[14] Yet this domesticized space is also configured as discursive. This intersection of gender and genre marks a notable shift in migration discourses: as one of few recent male-authored works that present migrant women as their central characters, "How to Beat a Child the Right and Proper Way" also broadens conversations about migrant experiences in a category of Caribbean literature that has been virtually synonymous with Caribbean women writers. Through its woman-centred poetics of performance, this story represents women as being at the core of critical conversations about migration, space, place, citizenship and belonging. In this way, Channer presents woman as the narrator of the nation, and thereby recuperates, like James, Caribbean women's central place in nationalist discourses.

I theorize yard, the Caribbean home space, as the location of a cultural economy that, in the renditions of the artistes and writers under consideration here, functions as a repository of a kind of capital – one that supersedes Western capitalism because of its capacity to facilitate Caribbean people's access to the benefits of modern capitalist systems while allowing them to retain wholesome cultural identities. The ideas in the Tinga Stewart and Chalkdust songs cited above reverberate in Channer's and Lovelace's performing fictions, projecting yard not just as a physical space where roots are planted and where familiar kinds of living are maintained, but also as a storehouse, a safety deposit box, where cultural traditions and habits are housed and from which Caribbean people can retrieve cultural valuables necessary for purchasing the products essential to survival in modern capitalist societies.[15] At the same time, these stories do not present the Caribbean home space as an unproblematic haven. Rather, the Caribbean, or yard, is a complicated physical and psychic locale that has the potential to both empower and marginalize the subject.

In this consideration of the significance of self-fashioning as central to migration experiences, I focus on how the self- representations that emerge from performance reinforce and complicate representations of yard culture. In its literal usage, "yard" refers to the open, outdoor space on which the house is built. It is a domestic space, a place of freedom, an informal space where children run freely, where adults lime, gossip and ponder topical issues. But "yard" is also a general reference to where West Indians live, as well as a place that implies ownership and belonging – hence the use of terms such as "mi gone a mi yard", "go a yu yard" and "yu think yu deh a yu yard" to reprimand inappropriate behaviour not fit for public and formal occasions and spaces. Taking all of the above meanings as a starting point, I theorize yard as a sociocultural space: the place of belonging, the place where culture is located and vice versa. The body inhabits yard as yard inhabits the body. In the examples of performing fiction discussed here, yard culture is presented as a "superior" culture, with the fictional works articulating its value and superiority through performance. And performance itself is a valorization of yard; performing yard is also the act of transplanting it into foreign spaces. On the other hand, performing another's culture constitutes a rejection, suppression or deferral of yard culture. Therefore, a few key questions guide the discussion that follows: To what extent does performance validate culture as it simultaneously focuses on the self as either an embodiment of the best cultural values or as a representation of dissonance with such values? What does the performance of self reveal about how yard is conceptualized, represented and traded by the characters in these stories? How does the chosen orature-performance structure of each story support the larger theme of the promotion of yard that the stories project?

Performing Another: "Joebell and America"

The author's choice of writing style, in this case the two-part structure and use of the stylistic features of picong, is the primary means by which "Joebell and America" discredits a migratory instinct centred on remaking the self through an erasure of West Indian identity. This misguided self-invention undermines the cultural valuables of yard, which, in this story, ironically thwarts Joebell's chances of access to the epicentre of Western capitalism. Through this stylistic turn to the kind of Caribbean culture that Chalkdust advocates should be taught in school, "Joebell and America" advances the idea that rootedness in yard culture is the most responsible and strategic move towards economic advancement. In this way, "Joebell and America" anticipates other yard-centred representations, including Channer's "How to Beat a Child the Right and Proper Way", which was published over two decades later.

   In her discussion of Negritude in Eastern Caribbean literature in *Clear Word and Third Sight*, Catherine John returns to one of the Negritude movement's central ideas: namely, that the extent of a black writer's investment in and successful use of orality is a major marker of his or her rootedness in a black diasporic consciousness. Of the three authors whose works she analyses in this context, John concludes that Lovelace, through his extensive and effective use of the oral tradition, "carries the thematic and aesthetic concerns of negritude furthest". John also suggests that Lovelace's Joebell reveals "the most developed individuality and the biggest connection to community".[16] Lovelace's effective use of West Indian orature in "Joebell and America" and in the rest of his oeuvre is indeed an excellent example of anglophone Caribbean writers' turn to orature-performance for the aesthetic tools of their fictions, and John's idea that Lovelace presents Joebell as an individualist is insightful, as is the claim that Joebell shows connection to community. It is this latter point that I find most provocative and worthy of further exploration.[17]

It is also here, in Joebell's relationship to community, that I believe a consideration of the kinds of performances that Lovelace deploys is most useful. Joebell's unsavouriness as a character lies in his individualism, which shows his connection to his community to be unwholesome, selective and exploitative, as is made explicit in the way he stages performances of another in order to "beat" the modern capitalist system. Locating "Joebell and America" within the specific performance tradition of Trinidadian picong – in other words, paying attention to the performativity of this story – unmasks Joebell as an anti-hero, an individualist, who slips in and out of different cultural performances solely on the basis of personal economic expediency.

The significance of making the distinction between shrewd economic decisions and the validation of local culture that emerges as admonition in Chalkdust's calypso is couched in the playful but piercing tease of picong, which Lovelace utilizes to underscore the value of yard culture. The representation of Joebell as one who denies or suspends yard culture, and at least temporarily replaces it with another hegemonic foreign culture, shows a clear synergy between Lovelace's fictional account and Chalkdust's song, in terms of both their shared location in the performance culture and the vision of migration that each projects. Chalkdust's clever reinterpretation of brain drain – from the movement of intellectuals and professionals from Trinidad to the rejection and devaluation of local culture – resonates with Lovelace's presentation of Joebell as a failed would-be migrant. Clearly, Joebell understands that travel to the United States is both a potentially viable option for someone like himself who "find that he seeing too much hell in Trinidad" and, as Chalkdust suggests, a completely acceptable way to "improve [one's] status . . . and pay". However, Joebell misunderstands the balancing act that successful migration demands and therefore miscalculates the terms of the cultural trade that must necessarily accompany such a migration.

In the first of the story's two parts, that told from a third-person point of view, the speaker builds on stories about Joebell's illegal activities in a way that harks back to the kind of playful attack on the opponent's character that would be part of a traditional picong exchange. Also as in such an exchange, Joebell's first-person narrative in the second part of the story is constructed as a reply that seeks to turn these jokes and insults around – in this case, onto the Americans at the airport – and to recover some dignity.

The irony in the title is the starting point for Lovelace's satirical representation of Joebell's ill-conceived relationship with yard culture. The evocative and ambiguous title "Joebell and America" initiates the suggestiveness that underlines this story. Once it becomes clear that the United States is not the setting and that Joebell's relationship with that country is primarily vicarious, the story becomes open to multiple interpretive possibilities and begs questions about the way America is used in the story. For example, the ironic use of the term "American" introduces the idea that this story is a joke on Joebell – that his schemes and trickery, especially his denial of yard culture, amount to nothing in the same way that he has had no concrete relationship with "America".

But beyond this, Lovelace's use of "America" in the story's title troubles the term "American" in the ambiguous tone of the calypsonian and puts on notice this story's engagement with the United States as a hegemonic space. Boyce Davies acknowledges the term "American" as one "synonymous with United States imperialistic identity" and argues that people of other locales in the continent of America may not want to claim the term because of its hegemonic history or might do so as a "tactical assertion" of the self.[18] Lovelace's use of "American' might well exemplify the kind of ambivalence around the term that Boyce Davies suggests. The ironic usage may also be a kind of tactical self-assertion, a subversive reclaiming of the continental space in a story that uses Joebell's relationship to culture as the basis for a validation of West Indian cultural values.

The story's opening builds on the title and playfully sets up Joebell as someone out of step with the terms of engagement in the marketplace of cultures:

> Joebell find that he seeing too much hell in Trinidad so he make up his mind to leave and go away. The place he find he should go is America, where everybody have a motor car and you could ski on snow and where it have seventy-five channels of colour television that never sign off and you could sit down and watch for days, all the boxing and wrestling and basketball, right there as it happening.[19]

Although the generic idea here is that, like most other people who migrate from the West Indies to the United States, Joebell is seeking entry into the capitalist economy, the speaker's representation of Joebell's fantasy of the United States sets him up as a naïve, lazy loafer who does not understand the difficulties of migration or the kind of work immigrants have to do to achieve the material comforts that Joebell seeks. The mention of "seventy-five channels of colour television that never sign off" and being able to "sit down and watch [television] for days" clearly implies almost childish delusion.

The speaker extends his characterization of Joebell's delusional understanding of "foreign" in the way he presents Joebell's plans to get out of Trinidad. After he learns that the one thousand dollars he was trying to use to bribe the policeman into giving him a clean criminal record could buy a United States passport, and that "the only ticklish thing is that [he] will have to talk Yankee", the narrator wickedly remarks, "Joebell smile, because if is one gift he have it is to talk languages, not Spanish and French and Italian and such, but he could talk English and American and Grenadian and Jamaican; and of all of them the one he love best is American. If that is the only problem, well, Joebell in America already" (112).

The final line of the above passage illustrates Joebell's understanding of the power of performance. But the mockery embedded in the speaker's ironic tone exposes Joebell's ignorance of its limits, and of the rules of cultural negotiation and trade. The emphasis on performance here is important. Part of the joke on Joebell is embedded in his idea that simply being able to pass himself off linguistically as "American" will get him out of his economic woes. The folly of this plan is reinforced in how quickly Joebell is pacified after he expresses doubts about the lack of resemblance between himself and the picture in the fraudulent passport. Joebell's salesman tells him, "Listen, in America every black face is the same to white people." The modicum of astuteness Joebell shows in his question, "Suppose I meet up a black immigration?", quickly fades when the salesman assures Joebell, "It aint have that many, but, if you see one stay far from him" (118–19). The fact that Joebell is satisfied with this explanation, which bases his entry into the United States on a convincing performance of 'American", reinforces the satirical tone of this story. The evocation of picong here creates a humour that takes the sharper critical edges off the representation of Joebell, but retains the idea of Joebell's performance of another as an imprudent disavowal of yard culture.

The last derisive turn in part one of this picong implies that Joebell approaches a moment of clarity in which he recognizes his performance as useless mimicry: "All the talk he talking big, Joebell just playing for time . . . and now he start figuring serious how he going to get through this one." The sense that he finally understands that he lives in a world beyond his fantasy of the power of performing another is soon dispelled when, instead of a rational strategy, Joebell starts

> feeling for that power, that craziness that sometimes take him over when he in a wappie game . . . he telling himself they can't trap him with any question because he grow up in America right there in Trinidad. . . . He know Tallahashie bridge and Rocktow mountain. He know Doris Day and Frank Sinatra. He know America. And Joebell settle himself down not bothering to remember anything, just calling up his power. (121)

The "power" that Joebell calls up is his perceived capacity to play another by performing American and, in so doing, outwit Americans. The irony of the short phrase "He know America", following as it does his list of places and people he has seen on television, reveals the mockery at the heart of this representation of Joebell. It is here that the narrative speaker's picong delivers its final punch line.

That there is a serious undertone in the narrator's seemingly light presentation of Joebell is perhaps most apparent in the details we receive about Joebell's mother's exasperation with his conduct and the lengths to which she goes to rehabilitate him. Again, the seriousness of Joebell's attitude to life is masked – if only partially – by the humour of picong: "If they have to give a medal for patience in Cunaripo, Miss Myrtle believe that the medal is hers just from the trials and tribulations she undergo with Joebell." And

Lovelace's use of the incremental, a stock feature of oral discourse, heightens the story's performativity and presents Joebell's situation as being both comical and serious:

> She talk to him. She ask his Uncle Floyd to talk to him. She go by the priest in Mount St Benedict to say a novena for him. She say the ninety-first psalm for him. She go by a obeah woman in Moruga to see what really happening to him. ... Joebell fly up in one big vexation with his mother for enticing him to go to the obeah woman: "Ma, what stupidness you trying to get me in? You know I don't believe in the negromancy business. What blight you want to fall on me now? That is why it so hard on me to win in gamble." ...
>
> But Miss Myrtle she pray and she pray and at last, praise God, the answer come, not as how she did want it – you can't get everything the way you want it – but, praise God, Joebell gone away. (114–15)

A few key issues important to my argument are underscored in this representation. The casting of Joebell as an anti-hero because of his frequent run-ins with the law is apparent. I am more interested in the humorous presentation of Joebell as one who disavows West Indian culture, as seen in his response to his mother's visit to the Obeah woman: "Ma, what stupidness you trying to get me in? You know I don't believe in the negromancy business. What blight you want to fall on me now?" It is not that disbelief in Obeah means a rejection of West Indian culture as a whole. Joebell's scepticism itself is less important than his reasoning for distancing himself from the practice: namely, that it makes it "so hard on [him] to win in gamble". Joebell, then, sees this longstanding cultural practice as a hindrance to progress in his capitalist endeavours. In fact, Joebell's statement suggests that he does believe in the power of Obeah, because he claims it prevents him from winning. If we read Obeah as a symbol of deep West Indian (African-derived) folk tradition, and gambling as a more culture-neutral pathway to wealth, then this example amplifies the picture of Joebell as someone who is willing to disavow yard culture whenever he perceives it as an obstacle to "progress". Another important point emerges from the irony in Miss Myrtle's response to the news that Joebell has gone to America: she praises God that he has gone away. She admits that this is not the way she wanted Joebell's turnaround to come, but she thanks God that life has changed for him. The problem is that Joebell has gone exactly the route that Miss Myrtle prayed against: he has gone to prison, not America, because of his misunderstanding of what performances have the purchasing power to guarantee him the kind of immigrant success that he seeks.

Joebell's Picong

Joebell's self-representation in part two of the story is a carnivalesque moment that emerges as a kind of inside-out version of picong. Joebell's reply to the speaker of part one – which, in the spirit of the picong tradition, he would typically be expected to use to recover his dignity – reinforces rather than contests the first speaker's representation of him, thereby bolstering the joke on Joebell. In traditional picong repartee, the singers reply to each other's challenges in a taunting fashion in the hope of recovering the upper hand. In other words, the respondent is supposed to give back what he got. Lovelace revises this tendency and instead turns what would have been Joebell's self-defence, by means of teasing his opponent, into a self-inflicted wound: his own affirmation of the mockery previously directed at him.

Joebell's introduction to his story in part two is one of the most significant examples of the kind of capital exchange that "Joebell and America" presents. Joebell opens with the retelling of his encounter with another black convict in the airport detention room. Of this incident, Catherine John writes, "Despite his plight, Joebell still expresses feelings of solidarity with his Black American brother. The Black Power handshake is a recognizable sign that situates Joebell's politics within a Pan-African context. The collective coming-to-consciousness that Césaire cites . . . is presumed in the Black world of Lovelace's short story."[20] Joebell's understanding of this history is, of course, apparent in the scene. But the encounter can only be read as an affirmation of community if we ignore other parts of the description: "As soon as I see him I say 'Oh God!' . . . He believe I want friends. I want to tell him, 'Listen, man, I love you. I really dig my people, but now is not the time to come and talk to me. Go and be friendly by those other people, they could *afford* to be friends with you'" (122; emphasis mine). What seems more important to Joebell in this moment is not brotherly love or black unity; it is his individual survival. His idea that the other people can "afford" to be friendly with the convict reveals Joebell's capitalist motivations as the overriding concern in this moment. The Black Power handshake does not come from Joebell; it is the other man, he reports, who "shake my hand in the Black Power sign". If in her description of a "coming-to-consciousness", John means a gaining of awareness, then Joebell clearly fits this description, understanding as he does that he is part of a larger, diasporic black collective. However, by Joebell's own admission, solidarity is not his concern in this moment; he wants to get out of trouble and get to the United States to reap its alluring material benefits. Therefore, the picture that he paints of himself here seems to be more of someone who is preoccupied with individual advancement, and not one with a strong sense of community.

In Joebell's understanding, knowledge is the bedrock of successful performance. The irony in his failure to perform successfully despite his claims of having knowledge of "Americans" and "America" underscores the story's larger point about which cultural products are marketable in the capitalist system that Joebell is trying to enter:

> The both of them know I lying ... they want to trap me plain for even me to see. So now is me, Joebell, and these two Yankees. And I waiting, 'cause I grow up on John Wayne and Gary Cooper and Audie Murphy and James Stewart and Jeff Chandler. I know the Dodgers and Phillies, the Redskins and the Dallas Cowboys.... I know Walt Frazier.... Really, in truth, I know America so much, I feel American. (123)

Lovelace's use of picong, and specifically of mockery, is especially effective in the section above. Here, Joebell's attempts at self-aggrandizement are consistent with the picong respondent's efforts to recover dignity in the second part of the exchange. However, the effect is of a turning of the joke back onto Joebell, and so he ends up being an object of ridicule: he believes he knows "America" enough to outwit "Americans", yet of course, the knowledge he boasts of is based on media representations. Moreover, the irony embedded in his claims is made starker by his repetition of "I know". Clearly Joebell does *not* know, and the third-person narrator's earlier presentation of Joebell as completely naïve is reinforced by Joebell's self-representation here. His insistence on knowledge of "America" – "I know America so much, I feel American" – also emphasizes his distance from a Trinidadian identity. It is therefore Lovelace's rendering of picong that allows this comical yet still harshly critical representation of Joebell as one who rejects yard.

Notably, Joebell's connection to West Indian culture only emerges when he is convinced that there is no longer any hope of making it out of the Caribbean and into the United States, and this happens with some reluctance on his part – before Joebell decides to be West Indian, he "think about getting on like an American, but I never see an American lose" (124). Here again, we see Joebell's acceptance of a construction of America that supports his desire for success and individual survival. Further, Joebell thinks about "making a performance like the British, steady, stiff upper lip . . . that didn't match, so I say I might as well take my losses like a West Indian, like a Trinidadian. I decide to sing." Thus, after all preferred performances fail, Joebell makes his way back to a Trinidadian identity. But not even this final choice is convincingly or fully West Indian. Joebell remains outward-looking: "Gonna take ma baby / Away on a trip / Gonna take ma baby / . . . To New Orleans" (123–24). While he has decided to sing like a Trinidadian, he still imagines being in the United States. John's point that Joebell references both Trinidad and America and "shows compassion for both" supports her larger argument about a black diasporic sensibility. But any "compassion" that Joebell shows for Trinidad comes only when it becomes useful as his fallback. It is only after he fails to pass himself off as belonging to some other place and culture that Joebell realizes that there is value in embracing his own. Ultimately, then, Joebell emerges through his own representation as one who consistently shows preference for a foreign identity, which leads him to remain in a state of "imagigration".[21] It becomes clear that the culture Joebell seeks to trade is not the currency most useful for access to and success in the Western system that he seeks to enter. Ironically, fashioning himself as American actually further removes him from "America". Lovelace's recourse here to the kind of irony that is characteristic of picong in modern calypso intersects with Chalkdust's similar turn on what constitutes brain drain. Both artists contend that it is a lack of commitment to yard culture, not the choice to physically leave a geographic space that constitutes disloyalty to yard.

Recasting the Immigrant Female Subject

With only a few exceptions, critical conversations about migrant female subjectivity have centred mostly on representations by Caribbean women writers.

Channner's "How to Beat a Child the Right and Proper Way" fills an important gap. Channer's choice to place a dominant female in the role of protagonist and narrator presents a kind of cultural transplanting that internationalizes the traditional domestic or yard-centred agency associated with Caribbean women. Moreover, the representation of woman in Channer's tale instantiates a veering away from the dislocated female subject that appears in works by writers such as Brand, Levy, Danticat, Chancy and others. Although the women in these works are mostly complex characters, some are defined largely by their experiences of loss, loneliness, cultural dislocation and traumatic memories of home. The radical turn that Channer's story presents can be set against Chancy's characterization of migration experiences as a form of exile. In *Searching for Safe Spaces*, Chancy describes exile as "the condition of consistent, continual displacement . . . the radical uprooting of all that one is and stands for". It is, she continues, "cruelly painful, for what one has lost is carried in this forced nomadism from one geographical space to another; all that one has lost remains 'over there', in that place once known as home".[22] Chancy's characterization of migration experiences accurately describes many representations of Caribbean migrants in the region's literature over the past several decades. Overall, the representations of female migrant subjects are varied and nuanced, and in those characterizations in which women's resilience is highlighted, their strength is often part of challenging circumstances. Ciselyn, the protagonist and storyteller in Channer's story, marks a departure from other literary representations and critical discourses by distancing herself from the more usual traumatized, displaced (albeit fortitudinous) subject to become instead a reconfigured one who, despite her acknowledgement of difficulties in the homeland, presents herself as successful agent and presents yard as a complicated space: a space in which culture marginalizes but also potentially empowers the female to take on the new "home" and a capitalist system – often viewed as terrifying – that she is able to "beat the right and proper way". Through a particularly skilful use of performance, Channer presents a female subject who tells a story not uncommon among West Indian immigrants: one of resiliency, agency and memories of home as a place that is simultaneously empowering and challenging. This is a story that presents the challenges of race, class and gender as a testament to the subject's agential actions.

This revised construction of the migrant female subject centres on how the purchasing power of West Indian cultural valuables engenders in the subject a different relationship with space in the migration location, one in which she inhabits and controls the otherwise threatening foreign space. Ciselyn is not traumatized by this foreign space, and she engages in negotiation only as a starting point: she ultimately resists creating a hybrid culture and instead explicitly promotes West Indian culture as the most valuable asset in her quest for economic success and social stability in her new migrant location.

In this story, the migrant's relationship with the home space is also reinterpreted because Ciselyn remembers yard from a position of agency. The prevailing critical narrative about the homes from which Caribbean women migrate is articulated in Carole Boyce Davies's position that "home is portrayed as a place of alienation and displacement".[23] "How to Beat a Child the Right and Proper Way" insists on a critical discourse in which the migrant female subject remembers and is affected by yard in more complicated ways. Ciselyn presents the Jamaica of the 1950s to 1970s as challenging for the black (dark-skinned) woman but also as a space where she was able to overcome obstacles by drawing on the same cultural valuables that, ironically, were set up to marginalize and even traumatize her. It is in Ciselyn's choice of performance, in her discarding of the academic strictures of the five-minute "how to" speech and her adoption of the imposing voice of a digressive, woman-centred storyteller, that she offers other ways of constructing and representing migrant female subjectivity. In this way, performance functions as the central battleground on which issues of power are contested and questions of legitimacy are engaged. It is Ciselyn's intrusiveness as a performer, the kinds of performance strategies she uses, and the way she reshapes the performance space that allow her to reinterpret the race, gender and class struggles that she experienced in Jamaica.

Noting the similarities between pre-1970s migration literature and literature produced in the late twentieth and early twenty- first centuries, Kezia Page suggests that "despite the differences in gender, location and historical moment, there are strong similarities between the writers at both ends of the continuum . . . a prevailing in-betweenity, of constantly negotiating what it means to be Caribbean in another place, as well as constantly attempting to reshape the migrant space".[24] Although I posit that in the end, there is a movement away from negotiation or "in-betweenity" in the sense that the subject does not locate herself between cultures, the cultural imposition for which I am arguing in my reading of Channer's story occurs as the end product of a subtle and subversive cultural takeover that is veiled as negotiation. In this regard, I have isolated a number of key steps that precede Ciselyn's eventual takeover. These include overt recognition of the power of the new space, gentle pushing against the established boundaries, explicit power brokerage or bargaining, and finally full, explicit cultural imposition. As I will argue, an examination of Ciselyn's manoeuvres in the classroom reveals a move towards a different kind of relationship between the migrant subject and the new living space that represents not a hostile takeover, but rather a gradual erosion of North American cultural hegemony. Ciselyn's imposition of yard culture on the classroom space and her disruption of the power structure are emblematic of this larger shift.

It is precisely Channer's choice of a particular form of orature, the way he reshapes the conventional scribal story as yard storytelling, that establishes Ciselyn as a different kind of migrant subject and thus reconfigures the Caribbean short story through a performance-driven poetics. Tapping into the inherent improvisational characteristics of storytelling in general and female Caribbean yard storytelling in particular, Channer revises, renews and exploits both conventional and yard storytelling to create a new form of the short story – a performing and performative fiction in which the worldview, voice and body of a migrant Caribbean citizenship is envisioned. As a result, because Ciselyn is so integral to the performance and therefore the form of the story, my analysis of form is deeply intertwined with my discussion of Ciselyn's performance.

"How to Beat a Child the Right and Proper Way" is from the outset a performance, a classroom speech, but it undergoes a change from a formal speech act to a less formal one (Jamaican yard storytelling) which draws upon different features of orality. This is of utmost significance to the critical intervention that Channer makes in migration discourses.[25] The story's plot, which unfolds through Ciselyn's revised "how to" speech, comprises a series of events that she recalls through multiple associational loops; the speech, and the story, are thus structured around her memory. Because memory is the primary structuring device, most of the events that Ciselyn relates are the result of digressions; it is, in fact, these digressions that end up constituting the story itself. Other stock storytelling features, particularly repetition – especially of terms such as "let me tell you", "anyway" and "by the way" – are central to Ciselyn's cultural imposition as well as her self-fashioning.

Just as the performance setting of the story and the way in which Ciselyn reconstructs that setting as her own performance space are central to this process of self-fashioning, the same may be said of the way she positions herself vis-à-vis yard. Ciselyn's performance space is, originally, the college classroom – a symbol of Western male intellectual hegemony. Her departure from the rules of the "how to" speech is the first indication of her disruptive immigrant presence. By breaking this cardinal rule of the classroom from the outset, she redefines the terms of engagement. She is able to engender a shift in the perception of migrant female subjectivity primarily because of her self-representation. Ciselyn exploits the storytelling phrases used in various traditions and in the Caribbean context to present herself as a dominant figure in a space where she is expected to defer to the professor and the larger academic system.

The opening of her speech reveals an initial acknowledgement of authority, which I am naming as the first stage in Ciselyn's move towards cultural imposition. She begins under the guise that she is abiding by the professor's performance rules: 'Good evening, fellow classmates. I'm very please to appear before you to present my five-minute 'how to' speech in Speech 112 this evening. I know many of you had a long day at work, so I am going to be brief and to the point. I had a day off today, but that don't mean I should go on and on just because my energy is up.' Although she begins within the prescribed framework, with the expected formal framing devices ("Good evening, fellow classmates"), true to the performance tradition of informal storytelling from which she will actually operate, after her opening sentence, Ciselyn undercuts the established rules by digressing to say that she had a day off and that she will not keep her classmates for long. At that moment, there is an intimation that she will be keeping them listening to her story far beyond the allotted time.

Ciselyn's second interaction with the professor marks the next stage in her pursuit of ultimate takeover, and a more extensive remaking of the performance space. The demand, framed as a request, that immediately follows her statement of her intention to be brief is: "By the way, professor, we could open the door? . . . And while you doing that can I ask you to give me a little break if I go over five minutes, please? I have a lot on my brain tonight" (94). Ciselyn guilefully orders the professor to open the door with the use of "we" in her question, which then turns into "while *you* are at it". Moreover, each time she addresses the professor, especially with regard to how the class time and space should be handled, Ciselyn further erodes his authority and, in so doing, claims more of the performance space, gradually turning the classroom into her "yard". After her initial request for "a little break" (she goes over five minutes), Ciselyn increases her control by negotiating with the professor to allow her to use time originally allotted to three other students: "By the way, professor, I see you giving me the signal that I'm over my time, but I should point out to you that neither Singh nor Avila nor Cumberbatch are here this evening to give their presentations, so you might as well give me their time" (106). Ciselyn has clearly moved away from more covert negotiations and towards a position closer to telling the professor what to do. "I should point out to you" also reverses the power hierarchy, and "you might as well" implies that the professor is not left with too many options.

The final stage of Ciselyn's erosion of the professor's power becomes apparent when her negotiations turn into a full takeover and she consolidates her control of the performance space: "Yes, professor . . . I see you giving me the signal again, but I can't stop now. I have to go on. Bear with me. Bear with me. This thing is too important. Way beyond this class" (119). Here, Ciselyn's skill as a performer and her positioning of herself as a power broker are apparent in her simultaneous assertion of authority and apparent deference. "Bear with me" appears twice, yet she tells the professor she "can't stop now" and that her story's importance extends "way beyond this class". So while on the one hand she asks for the extra time, her assertion that she "can't stop now" forecloses on further negotiations. Even more disruptive here is her declaration that what she has to say is of more value than what was intended for the class. In these examples, the digressiveness found in oral storytelling is foregrounded in the way in which Ciselyn's class assignment becomes a set of admonitions that she declares are more important than her original speech.

Scholars such as Boyce Davies and Chancy, whose writings on representations of migration experiences are referenced earlier in this chapter, also call attention to the way in which Euro-patriarchal power manifests in the multiple levels of marginalization of immigrant women of colour. Ciselyn subverts this power structure by drawing on other kinds of Jamaican orality to not only remake the performance space but also to undermine the professor's authority. She follows her request for more time with, "You're shaking your head. Consider it a graduation present. After this semester you won't have to see ol' Ciselyn again. You smiling now. You little devil you. You smile just like my youngest son" (94). What on the surface passes as a joke is Ciselyn's strategy for making further inroads into the power structure in the classroom. The professor is forced to play along with Ciselyn; he smiles at her comment. But her acknowledgement of that smile further wrests the power from him. He smiles, not just like her son, but like her "youngest son", a statement most likely intended to remind the professor of Ciselyn's seniority and construct him as a boy in her yard. Channer transforms the dramatic monologue by injecting the playfulness and humour of yard storytelling, where humour is often used to "spice up" the story, to convey important messages and to hold the audience's attention.

Additionally, Ciselyn tells her audience that the events she recalls took place in 1972, noting that "some of you never even born yet". Here, she draws on yard culture values to privilege age, not status (such as that of the professor) as the arbiter of power. Age thus moves from being a value to being a valuable; it buys Ciselyn agency in a space where a different system of empowerment is supposed to govern behaviour. She becomes the professor, the one who educates, and therefore projects yard values as not only worthy for classroom presentation, but important enough to replace what the professor and the system he represents define as education. And if we read the classroom space as representative of the larger cultural landscape of the United States, Ciselyn's exercise of power within that space epitomizes her somewhat dismissive approach to US power. Her performance in the classroom is the agency she claims as she negotiates the power structures of the larger, sociocultural North American space.

Like the female protagonists of many other literary representations, however, Ciselyn also sees her new immigrant home as a threatening space, ready to destroy what she implies are superior cultural values. Yet she is able to move beyond seeing the United States as a place where the immigrant is under constant cultural attack, and even beyond the idea that this is a place she has to fight against: for Ciselyn, this immigrant destination is a controllable space. Ciselyn's remark to the mother she encounters earlier that day, "Don't let America turn you into any fool. You don't come from here" (105), expresses her reconstruction of the image of "America". The reputation of the United States as "the land of opportunity" and its status as world leader are reframed in Ciselyn's suggestion that it can turn someone into "a fool". And by telling the woman, "You don't come from here", Ciselyn implies that being from a different place is a good thing, a status the woman should find empowering. In justifying her decision to change her topic, Ciselyn explains to the class: "When you look at the state of young people in this country today, there's a lot of parents who could benefit from knowing how to grow their children right" (106). Here, she moves from the idea that one can prevent oneself from becoming a "fool" in the United States to taking the higher ground by claiming a superior cultural tradition, one from which her new country can benefit.

It is also significant that in deciding to change her topic from "How to Make a Budget and Stick to It" to "How to Beat a Child the Right and Proper Way", Ciselyn replaces a quintessential "American" value with a West Indian one that she tells the class "is more beneficial to the world" (106) – the kind of "good West Indian discipline" that recurs in the threats of the male protagonist in Marlene NourbeSe Philip's novel *Harriet's Daughter*. For Ciselyn, then, negotiation does not constitute cultural oscillation or hybridization; rather, it is a path towards cultural imposition. This time, however, it is the immigrant – not the overpowering, First World migration destination – whose culture is being imposed. While the choice that Ciselyn makes is not novel in and of itself, Ciselyn's proselytizing impulse – and her use of performance to execute that mission – epitomizes the shift in representation that I am suggesting defines this story. What appears to be a lecture about discipline and survival is also Ciselyn's involvement in mythmaking: she is replacing "American" myth with "yard" myth.

While Ciselyn's rejection of the "how to" speech is itself significant, even more important is the particular way in which she restructures the assignment. Of the multiple oral devices that Ciselyn employs, it is her execution of digressiveness that most radically disrupts the classroom structure and the broader North American environment that this classroom represents, especially since the digressions become the story itself. Channer moves away from a genre that inherently requires brevity and a clear set of writing conventions, all intended to relay a focused and clear series of instructions, to one structured around the speaker's memory, in which the content is determined by interconnected stories and events. Because Ciselyn offers a presentation that is shaped by her memory as well as by an agenda serving her personal and cultural goals, what should have been a compact and structured set of instructions never emerges. Instead, the story turns out to be a set of principles, ostensibly about childrearing but in fact more about conquering modern Western capitalist systems while retaining one's cultural agency. The move from a prescribed "how to" speech to a looser, digressive tale also highlights the fluid relationship between orality and writing, and the performativity of this kind of fiction situated at the cusp of writing and speech.

Despite Ciselyn's sales pitch for yard culture, Tinga Stewart's line "all nation have dem boderation" reverberates in her performance. A shift in the concept of home is apparent in Ciselyn's presentation of Jamaica as a place with multiple, but surmountable, barriers. Although she seems to accurately recall the struggles she experienced in Jamaica, her performance places more emphasis on her representation of herself as an agent who has positively exploited the cultural values of yard, rather than on how the difficulties of her past have scarred her. The race- and class-based inequities in Jamaica are recurring features of Ciselyn's story, yet she always places herself in a superior position vis-à-vis these would-be barriers. For example, although the story of her professional success is told against the backdrop of a class-based education system that excluded her, it is her personal agency that Ciselyn foregrounds as the most prominent memory that she carries with her to the migrant location:

> I'm the last of all the eight [siblings], and I watch as all of my brothers and sisters turn twelve and my parents take them out of school and send them to a person in the area to learn a trade. But I didn't want a trade. I wanted a profession. From I was small I want to be something important. . . . I don't know where the ambition come from, but that is what I have inside me from I born.
>
> . . . It didn't look like life was going to work out like I want. Although teacher said I had the brain in primary school, my parents didn't have the money to pay for the exam to pass and go to high school. And even if I did pass the exam, who was going to pay for the uniform and the books?

> Plus, you know something? My parents never think it was important. None o' them never go to high school yet. And none o' them never know nobody that went to high school either. But for me to go and learn a trade like making hats or sewing clothes was a normal thing. (108)

In the scenario that she lays out, Ciselyn sets herself apart not just from her family but also from an entire cultural orientation. She decided for herself that her path would be different – and better – than what her society's value system dictated was her designated place. Furthermore, as part of her storytelling strategy, Ciselyn does not relate this part of her life story to bemoan the difficulties of an inequitable postcolonial socio-economic system. As the story progresses, it becomes clear that this is simply the backdrop against which she presents herself as an extraordinary woman who has achieved in spite of the systemic obstacles.

That picture of exceptional strength emerges when Ciselyn relates how she managed to move from a blue-collar job in a factory to a clerical position in an accountant's office and later to supervisor: "But believe you me, I only spent five years on the factory floor before I got an office job." She explains how she "put away a little money to take some correspondence course" and passed five subjects, and although she did not pass English, she makes sure to point out that she "get distinction for maths" (109). The difficult journey to a white-collar position and to the middle class is again framed as a testament to Ciselyn's capacity to mine the most useful values of her culture:

> When I get my results, I go to work extra early the next morning and wait for Mr Parnell. . . . I make sure I put myself together spic-and-span, and when I see him step out o' him blue Cortina I go up to him and show him the paper with the passes I got.
>
> He said, "Miss Thompson. Congratulations. I'm so proud of you. Keep it up."
>
> Anyway, I said, "I don't have anymore to keep up, sir. I pass my subjects now. What I want is to apply for a office job. But I know the people who work up there won't give me a chance because I work in the plant and I'm not fair skin. . . . But I know you as a fair man . . . so I come to talk to you."
>
> Mr Parnell face turn red and then him start to laugh. . . . I just catch him by surprise. (110)

Ciselyn presents herself here as a woman who is so agential that in a society in which her gender, colour and class render her among the most marginalized, even the white Englishman who owns the factory where she is employed in a blue-collar position is susceptible to her careful strategizing. Ciselyn's representation of her negotiation with Mr Parnell consolidates her framing of the challenges she has surmounted; she provides the context within which the audience must read her actions. As Ciselyn relates the story, she told Mr Parnell that she knew that others would prevent her from being promoted because of race and class barriers and, more disarmingly, that she knew he was different, "a fair man". By showing how she put Mr Parnell in a position that made it virtually impossible for him to deny her a job, Ciselyn presents herself as having wrested power from her employer: "Mr Parnell face turn red . . . I just catch him by surprise." And in describing how she forced Mr Parnell to admit there was a vacancy, Ciselyn presents herself as an aggressive negotiator: "As long as it have to do with maths, I can do it. Just let me watch somebody do it for a week. When the week done, I want you to give me a test. I don't want anybody else to gi' me the test" (110).

At the end of this account, Ciselyn's bold moves force Mr Parnell to "hold down him head" in embarrassment and in admission of the unjust system designed to keep one such as Ciselyn in her place. However, what Ciselyn is emphasizing in this story is not the obstacles that women such as her face in Jamaica, but rather the fortitude that Jamaican women are reputed to possess. Thus rather than functioning as a traumatic environment that remains in Ciselyn's itinerant body, Jamaica is cast as the place where Ciselyn did her dress rehearsal for access to an even more demanding and potentially marginalizing capitalist system. Ciselyn's reconstruction of her conversation with Mr Parnell is an important element in the performativity of this story and the interaction between form and meaning. Her inclusion of only brief responses from Mr Parnell, set against her own verbosity, underscores the strength and boldness of a woman who never stayed in her designated place.

The sense of cultural superiority that Ciselyn projects, and that she represents through notions of superior parenting, is the point at which her conquest of both cultural contexts – Jamaica and the United States – converges. Ciselyn concludes that her daughter Karen has internalized society's colour prejudices: she reads and represents her daughter's disregard for her as a result of the colour-based system in which she is parenting a child of a much lighter complexion. Having got disapproving looks from Karen's schoolmates, and having been asked by one of the children if she is Karen's mother's friend, Ciselyn is deflated by perceptions of her black body. She tells her professor and classmates that her hair was "hard to manage", that her cheeks were "pronounced", "unladylike" and "tough" and that she admitted to herself, "You know you really, really black? Why you bother even try with makeup base? That kind o' black can't hide" (129). The deep psychological impact of the colonially derived "positional" inferiority[26] that defines Jamaican society is laid bare as momentarily crippling even for someone with Ciselyn's strength and resilience. But while she admits to this brief surrender to the debilitating class system, her understanding of the dangers of poor parenting trumps the few hours of depression she admits to experiencing. It is that same day that Karen and her friends show their disregard for her and, after a short period of self-loathing, that Ciselyn beats her daughter and recovers her position as a strong and forceful parent. From then on, Ciselyn sets Karen on a path to the kind of professional success that she celebrated on the day she tells the story to her classmates and professor.

Ciselyn's strategic placement of this story – the defining moment in her daughter's life, which she positions against the backdrop of her own feelings of defeat by a racialized society – projects her exceptionality. The dramatic climax of the day is Ciselyn's assertion of herself as a parent who is able to control a child whom society deems superior because of her lighter skin. Here, Ciselyn underscores the triumph of her individual strength over a racist system. Her beating and subduing of Karen – whose light-skinned privilege casts a different light on teenage rebellion – represents her conquest of this oppressive, racialized society. Further, Ciselyn sets her daughter's success under the guidance of a black mother against the destructive path and eventual death of a friend of Karen's, a light-skinned girl with parents of a higher social class. Ciselyn's inclusion in the story of the death of Karen's higher-class friend exemplifies the melodramatic tendencies of oral (yard) storytelling.

In addition to facilitating a shift in the discourse on migrant subjectivity, Ciselyn's representation of herself and her experiences in Jamaica and the United States also reveals the subversive capacity of performance. While her digressions and her organization of the story clearly project an agential migrant subject, her digressive manoeuvres also betray some insecurity, revealed in the way she uses some of these digressions to include seemingly irrelevant details that continually establish her personhood. For example, early in the speech, when she explains the reason for her change of topic, she adds, "I was in a mood where not a thing was going to bother me, because I was coming from a luncheon for my daughter Karen. I can't really remember the place. Fancy place though. When you walk in you see class. . . . Fancy name. . . . French" (95). Similarly, as she describes the mother she encountered and explains why she assumed the woman was Italian, she informs the class, "I'm not so good with the European setup. . . . But that don't mean I don't know the continent though, you know. My son Andrew . . . the bond lawyer . . . send me over there about six or seven times a'ready" (104). And about her neighborhood in Jamaica, she explains, "We had moved up to Havendale. . . . In those days, is only bank manager and people like that use to live up there. Lawyer, doctor, politician, businesspeople" (113). Each of these examples reveals a subtextual anxiety about personhood, and these digressions are evidence of Ciselyn's efforts to legitimize herself against the various constructions of Other – immigrant, black, female, older student – that the two societies in which she has lived seek to place her. These efforts highlight the story's engagement with migration as a problematic experience, even as it presents a migrant subject who is in many respects an agent, and who has taken from one society a set of cultural valuables that have guaranteed her prosperity in both societies. Ironically, it is the same culture that places Ciselyn in a lower stratum that also gives her the values and agency to defeat that culture's less empowering traditions.

Most of Ciselyn's uses of stock phrases such as "let me tell you", "listen to me" and "believe you me" emphasize her effectiveness as a parent and make the case for "beating a child the right and proper way" as the best way to save a girl from hardship. For example, as a way of establishing unconditional parental authority, one of the core values of the larger cultural model she represents, Ciselyn says, "Because let me tell you, I'm the kind of mother who will discipline a child anywhere anytime" (125). She also presents herself as a parent who knows all there is to know about proper parenting: "For let me tell you – when your child has you in the kind o' position like Karen had me, you're her slave for life . . . and whatever they want to do, they do" (141). This example shows one of several instances in which Ciselyn uses storytelling strategies to set herself up as an authority figure in the classroom, to claim dominance and superiority in a space where, as an immigrant, woman and older student, she could well be perceived as the lowest in the academic hierarchy. But here Ciselyn establishes that she knows more about effective parenting than her classmates and her professor do.

Perhaps most significant, however, is the way Ciselyn uses these storytelling strategies as her final rhetorical move to call attention to her ultimate success. In reference to Karen's behaviour after the beating, she explains, "Let me tell you something. You think I had any real trouble with Karen after I straighten her out that night? No sir. You think I had to give her something even close to that again? Not at all" (147–48). And she ends the story with, "After that, let me tell you, she see everything my way" (148). Presenting this ending as an unequivocal triumph for herself and her decision to "beat" Karen not only cements Ciselyn's emphasis on herself as a particular kind of mother but also underscores her presence as an embodiment of authority in this classroom, her performance space, and, by extension, in the larger United States culture. By beating her daughter, Ciselyn is able to instill in her the valuables, discipline and various behaviours that ensure entry and success in her profession, which – not surprisingly, given the yard storyteller's boastfulness – turns out to be one at the very top of the capitalist system: J.P. Morgan Chase. Ultimately, then, Ciselyn's culturally determined parenting style privileges her as a subject capable of surmounting systemic barriers. She passes these values on – in her story and in her family, as disciplinarian – as her cultural legacy, using performance both to validate them and to impose them on the audience she commandeers.

To avoid oversimplifying the validation of yard in these stories, it seems useful to return to the guiding questions of this chapter. To what extent does performance validate culture as it simultaneously focuses on the self as either an embodiment of the best cultural values or as a representation of dissonance with such values? What does the performance of self reveal about how culture is traded by the characters in these stories? None of the works being analysed here – songs or stories – explicitly projects yard as safe haven, where the subjects are always protected and their personhood always affirmed. Yard is a place the subject wants, and sometimes needs, to leave in order to use yard valuables to become agents in modern capitalist systems.

At the same time, both stories discussed in this chapter suggest that some responses to the questions about location and identity that they engage are available in the performances of their subjects – specifically, in the identities their subjects claim and disavow through performance. These works also suggest that self-fashioning is an elemental component of cultural trade; in both stories, it is through the characters' performances of particular selves that the perspectives on cultural valuables are most clearly elaborated. By showing how Joebell's attempts to pass as "American" undermine his ambitions and how his (re)construction of himself as another obliterates or delays his chances of gaining material success, "Joebell and America" illustrates at the very least what types of cultural performances do not have the purchasing power to allow the kind of access to wealth that Joebell seeks. On the other hand, Ciselyn's self-representation and her counter-hegemonic presence in the classroom yield her the space to recover and enact a particular brand of Caribbean performance that in turn makes her claim of Caribbean cultural superiority somewhat credible.

In his essay "Maps Made in the Heart", Edward Baugh notes that "the Caribbean, we have heard it said, is not so much a place as an idea, and, we may add, a passion, a set of variable desires".[27] From this more abstract sense of what constitutes Caribbeanness, one might conclude that Baugh – along with some others, such as Antonio Benítez-Rojo, whom Baugh quotes extensively in his essay – is reconciled to the idea that the Caribbean transcends a physical location. However, Baugh's pivot back to the importance of geography exemplifies the problematics of Caribbean identity and identification. Baugh continues,

> Yet we cannot break free of geography and the sense of place, even if we think only metaphorically and metaphysically, and in terms of "maps made in the heart".... One's identity is, in more than one sense, one's sense of one's place. Who I am is a function of where I am, or where I think I am.... the desire, however suppressed, for a sense of roots, a sense of one's particular ground, is ineradicable.[28]

That "sense of roots" remains a crucial undercurrent in both stories. Joebell is somewhat rootless as he sets his sights on material gains as his ultimate desire, while Ciselyn pursues similar desires with an unyielding sense of the geographic and psychic places where she belongs or where she is rooted.

In the presentation of Joebell and Ciselyn, therefore, Lovelace and Channer demonstrate Baugh's investment in the importance of roots; yet these stories insist on rootedness not grounded in place as geography, at least not directly. Rather, they locate home or yard in the performance of culture. Joebell, though physically located in the Caribbean, performs "foreign" to his detriment, and falls back on West Indian culture only when that performance fails as a literal passport to America. Ciselyn, who is physically located in a foreign space, embodies and enacts a Caribbean identity. From these stories by Lovelace and Channer comes a sense of Caribbeanness that more closely resembles Baugh's (and Benítez-Rojo's) more metaphysical definition of home. And in these representations, even in Lovelace's story with its Caribbean setting, home is comprised of a set of valuables that include cultural habits, beliefs and values that are housed in the body of the Caribbean person and are retrievable as performances. Lovelace and Channer suggest, through Joebell's and Ciselyn's performances, that the Caribbean or yard is located in the bodies of itinerant Caribbean people. Channer's story, in particular, troubles the notion that the United States and other migrant locations are hybrid homes where migrants such as Ciselyn live between cultures. Both stories also move beyond engaging with definitions of home; they, like the songs discussed earlier in this chapter, place a value judgment on Caribbeanness, suggesting that it is by embracing and performing this culture that the characters can most effectively exploit important purchasing power.

Afterword

THE CLAIM I MAKE for a poetics of performance as the guiding creative and ideological impetus of performing fiction raises a number of questions, a few of which I will consider in these closing reflections. First, to what extent are these texts in some way representative of a trend in anglophone Caribbean literature? In the contemplations that follow, I will highlight a number of other post-1950s works of fiction that could buttress the argument I have made in this work. By offering a brief sketch of the variety of ways in which West Indian fiction has been shaped by orality and orature, I am suggesting that the particular forms of performing fiction discussed in this book epitomize the many ways in which writers enter what Gordon Rohlehr refers to as a "continuum that exists between the living oral tradition and the growing scribal one".[1]

A related consideration is how current critical discourses about Caribbean fiction have reckoned with the ways in which the confluence of oral and written traditions has shaped fiction from and about the region. Taking for granted that the case I make in the foregoing discussion for a poetics of performance finds validation in other works, and that this book finds scholarly kinship in extant criticism, it seems useful to consider the implications for critical engagements with these fictions. With this in mind, I will close with some preliminary considerations that address the following questions: How should the existence of this established and growing genre impact or alter critical approaches to the study of anglophone Caribbean fiction? How should or does the presence of these works inform reading strategies and critical praxis?

In the introduction to this book, I noted that the poetics of performance is part of a more extensive and sustained engagement with what it means to be a nation, even as conceptions of nationhood have come to include diasporic communities and relationality in what is now termed the age of high globalization. I have also suggested that this claim to nationhood expresses itself through a turn to indigenous expressive culture for the rhetorical strategies by which that nation and the values it extols are represented and interrogated. Nadia Ellis's observation that "the nation . . . comes under much scrutiny in the work of recent critics of Caribbean literature"[2] speaks to a responsiveness to the body of literature that consistently engages the conceptions and articulations of nationhood.[3] This connection between creative works and nationhood implies a certain awareness and artistic activism on the part of writers who have harnessed the creole performance culture for their expressive resources. Given the significant extent to which orality shapes both the works I have included here and other fiction from the region, it is conceivable that the nation is not only scrutinized but also claimed, in literature, through certain writers' turn to the creole culture for the performance modes that become the means of their literary creations.

A survey of post-1950s anglophone Caribbean fiction shows a number of critical moments in the establishment of a poetics grounded in the region's performance culture. In the 1970s, and even more so from the 1980s onward, Caribbean literature realized another important expansion: the publication of several works by women writers from across the region. Since then, anglophone Caribbean literature has been virtually dominated by women writers, both at home and in the diaspora. In their introduction to the anthology *Her True-True Name*, Pamela Mordecai and Betty Wilson mark 1980 as the time after which a "remarkable volume of work" was produced by Caribbean women writers. Noting "the freedom and authority of the woman's voice" as a defining feature of fiction published by this growing cadre of women writers, Mordecai and Wilson also suggest that "the shape of the novel, as explored by Caribbean women, [is not] restricted".[4] Further, they attest that Caribbean women not only produced a substantial body of writing but also inscribed a distinctly Caribbean speaking voice onto the written page, one of several ways in which they changed the shape of traditional fiction. The post-1970s era of anglophone Caribbean literature therefore ushered in a reawakening that was led by, though not limited to, women writers. Novels and short stories by Merle Hodge, Olive Senior and Erna Brodber are among the pivotal works of this period. Arguably, this second wave of Caribbean writing established the creole-speaking voice, along with various performance modes, as a mainstay of narration in anglophone Caribbean fiction.

Merle Hodge's landmark work *Crick Crack, Monkey* (1970) is a leading text within this group of fiction shaped by orature that reflects how the Caribbean nation is simultaneously claimed, scrutinized, and has its values called into question. This novel, often lauded for its complex representation of female experiences in the postcolonial Caribbean, is also distinctive for its deployment of a Caribbean creole voice as the mode of narration and for its overall linguistic innovations. The author's use of *crick crack*, a framing device for storytelling in the Eastern Caribbean, locates the novel in an oral tradition. Therefore, in the author's choice of both title and mode of narration, *Crick Crack, Monkey* puts orature on notice and signals the significant influence of the oral tradition on West Indian fiction, which was, by 1970, well on its way to having a distinctive tradition. In its presentation of Tantie and Aunt Beatrice as flawed characters, this novel interrogates elements of both the creole and Euro-derived cultures, while also clearly foregrounding the creole expressive culture through its novelistic techniques. Simon Gikandi describes *Crick Crack, Monkey* as

> the first major novel by a postcolonial West Indian woman writer to problematize and foreground questions of difference and the quest for a voice in a social context that denied social expression to the colonized self. . . . The voice was, in radically contrasting ways, an instrument of struggle. [and] in terms of narrative, the recovery of voice becomes one way through which unspoken and repressed experiences can be represented.[5]

This notion of voice as a means of reclaiming marginalized cultural practices that have nonetheless stubbornly persisted and thrived is a centrepiece of postcolonial discourses. Furthermore, because *Crick Crack, Monkey* also draws on the creative resources of multiple Caribbean cultures, its pioneering contributions extend beyond protest literature; in this way, the work epitomizes the complex relationship between cultures and modes of representation that have come to define performing fiction. Thus, because of its critical turn to local cultures for the means of unpacking multi-layered, complex Caribbean experiences, *Crick Crack, Monkey* marks a groundbreaking literary juncture in the development of the poetics of performance for which I have argued.

Olive Senior, one of the most celebrated architects of this poetics of performance, presents a rich corpus that I have analysed elsewhere.[6] In response to Charles Rowell's question "What would you say are the probable forces, experiences or individuals that motivated you to become and shaped you as a writer – a poet and a fictionist?", Senior responds: "My major influence then was the oral tradition – storytelling, 'hot' preaching, praying and testifying (for religious influence was strong), concerts, 'tea-meetings' and so on."[7] Senior also affirms her reliance on the creole expressive culture for her oral-literary modes in her observation that "written stories, like the oral, can be formed out of the dramatic substance of everyday lives".[8] By including "dramatic substance" in her reflections here, Senior also attends to the performative as fundamental to the approach to fiction writing that she and others have adopted.

Senior's oeuvre, particularly her short story collections *Summer Lightning* (1986), *Arrival of the Snake-Woman* (1989) and *Discerner of Hearts* (1995), not only eloquently attests to the approach to writing she outlines in the above quotations, but also stands as a selection of some of the best examples of a body of literature grounded in what Michael Bucknor refers to as "grung" or "grounded poetics".[9] Bucknor's use of these terms evokes a subaltern poetics. *Grung*, creole for both "dirt"/"earth" and "farm", locates Senior's aesthetics firmly in the local and primarily working-class culture. "Grounded", with its suggestion of rootedness, implies a way of writing that remembers and recalls its creole sources. The stories in each of these collections inscribe the creole-speaking voices of girls, domestic helpers and other workers, voices which are familiar to anyone conversant with Caribbean performance cultures. Senior's characters literally stage performances in which they use gossip, conversation and a range of storytelling modes and strategies to represent the worldviews and sensibilities of Caribbean subalterns. By using different forms of orature as discursive tools, these characters contemplate urgent questions, challenge orthodoxies and expose cherished remnants of colonialism such as enduring class structures. In Senior's poignant stories, the simultaneous marginalization and agency of girls and women stand as one of the most vivid instantiations of a poetics moulded by the expressive systems of the creole culture.

Also published in the 1980s, Erna Brodber's first three novels evidence other points at which West Indian writers enter the oral-scribal continuum.

Drawing on a diverse range of oral and scribal sources, and including several identifiable oral forms and linguistic registers, Brodber's novels are some of the most richly textured examples of orally inflected fiction of the late twentieth century. Brodber's first novel, *Jane and Louisa Will Soon Come Home* (1980), uses a third-person voice interspersed with songs as a mode of narration. Some of the story is also written as a play, and dialogue in various creole registers is seamlessly interwoven into the narrative. Simultaneously, there are multiple voices engaging in a participatory narration similar to that used by Lovelace in his novel *Salt*.[10] Finally, in terms of locating this novel in an oral tradition, perhaps most noticeable of all is its title, which is the first line of the chorus of a well-known song for a children's game.

Myal (1988), Brodber's second novel, which has attracted much critical attention largely for its espousal of an African-derived Caribbean spirituality, is told in the person-to-person style of storytelling that Olive Senior has used extensively in her short stories. The tone and structure of *Myal* are those of the creole-speaking interlocutor who draws on a range of storytelling modes and oral forms. Brodber's third novel, *Louisiana* (1994), is one of the most intricately crafted multi-voiced, oral-scribal novels of the post-1950s era. With its leitmotif, "A who sey Sammy dead", as well as the use of Bible verses, conversations, songs and multiple other oral forms, *Louisiana* inscribes the oral-scribal synergy that defines contemporary Caribbean fictions.

Three of the texts that I have analysed in this book – those written by Channer, James and John – were published after the year 2000. Not surprisingly, the twenty-first century has seen a groundswell of fiction whose writers have claimed and built upon an oral-literary tradition that has shaped their artistic creations in diverse ways. Two works by Jamaican writers, Curdella Forbes and Paulette Ramsay, published around the turn of this century, are especially noteworthy. Remarkably, both works draw on a specifically rural Jamaican performance culture from the 1960s and 1970s. In *Aunt Jen* (2002), Ramsay reframes the epistolary form, long established in the British literary tradition, with the creole-speaking voice of Sunshine, a young female. Intertwined with Sunshine's letters is an array of oral forms – proverbs, prayers, songs, anecdotes – that successfully foreground the speakerly orientation of this novella, thereby complicating the oral-scribal intersection in unique ways. By using a creole voice that draws on multiple oral modes, Ramsay's character speaks the letter onto the page, crisscrossing orality and writing in a way that extends this centuries-old literary form in a specifically Caribbean fashion.

Curdella Forbes's story collection *Songs of Silence* (2002), published in the same year as Ramsay's novella but written in a different style, illustrates the variability of the kind of oral-scribal fiction that now constitutes the Caribbean literary canon. The inclusion of both "song" and "silence" in the title evokes listening as an essential component of the relationship that readers will be compelled to establish with this work. As described by a reviewer, the stories in this collection are "held together by the sure and simple voice of a child . . . [and] interspersed with the whisper of adult reflection".[11] The use of "voice" and "whisper" here underscores the prominence of orality in this work. Forbes's invented creole locates *Songs of Silence* within the tradition begun by early writers of performing fiction such as Reid and Selvon and later extended by poets including Lorna Goodison, Pamela Mordecai and Edward Baugh, to produce literary language that moves across and combines multiple Englishes. The performativity of this work is established through an artful integration of songs, idiomatic expressions, prayers, proverbs and other oral forms. Thus, inscribed on the pages of *Songs of Silence* is the richness and variety of Jamaican folk orality and the folk sensibilities that helped shape these stories.

The acceleration of a performance-driven aesthetic that has taken place in twenty-first-century fiction is also evident in English-language Caribbean novels by authors from outside the anglophone Caribbean. The most prominent and celebrated example of this is Junot Diaz's *The Brief Wondrous Life of Oscar Wao* (2008). Diaz's novel is a brilliant example of what Maureen Warner-Lewis refers to as "linguistic extravaganza".[12] Written in English but with Spanish words and phrases integrated throughout, this work demonstrates the growing acknowledgement of Spanglish as a prominent part of the linguistic landscape of the United States. Traversing the cultures of the United States and the Dominican Republic, this novel, through its performativity, employs a literary aesthetic that captures the fluidity that defines migrant experiences. Its shifting narrative points of view make possible an inscription of multiple voices, perspectives, cultures and modes of representation. The innovations of Diaz's novel extend beyond the linguistic dimension to incorporate a wide range of Caribbean performances. For example, its narrative voices signify upon the sounds and style of the carnival mas band, with its many and varied performance modes. In this work, as Michael Niblett notes, "Caribbean myths and legends are articulated alongside references to US pop culture, particularly comic books and graphic novels".[13] By illustrating the tension between itinerant and located Caribbean identities through style, Diaz places his work within an established poetics of performance for Caribbean literatures written in English.

It is beyond question that a poetics of performance that has guided Caribbean fictions since the mid-twentieth century is now a core feature of this literary tradition, and that the performative ethos that remains an enduring feature of Caribbean societies is now firmly established as the lifeblood of these works. There are several questions that logically follow from this. Perhaps the most significant of these is, how do readers – including and perhaps especially non-Caribbean ones – understand the aesthetics, practices and range of performing fiction, and how have critics been responding to this dynamic body of work?

Caribbean critics and theorists have taken note of the need for a critical praxis that attends to non-scribal and performative elements in the literature. Maureen Warner-Lewis opens her essay "Samuel Selvon's Linguistic Extravaganza: *Moses Ascending*" with the observation that "Errol Hill's suggested paradigm of Trinidad carnival, as a model for both moulding and *interpreting* the Trinidad theatre, is particularly apt for appreciating certain distinguishing artistic features of Selvon's oeuvre" (emphasis mine). Warner-Lewis goes on to lay out specific features of calypso and carnival that define Selvon's works. These include the "episodic narrative structure", the 'humorously ironic twist" at the end of calypsos and the "bands which together cohere to form the macrocosmic festival, Carnival".[14] Apart from highlighting the performance-driven structural features of Selvon's works, by including interpretation, Warner-Lewis gestures to the idea that engagement with and appreciation of Selvon's works must include attentiveness to these extra-literary forms through which the stories are told and by which they are structured. Because the sounds and sights that such performance modes integrate into these stories impact how readers experience them, it is imperative that these oral forms also influence the reception of oral-literary works and thus become central to the hermeneutical process.

Kenneth Ramchand's discussion of Brathwaite's distinction between reading literature and watching live performances underscores the fact that performing fiction occupies a space between the two in terms of the ways we tend to experience these forms and therefore requires different critical approaches: "Reading is an isolated, individualistic expression. The oral tradition, on the other hand, makes demands not only on the poet but also on the audience to complete the community: the noise and sounds that the poet makes are responded to by the audience and are returned to him. Hence we have the creation of a continuum where the meaning truly resides."[15] Though a reader-text relationship for any literary work is usually a one-to-one relationship, for performing fiction there is a middle person of sorts. Because writers of performing fiction inscribe performances into their work, reading these fictions is not quite the "isolated experience" to which Brathwaite refers. Since these written works are grounded in orality, they require critical approaches that similarly bridge orality and writing. Although the reader may have a text in hand and is ostensibly isolated, the performativity of the work renders him or her a quasi-audience member who is called upon to respond in the manner of an audience listening to a calypsonian, a storyteller or a dancehall DJ, for example. It is only by interacting with the text in a more active manner that the reader/audience can approach meaningful interpretations of performing fiction. The collaboration between teller and listener to which Olive Senior refers must, to some degree, also define the relationship that readers establish with performing fiction.[16]

As I have noted in the introduction to this study, Gordon Rohlehr has offered one of the most explicit acknowledgements of the need for a performance-driven critical praxis. To reiterate, he notes: "When [Selvon's works] are read aloud to a group, and there is an interplay between narrator and audience, they yield up ironies and subtleties which one can miss when simply reading the words on the page.... Criticism of works which are meant to be performed can never be purely *literary* criticism, although it may borrow some of the methods of literary criticism."[17] In his suggestion of "ironies and subtleties which one can miss when simply reading the words", Rohlehr implies that an attentiveness to performativity in reading Selvon's work and, by extension, performing fiction not only enhances the reading experience but is in fact essential to the interpretation of the text. The approach that Rohlehr proposes is, like the texts under consideration here, an amalgam of literary and performative perspectives.

Rohlehr's reference to Louise Bennett's poetry to illustrate his idea is particularly useful. He suggests that her poetry "depends so much on tones of voice, on the fluidity of the voice . . . that one ought to comment on the words in audible motion, rather than in their comparatively frozen form on the page".[18] The phrase "words in audible motion" suggests performativity and activity that extend beyond the relatively static existence of words on the page and transcend the typical reader-text interaction. Additionally, the reader needs to tap into his or her interpretive imagination to see the body in action, since part of the purpose of words in performing fiction is to dramatize stories in ways that make the characters' actions, and therefore their bodies, important to meaning in ways that are similar to our interpretive relationship with actors on a stage.

Two examples from Lovelace's oeuvre that are discussed in previous chapters of this study illustrate this point. I have argued that in *The Dragon Can't Dance*, the reader/audience must tune in to the features of calypso that Lovelace exploits in order to gain access to the "ironies and subtleties" of the work. This novel also exemplifies Rohlehr's point that "as products of the carnivalesque frame of mind, [calypsos] are concerned with ceaseless masking and unmasking, in which stereotypes may be simultaneously celebrated and demolished".[19] When readers pay attention to the carnivalesque features of the novel, they can move beyond the idea that Lovelace objectifies and mocks women, and can appreciate the novel's sympathetic and in some instances celebratory treatment of women. Attentiveness to double entendre, particularly in Lovelace's representation of Sylvia, is especially effective in reading feminist undercurrents in *The Dragon Can't Dance*. Similarly, it is essential to read "Joebell and America" as picong and to follow the twists and turns of the extended joke in order to hear the validation of yard culture that this story highlights in its representation of Joebell's failed migration efforts.

Colin Channer's Ciselyn, whose narrative constitutes "How to Beat a Child the Right and Proper Way", draws on multiple storytelling strategies to execute a story that extols the values of yard culture by engaging in cultural imposition, thereby challenging United States hegemony. However, when the reader/audience attends to the specific storytelling features she uses, it becomes apparent that beneath her exterior of agency and fortitude, Ciselyn also has anxieties about her status as an older student whose limited access to college education would render her marginal in this academic context. Ciselyn's choice of storytelling strategies – for example, the recurrent use of the authoritative "let me tell you" and "listen to me" – allows her to establish a kind of culture-specific authority based on her age and experience in order to place herself above her classmates and professor. However, simply reading the text on the page does not get the audience far enough to unpack these subtleties. Paying attention to Ciselyn's tone and imagining her body language – attuning oneself to the key elements of performativity – enables an appreciation of the story as a multilayered work that presents the migrant female subject in complex and nuanced ways.

The growing awareness among scholars of the importance of adopting critical practices that take performance into account shows that the subaltern-infused poetics does not only shape Caribbean fictions. Literary criticism, with its European origins and totalizing impulses, has also been reframed, since performing fiction demands, and is gradually receiving, new kinds of criticism. This has led to more holistic and inclusive critical theories and praxes that look to the culture of the folk for some of their hermeneutical tools. Thus, the development of coherent and explicit critical models is an important next step in this ongoing creative and scholarly element of the claim to nationhood.

Notes

Introduction

1. Calypso and carnival were suppressed at various points during the colonial era when black people's participation in the festivities increased and the celebrations were regarded as a threat to public order. Reggae, which emerged in Jamaica in the late 1960s and early 1970s, was often frowned upon, though not actually banned, before it gained international recognition. For a detailed account of the efforts to suppress carnival and calypso in post-emancipation Trinidad, see Andrew Pearse, "Carnival in Nineteenth-Century Trinidad", *Caribbean Quarterly* 4, nos. 3–4 (1956): 175–93.
2. I find Antonio Benítez-Rojo's definition of poetics useful in articulating my own use of the term to describe the kinds of prose fiction under consideration here. The elements that he includes in his delineation of poetics – structure, theme, character, conflict, technique and language – capture the encompassing way in which I use the term here. In other words, I am suggesting that performance shapes the fictions in their totality. See Benítez-Rojo, "Three Words Toward Creolization", in *Caribbean Creolization: Reflections on the Cultural Dynamics of Language, Literature, and Identity*, ed. Kathleen M. Balutansky and Marie-Agnès Sourieau (Kingston: University of the West Indies Press, 1998), 53–61.
3. Maureen Warner-Lewis, "Orality in Caribbean Culture" (lecture, Caribbean Worldview Series, University of the West Indies, Mona, 1995).
4. Ngũgĩ wa Thiong'o, *Penpoints, Gunpoints, and Dreams: Towards a Critical Theory of the Arts and the State in Africa* (Oxford: Oxford University Press, 1998), 105.
5. That connection between the significance of performance in all forms of orature is underscored in Ngũgĩ's point that "performance was what made the oral imaginative product so very powerful, be it a riddle a proverb, a story, a poem, myth or legend. It was in performance and the conditions surrounding it that

a well-developed system of oral aesthetics was perpetually developed." Ngũgĩ contends that "the oral text [or specific forms of orature] . . . becomes realizable in its fullest dimension as a work of creative imagination only in performance" (*Penpoints*, 109–11). He further states, "Performance is what distinguishes orature from literature, even in the most obvious way: when you are reading a novel, you don't need a performance". While making clear that performance and orature are not synonymous, Ngũgĩ also calls attention to the close relationship between the two. See, Ngũgĩ wa Thiong'o, interview with Charles Cantalupo, in *Ngũgĩ wa Thiong'o Speaks: Interviews with the Kenyan Writer*, ed. Reinhard Sander and Bernth Lindfors (Trenton, NJ: Africa World Press, 2006), 4.

6. See M.M. Bakhtin, *The Dialogic Imagination: Four Essays*, ed. Michael Holquist, trans. Carryl Emerson and Michael Holquist (Austin: University of Texas Press, 1981).

7. Sylvia Wynter, "Novel and History, Plot and Plantation", *Savacou* 5 (June 1971): 97.

8. Mervyn Morris. "Printing the Performance", in *Is English We Speaking* (Kingston: Ian Randle, 1999), 45.

9. Richard Schechner, *Between Theater and Anthropology* (Philadelphia: University of Pennsylvania Press, 1985), 35.

10. Several scholars of performance studies have written extensively about the relationship between performance and resistance. Marvin Carlson, for example, notes that "the body in performance provides not only alternative ways of knowing but a necessary subversion of the dominant symbolic order". Carlson also cites Sally Potter, who suggests that live performance always possesses a subversive and threatening quality. See Marvin Carlson, *Performance: A Critical Introduction* (New York: Routledge, 1996), 169.

11. Benítez-Rojo has also characterized Caribbean texts as performative, suggesting that "the Caribbean text . . . is a consummate performer" and further noting that the Caribbean novel in particular has "a will to set itself up at all costs as a total performance". He cites examples such as circus acts, concerts and carnival dances to explain the kind of performer he has in mind. Benítez-Rojo is referring to Caribbean texts' inherent propensity for spectacle, their intrinsic carnivalesque qualities that connect them to the similarly carnivalesque Caribbean culture. See Antonio Benítez-Rojo, *The Repeating Island: The Caribbean and the Postmodern Perspective*, 2nd ed., trans. James E. Maraniss (Durham: Duke University Press, 1996), 218, 221.

12. Curdella Forbes makes a similar point in her introduction to *From Nation to Diaspora*. However, that work theorizes gender in works by Samuel Selvon and George Lamming, and does not pursue a literary aesthetic as its primary focus.

See Forbes, *From Nation to Diaspora* (Kingston: University of the West Indies Press, 2005), 10.

13. For example, Edward Baugh famously characterized this engagement with the past as "the West Indian Writer and his quarrel with history" in his essay of the same name. More recently, Alison Donnell has argued that "the most important debates with which Caribbean writers have persistently engaged have been those concerning history". See Baugh, "The West Indian Writer and His Quarrel with History", *Tapia* 7, no. 8 (20 February 1977): 6–7; Alison Donnell, *Twentieth-Century Caribbean Literature: Critical Moments in Anglophone Literary History* (London: Routledge, 2006), 1.

14. I borrow this term from Antonio Benítez-Rojo, who uses the term "repeating island" to describe the cultural synergies among Caribbean islands. See Benítez-Rojo, *Repeating Island*.

15. Kamau Brathwaite, "Jazz and the West Indian Novel", in *Roots* (Ann Arbor: University of Michigan Press, 1993), 55–110.

16. Édouard Glissant, *Caribbean Discourse: Selected Essays*, trans. J. Michael Dash (Charlottesville: University of Virginia Press, 1999), 147.

17. Kwame Dawes, *Natural Mysticism: Towards a New Reggae Aesthetic in Caribbean Writing* (Leeds: Peepal Tree, 1999); Benítez-Rojo, *Repeating Island*.

18. Evelyn O'Callaghan, *Woman Version: Theoretical Approaches to West Indian Fiction by Women* (New York: St Martin's Press, 1993); Marlene NourbeSe Philip, *A Genealogy of Resist* Marlene NourbeSe Philip, *A Genealogy of Resistance and Other Essays* (Toronto: Mercury, 1997), 48, 51.

19. Gordon Rohlehr, "Literature and the Folk", in *My Strangled City and Other Essays* (Port of Spain: Longman, 1992), 68.

20. See Maureen Warner-Lewis, "Samuel Selvon's Linguistic Extravaganza: *Moses Ascending*", *Caribbean Quarterly* 28, no. 4 (December 1982): 60–69; Funso Aiyejina, "Unmasking the Chantwell Narrator in Earl Lovelace's Fiction", *Anthurium: A Caribbean Studies Journal* 3, no. 2 (2005): 1–10.

21. Maria Grazia Sindoni, *Creolizing Culture: A Study on Sam Selvon's Work* (New Delhi: Atlantic, 2006), xxi, 236.

22. Silvio Torres-Saillant makes a similar claim that "literatures written in European languages in the Caribbean area constitute a regionally unified and socicaesthetic corpus with its own identity". See Torres-Saillant, *Caribbean Poetics: Toward an Aesthetic of West Indian Literature* (Cambridge: Cambridge University Press, 1997), xi.

23. See Peter A. Roberts, *From Oral to Literate Culture: Colonial Experience in the English West Indies* (Kingston: University of the West Indies Press, 1997), especially chapter 3.

24. Walter D. Mignolo, *Local Histories/Global Designs: Coloniality, Subaltern Knowledges, and Border Thinking* (Princeton: Princeton University Press, 2000).
25. Ibid., 6.
26. Michel Foucault, "Two Lectures", in *Power/Knowledge: Selected Interviews and Other Writings, 1972–1977*, ed. Colin Gordon; trans. Colin Gordon et al. (New York: Pantheon, 1980), 81.
27. In this regard, Kwame Dawes's articulation of the political significance of what he terms "the new literatures" captures the ways in which subordinate knowledge and creolized expressive tools have "piped their way" into the written text: "The new literature had to both find the language and forms with which to contend with current realities . . . [and] had to find a poetic and aesthetic articulation that emerged not merely from a progression of the literary tradition but represented a qualitative shift from an anti-colonial literature . . . to postcolonial writing rooted in our way of seeing and speaking." See Dawes, *Natural Mysticism*, 57.
28. See Anthony Boxill, "The Beginnings to 1929", in *West Indian Literature*, ed. Bruce King (London: Macmillan, 1995), 27–37; Reinhard Sander, "The Thirties and the Forties", in King, *West Indian Literature*, 38–50.
29. Baugh, "West Indian Writer".

Chapter 1

1. See, for example, Ruth Finnegan, *Oral Poetry: Its Nature, Significance and Social Context* (Cambridge: Cambridge University Press, 1977); Walter J. Ong, *Orality and Literacy* (London: Routledge, 2002); Warner-Lewis, "Orality in Caribbean Culture"; Penny Fielding, *Writing and Orality: Nationality, Culture and Nineteenth-Century Scottish Fiction* (Oxford: Clarendon, 1996); Carolyn Cooper, *Noises in the Blood: Orality, Gender, and the "Vulgar" Body of Jamaican Popular Culture* (London: Macmillan, 1994); and Kenneth Ramchand, "The Fate of Writing in the West Indies: Reflections on Oral and Written Literature", *Caribbean Review* 11, no. 4 (1982): 16–41.
2. Mervyn Morris, introduction to *New Day*, by V.S. Reid (London: Heinemann, 1973). Since Morris's 1973 essay, several Jamaican novelists have used creole as their language of narration.
3. R.B. Le Page, "Dialect in West Indian Literature", in *Critics on Caribbean Literature*, ed. Edward Baugh (New York: St Martin's Press, 1978), 123.
4. Kenneth Ramchand, *The West Indian Novel and Its Background* (New York: Barnes and Noble, 1970), 73, 114.
5. Merle Hodge, "Language Use and West Indian Literary Criticism", in *The Routledge

Companion to Anglophone Caribbean Literature, ed. Michael A. Bucknor and Alison Donnell (New York: Routledge, 2011), 470.
6. Rhonda Cobham-Sander argues that "the styles . . . were developed during overlapping historical periods' and suggests that "a chronological consideration is misleading". Ramchand himself retreats somewhat from his idea that there has been a clear line of progression in the way in which West Indian writers have included creole in their fiction. He notes that "writers like V.S. Naipaul achieve effects of incongruity by exploiting the differences between the two voices". Considering that much of Naipaul's works were published after 1950 when, as Ramchand and others have suggested, the earlier distance and difference between narrators' and characters' voices was for the most part narrowed, this example from Ramchand clearly illustrates the greater shift over time and the diverse ways in which different writers use creole in their fictions. See Rhonda Cobham-Sander, "The Creative Writer and West Indian Society: Jamaica 1900–1950" (PhD diss., University of St Andrews, 1981), 185; Ramchand, *West Indian Novel*, 79.
7. Maureen Warner-Lewis, "Language Use in West Indian Literature", in *A History of Literature in the Caribbean*, vol. 2, ed. A. James Arnold (Philadelphia: John Benjamins, 2001), 27; Ramchand, *West Indian Novel*, 73–90.
8. Hodge, "Language Use", 475.
9. Jamaica Kincaid, "Girl', in *At the Bottom of the River* (New York: Farrar Straus, 1984), 5
10. Stuart M. Hall, "Lamming, Selvon and Some Trends in the W.I. Novel", *Bim* 6, no. 23 (1955): 172.
11. Edward Baugh, "Tribute to Vic Reid", *Journal of West Indian Literature* 2, no. 1 (1987): 2.
12. Hall, "Lamming", 172
13. Le Page, "Dialect in West Indian Literature", 129.
14. P.M.S., review of *New Day*, *Caribbean Quarterly* 1, no. 1 (1949): 132.
15. Ramchand, *West Indian Novel*, 77.
16. Le Page, "Dialect", 129.
17. Michael Cooke, "V.S. (Vic) Reid", in *Dictionary of Literary Biography*, vol. 125, *Twentieth-Century Caribbean and Black African Writers*, ed. Bernth Lindfors and Reinhard Sander (London: Bruccoli Clark Layman, 1993), 257.
18. Baugh, "Tribute", 1.
19. Warner-Lewis, "Language Use", 30.
20. Ibid.
21. See Erna Brodber, "Where Are All the Others?", in Balutansky and Sourieau, eds., *Caribbean Creolization*, 68–75.
22. Ramchand, *West Indian Novel*, 100.

23. Ibid., 101.
24. Ibid., 78.
25. Bruce Hamilton, review of *The Lonely Londoners*, Bim 7, no. 25 (1957): 61.
26. Ramchand, *West Indian Novel*, 90.
27. Hamilton, review, 62.
28. Ramchand, *West Indian Novel*, 90.
29. Rohlehr, "Literature and the Folk", 68.
30. Sindoni, *Creolizing Culture*, 81.
31. Forbes includes "ballads, movements, episodes, litanies of ritual, contrapuntal verbal performances" among the forms of music that shape *The Lonely Londoners*. See Forbes, *From Nation to Diaspora*, 88.
32. V.S. Reid, *New Day* (Chatham, NJ: Chatham Bookseller, 1972), 3, 5. Further citations of this work are given in the text.
33. Warner-Lewis, "Language Use", 25.
34. Hall, "Lamming", 172.
35. Baugh, "Tribute", 2.
36. See Michael Bucknor's essay "Olive Senior: 'Grung'/Ground(ed) Poetics: 'The Voice from the Bottom of the Well'", in Bucknor and Donnell, eds., *Routledge Companion*, 85–91.
37. Baugh, "Tribute", 2.
38. See Forbes, *From Nation to Diaspora*, 77–108.

Chapter 2

1. Philip Nanton makes a similar point when he notes that analysts have mostly used continuum theory as the framework within which to incorporate oral and written traditions. See Nanton, "Making Space for Orality on Its Own Terms", in *The Pressures of the Text: Orality, Texts, and the Telling of Tales*, ed. Stewart Brown (Birmingham: University of Birmingham Press, 1995), 83–90.
2. Glissant, *Caribbean Discourse*, 147, 137.
3. See Henry G. Murray, *Manners and Customs of the Country a Generation Ago: Tom Kittle's Wake* (Kingston: E. Jordan, 1877).
4. Cooper, *Noises in the Blood*, 2.
5. I use "stories" to refer specifically to oral tales, while I use "narrative" to mean a particular representation of events or ideas, an ideological construct.
6. Kamau Brathwaite, *History of the Voice: The Development of Nation Language in Anglophone Caribbean Poetry* (London: New Beacon, 1984). See also Carolyn

Cooper and Hubert Devonish, "A Tale of Two States: Language, Lit/orature and the Two Jamaicas", in Brown, *Pressures of the Text*, 60–74.

7. Belinda Edmondson, *Caribbean Middlebrow: Leisure, Culture, and the Middle Class* (Ithaca: Cornell University Press, 2009), 2.

8. In laying out the key concerns of *Twentieth-Century Caribbean Literature*, Donnell notes, "I wish to discuss the ways in which at certain critical moments the 'nationalist', the 'resistant', the 'oppressed' and the 'displaced' have been constructed as bona fide figures of Caribbeanness and how, in these moments, only they have been allowed to occupy the place of the ethical or the redemptive subject. I also want to examine the consequences that these strategic investments have had on the opening up of new critical pathways and the foreclosure of others" (6).

9. Kim Robinson-Walcott, *Out of Order! Anthony Winkler and White West Indian Writing* (Kingston: University of the West Indies Press, 2006), 2. Noting that Winkler "has often been taken by newcomers to his novels to be black" (9), Robinson-Walcott argues that Winkler's representation of blacks and blackness is one key element in the stark difference between Winkler's writing and a substantial body of literature produced by other white West Indian writers.

10. Karin Barber, "Literacy, Improvisation and the Public in Yoruba Popular Theatre", in Brown, *Pressures of the Text*, 6.

11. It is important to acknowledge that Caribbean scholars and creative writers, especially the latter, do offer complex representations. My point is that because orality is such a central subject in *Unburnable*, its complex treatment is more apparent.

12. Merle Collins, *The Colour of Forgetting* (London: Virago, 1995). Further citations of this work are given in the text.

13. Marie-Elena John, *Unburnable* (New York: Amistad, 2007), 88. Further citations of this work are given in the text.

14. Richard Bauman theorizes "responsibility to an audience" as essential to actions that may be defined as performance. See his *Verbal Art as Performance* (Prospect Heights, IL: Waveland, 1977), 34.

15. Dipesh Chakrabarty, "Postcoloniality and the Artifice of History: Who Speaks for 'Indian' Pasts", *Representations* 37 (Winter 1992): 1.

16. Pierre Nora, "Between Memory and History: Les Lieux de Mémoire", *Representations* 26 (1989): 8.

17. Yosef Hayim Yerushalmi, *Zakhor: Jewish History and Jewish Memory* (Seattle: University of Washington Press, 1982), 5.

18. Joseph Roach, *Cities of the Dead: Circum-Atlantic Performance* (New York: Columbia University Press, 1996), 2.

19. Collins, *Colour of Forgetting*, 13.

20. Chakrabarty "Postcoloniality",1.

21. Paul Connerton, *How Societies Remember* (Cambridge: Cambridge University Press, 2003), 19.
22. Catherine A. John, *Clear Word and Third Sight: Folk Groundings and Diasporic Consciousness in African Caribbean Writing* (Durham: Duke University Press, 2003), 2.
23. See Collins's first novel, *Angel* (London: Women's Press, 1987).
24. Maurice Halbwachs, *On Collective Memory* (Chicago: University of Chicago Press, 1992), 38.
25. Ibid., 182.
26. Nana Wilson-Tagoe, "Myth, Ritual and Song as 'Counter Texts' in Three Plays of Derek Walcott", in Brown, *Pressures of the Text*, 28–29.
27. In Erna Brodber's *Myal* (London: New Beacon, 1988), Reverend Simpson terms "exorcise and replace" as the primary aim of the education and religious systems of the postcolonial context that serves as the setting for this novel.
28. This is a direct reference to Nanton's essay "Making Space for Orality", in which Nanton makes a compelling case for discussion of orality outside of continuum theory.

Chapter 3

1. Donette Francis, *Fictions of Feminine Citizenship: Sexuality and the Nation in Contemporary Caribbean Literature* (New York: Palgrave Macmillan, 2010).
2. Patricia Mohammed, "Rethinking Caribbean Difference", *Feminist Review* 59 (Summer 1998): 2.
3. Hilary McD. Beckles, "Historicizing Slavery in West Indian Feminisms", *Feminist Review* 59 (Summer 1998): 48.
4. Forbes presents a full discussion of the intersections between the "making" of the West Indian literary canon, reading conventions, the role of nationalist writers in shaping literary representation and the way in which such literary works were read. See Forbes, *From Nation to Diaspora*, 5.
5. For many years, one of the stock expressions in Caribbean literary discourse has been the notion of the "voiceless woman". Davies and Fido define voicelessness as "the historical absence of the woman writer's text . . . [and] silence: the inability to express a position in the language of the 'master' as well as textual construction of woman as silent. Voicelessness also denotes articulation that goes unheard." Carole Boyce Davies and Elaine Savory Fido, introduction to *Out of the Kumbla: Caribbean Women and Literature* (Trenton: Africa World Press, 1990), 1.

6. Belinda Edmondson, *Making Men: Gender, Literary Authority, and Women's Writing in Caribbean Narrative* (Durham: Duke University Press, 1999), 5–6.
7. Forbes, *From Nation to Diaspora*, 2.
8. Ibid., 3.
9. Mohammed, "Rethinking Caribbean Difference", 8.
10. Beckles, "Historicizing Slavery", 35. Mohammed's analysis of Lady Nugent's documented observations about women provides useful insights into the ways in which differing definitions of black and white womanhood appear during slavery. See Patricia Mohammed, "Nuancing the Feminist Discourse in the Caribbean", *Social and Economic Studies* 43, no. 3 (1994): 135–67.
11. Forbes, *From Nation to Diaspora*, 35.
12. Rawwida Baksh-Soodeen, "Issues of Difference in Contemporary Caribbean Feminism", *Feminist Review* 59 (Summer 1998): 78.
13. Here I use the term "coloured" in the way Edward (Kamau) Brathwaite used it in his documentation of the categorization of people of mixed race (mostly black and white then) in Jamaica between 1770 and 1820. See Edward Brathwaite, *The Development of a Creole Society in Jamaica, 1770–1820* (Oxford: Oxford University Press, 1978), ch. 12.
14. Baksh-Soodeen also notes that "the notion of woman as worker", which has been consistently ascribed to black women, "was also true for the Indian woman under the system of indentureship". This example illustrates the kinds of overlaps that exist among different groups of women as well as the need for a more inclusive approach to conceptions of womanhood. See Baksh-Soodeen, "Issues of Difference", 79.
15. Beckles argues that "the stereotyped armed and deadly 'rebel woman' was singled out and promoted as a heroine within the struggle against slavery and patriarchy", noting that this approach, paradoxically, has not yielded the most illuminating revisionary work on women's participation in anti-slavery activities. He writes that "the process for selection in this status resulted in the exclusion of other types of less well-documented rebellious women whose oppositional politics remains textually suppressed". Beckles, "Historicizing Slavery", 47.
16. Beckles cites the memoirs of Michel de Cunes, which describe armed resistance of native women when the Spanish landed in St Croix and Guadeloupe. In this account, women are described as being "armed to the teeth". Beckles, "Historicizing Slavery", 38.
17. Lucille Mathurin Mair, *A Historical Study of Women in Jamaica, 1655–1814*, ed. Hilary McD. Beckles and Verene A. Shepherd (Kingston: University of the West Indies Press, 2006), 234.

18. Ibid., 235.
19. Ibid. In the chapter "The Black Woman: Agency, Identity and Voice", Mair cites primary sources that provide compelling examples of enslaved women's relentless use of various modes of rebellion, including court battles, extended lactation periods, feigned illness and, importantly, songs that mocked, critiqued and ridiculed the plantation system. Ibid., 234–37.
20. See Denise Hughes-Tafen, "Women, Theatre and Calypso in the English-Speaking Caribbean", *Feminist Review* 84 (2006): 48–66. This work examines the participation of Singing Sandra and Queen Ivena, two female calypsonians, in nationalist conversations.
21. Patricia Mohammed notes that an "anti-colonial militancy [among women] in India was conveyed to Trinidad through the medium of the newspapers" and that "both in India and the West Indies, Indian women were inside and outside the political struggle". One key area that Mohammed highlights is Indian women's centrality in counteracting "the 'westernizing' influences of the colonizer". Mohammed's research and her unearthing of the exclusion of Indian women from conversations about West Indian womanhood, particularly women's political engagement, legitimize the inclusive theorization of womanhood that emerges from my analysis in this chapter. Mohammed, "Towards an Indigenous Feminist Theorizing in the Caribbean", *Feminist Review* 59 (Summer 1998): 13.
22. By "conventional conceptions of womanhood", I mean the proclaimed Eurocentric ideal of female respectability, such as that addressed in the chapter "Colonial Legacies, Gender Indentity, and Black Female Writing in the Diaspora" in John's *Clear Word and Third Sight*, 43–73.
23. These laws were passed in 1917 and remained in place until 1951.
24. Marjorie Thorpe, introduction to *The Wine of Astonishment*, by Earl Lovelace (Oxford: Heinemann, 1986), viii.
25. Forbes argues in *From Nation to Diaspora* that "given the nature of nationalism as an intrinsically totalizing world view, the focus was on those issues that affected the society macrocosmically, with a concomitant 'unreading' . . . of microcosmic differences, processes and relations. . . . It was in this context that gender remained unread, even though it was inevitably and in some cases deliberately and ideologically written in the fictions" (5). Forbes also includes Lovelace in a list of writers she describes as "arch-nationalists" (13).
26. In *Growing in the Dark*, for example, Lovelace argues that the retrieval of personood involves "a new valuing of the human person, a new respect for life, a new appreciation for the need to trust, that affirms for us the need for fair play and respect that goes beyond colour, class, race and creed". The absence of gender from this list is part of a broader gender-neutral orientation of nationalist discourses.

See Lovelace, *Growing in the Dark: Selected Essays*, ed. Funso Aiyejina (San Juan, Trinidad: Lexicon, 2003), xiv.
27. Marlon James's first novel is *John Crow's Devil* (Brooklyn: Akashic, 2012).
28. Hughes-Tafen cites the work of Carole Maison-Bishop, who points out that in the 1800s, women, especially those considered "disreputable", dominated calypso. See Hughes-Tafen, "Women, Theatre and Calypso" 48–66.
29. See Carole Boyce Davies, "Woman Is a Nation", in Davies and Fido, eds., *Out of the Kumbla*, 165–94.
30. Lady Saw's recent remake of Gyptian's "Hold Yuh", in which she focuses on the male anatomy in much more explicit ways than Gyptian focuses on the female's, is an excellent example of the way that men continue to dominate the terms of the conversation about women and sexuality.
31. Francis, *Fictions of Feminine Citizenship*, 4.
32. See M.M. Bakhtin, "Epic and the Novel: Toward a Methodology for the Study of the Novel", in *Dialogic Imagination*, 3–40.
33. Julia Kristeva, *Desire in Language: A Semiotics Approach to Literature and Art*, ed. Leon S. Roudiez; trans. Thomas Gora, Alice Jardine and Leon S. Roudiez (New York: Columbia University Press, 1980), 64–65; See also Bakhtin, *Dialogic Imagination*, 410, 411.
34. The chantwell figure in Trinidadian oral tradition dates back to the nineteenth century, emerging in the 1840s as a verbal artiste who was part of stickfighting street gangs. As a member of the gang, his role was that of a soloist and spokesman for the group. His responsibilities included haranguing stickfighters into action and encouraging them to maintain their courage. The chantwell eventually became a kind of storyteller, critic and commentator, reminiscent of the African griot, and is a forerunner of the calypsonian. See Aiyejina, "Unmasking", 2.
35. Aiyejina, "Unmasking", 1.
36. Earl Lovelace, *The Wine of Astonishment* (Oxford: Heinemann, 1986), 1. Further citations of this work are given in the text.
37. Marlon James, *The Book of Night Women* (New York: Riverhead, 2009), 3. Further citations of this work are given in the text.
38. Richard Bauman refers to performance as "situated behavior, situated within and rendered meaningful with reference to relevant context". The specific context within which this frame is situated is the formal (and sometimes informal) storytelling performance context of the Caribbean that was born out of plantation experiences. *Verbal Art* 27.
39. Ibid., 9–10.
40. Kamau Brathwaite discusses "nation language" as one of the significant features of a uniquely Caribbean creole society in *History of the Voice*. For discussion of the

impact of Caribbean creole languages on fiction from the region, see Ramchand, *West Indian Novel*, and Warner-Lewis, "Language Use".

41. A "cuss-out" is a public quarrel in which the speaker/tracer engages in a verbal battle with an opponent. Often in a cuss-out, the abuse is one-sided. The people involved are usually women.
42. Chantwells are the performers from whom calypsonians descended. They were men who engaged in verbal battles as part of their role as stickfighters.
43. See Beckles, "Historicizing Slavery", 34–56.
44. Forbes, *From Nation to Diaspora*, 19.
45. Ibid.
46. Ibid., 20.
47. Sandhya Shetty, "Masculinity, National Identity, and the Feminine Voice in *The Wine of Astonishment*", *Journal of Commonwealth Literature* 29, no. 1 (March 1994): 76.
48. Shetty, "Masculinity", 68.
49. See Forbes, *From Nation to Diaspora*, 35.
50. See Edmondson, *Making Men*, 58–78.
51. See Claudia Tate's interview with Audre Lorde in *Black Women Writers at Work*, ed. Claudia Tate (New York: Continuum, 1984), 106–7.
52. See John, *Clear Word and Third Sight*, especially chapter 2, for a useful discussion of the different models of womanhood available to, and imposed upon, women in Caribbean and larger African diasporic contexts.
53. Mohammed's discussion of Lady Nugent's observation about enslaved women provides a context for the genesis of these views, which have persisted long after the end of slavery. See Mohammed, "Nuancing the Feminist Discourse".
54. In the Jamaican culture, a man referred to as "bwoy" is almost always a sign of disrespect and is rarely considered flattering in the way "girl" used in reference to a woman might be.
55. Francis, *Fictions of Feminine Citizenship*, 6.
56. Carolyn Cooper, introduction to *Sound Clash: Jamaican Dancehall Culture at Large* (New York: Palgrave Macmillan, 2004), 3–4.
57. By all indications, official society's knowledge of and attention to pedophilia is virtually non-existent. For a discussion of the limited attention paid to this issue, see "Jamaica's Hidden Paedophilia Problem", *Jamaica Gleaner*, 23 January 2011, http://jamaica-gleaner.com/gleaner/20110123/lead/lead61.html.
58. For an analysis of "Ramping Shop" that goes beyond the hype and superficial critique, see Carolyn Cooper's article "Is 'Rampin' Shop' Erotic in English?", *Jamaica Gleaner*, 22 February 2009, http://jamaica-gleaner.com/gleaner/20090222/cleisure/cleisure6.html.

59. Although men still control the dancehall in terms of sheer numbers as well as by continuing to shape its discourse, my point is that this dominance has not gone unchallenged by female dancehall artistes.
60. In her introduction to *Sound Clash*, Cooper restates her position that dancehall provides a space for women "to claim a self-pleasuring sexual identity that may even be explicitly homoerotic" and asserts that "Jamaican dancehall culture ... is best understood as a potentially liberating space" (17).
61. "Women Will Rule the World", which opens chapter 4, is a classic example of this kind of calypso.
62. Discussions about how the desecration of the female body revealed the brutality of slavery abound. Here, I want to attend to how this fictional representation links the two factors with regard to female agency and power.

Chapter 4

1. Full lyrics are available at http://www.mustrad.org.uk/articles/calypso.htm.
2. Rohlehr traces the roots of these hostile tendencies to nineteenth-century "cariso songs, as well as the ribald music which accompanied the quelbay dancers of the 1880s". See Rohlehr, "'Man Talking to Man': Calypso and Social Confrontation in Trinidad, 1970 to 1984", *Caribbean Quarterly* 31, no. 2 (1985): 1–2.
3. I use the singular "calypso" in reference to the genre and the plural "calypsos" to mean songs within that genre.
4. Funso Aiyejina, introduction to Lovelace, *Growing in the Dark*, xiv.
5. In a recent discussion with a group of undergraduate students, Lovelace explicitly stated his sustained concern for and interest in black men in particular and non-European men in general. He bases this concern on the challenges these men have faced in meeting the demands of manhood, even as they are marginalized within Euro-patriarchal systems (Amherst College, March 2012).
6. Forbes, *From Nation to Diaspora*, 58.
7. Linden Lewis, "Masculinity and *The Dragon Can t Dance*: Reading Lovelace Discursively", in *Feminist Review* 59 (Summer 1998): 164.
8. See Funso Aiyejina's lecture, "Decolonising Myth: From Esu to Bacchanal Aesthetics," at: http://sta.uwi.edu/uwitoday/archive/october_2009/article12.asp.
9. Gordon Rohlehr, *Calypso and Society in Pre-independence Trinidad* (Port of Spain: Gordon Rohlehr, 1990), 164.
10. Gordon Rohlehr, "The Calypsonian as Artist: Freedom and Responsibility", in *A Scuffling of Islands: Essays on Calypso* (San Juan, Trinidad: Lexicon, 2004), 167.
11. Ibid., 164.

12. Rohlehr, "'Man Talking to Man'", 1.
13. M.M. Bakhtin, *Rabelais and His World*, trans. Hélène Iswolsky (Cambridge: MIT Press, 1968), 11.
14. Rohlehr, "Calypsonian as Artist", 168.
15. Ibid., 167.
16. Merle Hodge, "The Shadow of the Whip: A Comment on Male-Female Relations in the Caribbean", in *Is Massa Day Dead? Black Moods in the Caribbean*, ed. Orde Coombs (New York: Anchor, 1974), 116.
17. The "man of words" is highly valued for his verbal dexterity, which is demonstrated in many formal and informal settings including churches, political platforms, dancehalls, rum bars and construction sites. As Michael Bucknor notes, such use of orality often involves a "prevalence of bombast, exaggeration and a self-conscious attention to [men's] own virtuosity". It is not surprising, then, that calypso, one of the Caribbean's oldest and most popular genres of orature, functions as a site of masculine self-assertion and resistance. See Michael Bucknor, "Staging Seduction: Masculine Performance or the Art of Sex in Colin Channer's Reggae Romance *Waiting in Vain?*", *Interventions: The International Journal of Postcolonial Studies* 6, no. 1 (2004): 69.
18. Rohlehr, *Calypso and Society*, 54. According to Funso Aiyejina, "the chantwell functioned as a soloist and the other members of the gang as the chorus". He quotes Rohlehr, who writes that the chantwell, as the "possessor of the word and as a spokesman for the group, occupied a position of supreme importance" (*Calypso and Society*, 52), and continues that "the performance of the chantwell would go on to form the foundation of the calypso art". See Aiyejina, "Unmasking", 1.
19. As Rohlehr indicates, "the stick represented the phallus", and often a woman was the prize for the stickfighter's display of valiance. Logically, then, "the woman was transmuted from being the passionate prize . . . which crowned triumphant warriorhood into property . . . or antagonist against whom the male . . . fought out the battles that tested, affirmed and reaffirmed his masculinity". Gordon Rohlehr, "I Lawa: The Construction of Masculinity in Trinidad and Tobago Calypso", in *Interrogating Caribbean Masculinities: Theoretical and Emprical Analyses*, ed. Rhoda E. Reddock (Kingston: University of the West Indies Press, 2004), 327–28.
20. Forbes, *From Nation to Disapora*, 55. See also Davies, "Woman Is a Nation", 165–94.
21. Forbes, *From Nation to Diaspora*, 55.
22. "Bad John" is a term specific to Trinidad and is used to mean "hooligan", the kind of urban or urban-styled male whose aggressive demeanor and violent acts inject fear into communities.
23. Peter Nazareth, review of *The Dragon Can't Dance*, *World Literature Today* 56, no. 2 (1982): 394.

24. Kenneth Ramchand names Selvon's short story "Brackley and the Bed" as a work in which the narrator takes up the stance of calypsonian and ballad maker.
25. Aiyejina, "Unmasking", 3.
26. Rohlehr, "Construction of Masculinity", 355.
27. Earl Lovelace, *The Dragon Can't Dance* (London: Faber, 1979), 5. Further citations of this work are given in the text.
28. Aiyejina, introduction to *Growing in the Dark*, xv.
29. A few significant lines include "Who is Sylvia? What is she, / that all our swains commend her? / Holy, fair and wise is she / the heavens such grace did lend her". See act 4, scene 2 in William Shakespeare, *The Two Gentlemen of Verona*, edited by Roger Warren (Oxford: Oxford University Press, 2008).
30. Aiyejina, introduction to *Growing in the Dark*, xi.
31. The representation of woman as dangerous is a recurring theme in calypsos. A few notable examples are King Radio's "Matilda" (1938), whose title character "take me money and run Venezuela"; "Man Smart, Woman Smarter" (1936), also by King Radio; and Mighty Sparrow's "Obeah Wedding" (1966).
32. In this example, Lovelace's representation of the female subject is akin to Black Stalin's "No Woman No", in which the woman is valued and celebrated for more than her sexuality.
33. Benítez-Rojo *Repeating Island*, 29.
34. I am using "tracing" in the specifically Caribbean sense to mean extended verbal abuse.

Chapter 5

1. See Edward Baugh, *Derek Walcott* (New York: Cambridge University Press, 2006), 153.
2. Kemlin Laurence includes picong among a number of "loan-words" from the Spanish language that "enjoy great currency and popularity in all levels of Trinidadian speech". Laurence explains further that "in [Trinidadian speech] *picón* is particularly associated with the singing contests of the *velorio de cruz* (cross wake, Patois *veille croix*). During the course of the cross wake the principal singers, drawing upon an established corpus of material which is either religious (mainly Biblical) or historico-geographical (e.g., the discovery of the New World) in nature, engage in a sort of verbal duel carried out in song." Kemlin Laurence, "Trinidad English: The Origin of 'Mamaguy' and 'Picong'", *Caribbean Quarterly* 17, no. 2 (1971): 36–38.

3. Laurence, "Origin of 'Mamaguy' and 'Picong'", 37.
4. One of the most celebrated examples of this form of picong is the legendary duel between the Mighty Sparrow and Lord Melody performed in 1957.
5. Colin Channer, "How to Beat a Child the Right and Proper Way", in *Iron Balloons: Hit Fiction from Jamaica's Calabash Workshop* (Akashic Books, 2006), 94. Further citations of this work are given in the text.
6. Kezia Page uses the term "reshape the migrant space" in her discussion of the impact of home cultures on diasporic space. See Page, *Transnational Negotiations in Caribbean Diasporic Literature: Remitting the Text* (New York: Routledge, 2011), 15.
7. I use "spread out" here in the colloquial Jamaican sense. Louise Bennett discusses how one woman telling the other to "spread out, dress up / woman a come" was the catalyst for her distinguished career as a poet who used West Indian orature. This kind of "spreading out" refers to the physical taking over of space. In this context, the term takes its meaning from the literal spreading out that working-class women tend to do in spaces such as the market or in their yards as they gossip.
8. Evelyn O'Callaghan's discussion of the way England is "revisioned" in V.S. Naipaul's *The Enigma of Arrival* as "appropriation in reverse" is a useful characterization of representations of migration experiences that add another layer to the ways in which home and metropole are characterized in fiction. See O'Callaghan, "Exile and West Indian Writing", in *Caribbean Cultural Identities*, ed. Glyne Griffith (Lewisburg, PA: Bucknell University Press, 2001), 84.
9. I use "foreign" in the creole sense, in which it is a generic term for all places outside of the Caribbean.
10. Page, *Transnational Negotiations*, 7.
11. Carole Boyce Davies, *Black Women, Writing and Identity: Migrations of the Subject*. (New York: Routledge, 1994); Myriam Chancy, *Searching for Safe Spaces: Afro-Caribbean Women Writers in Exile* (Philadelphia: Temple University Press, 1997).
12. Donnell, *Twentieth-Century Caribbean Literature*.
13. Kezia Page argues that a "two-place gaze" is warranted in order to paint a fuller picture of migration experiences. Alison Donnell notes that diasporic experiences dominate Caribbean literary discourse. See Page, *Transnational Negotiations*; Donnell, *Twentieth-Century Caribbean Literature*.
14. This representation of cultural imposition as a survival strategy is anticipated in earlier migrant literature such as Selvon's *Lonely Londoners*; the character Tanty in that work changes how business is conducted by introducing "trust" (credit) to the storekeeper in London. Yet although Tanty stands out as one of the most wholesome characters in *Lonely Londoners*, she is not one of the ostensible main characters.
15. Here, I use "valuables" instead of "values" because I want to focus on the text's

presentation of the economic value of Caribbean cultures. Yet I am also interested in values in the way we tend to use the term to refer to beliefs and practices that guide how people live.

16. John, *Clear Word and Third Sight*, 111.
17. It is important to note that John discusses "Joebell and America" specifically within the context of diasporic connections in Caribbean fictions, and that in the chapter in which she analyses Lovelace's work she establishes a hierarchy of Caribbean writers that includes Kincaid, Hodge and Lovelace.
18. Davies, *Black Women*, 6, 9.
19. Earl Lovelace, "Joebell and America", in *A Brief Conversion, and Other Stories* (Oxford: Heinemann, 1988), 111. Further citations of this work are given in the text.
20. John, *Clear Word and Third Sight*, 104.
21. I borrow this term from Erold Bailey (oral communication).
22. Chancy defines exile not simply as "the expulsion of individuals through overt, political, governmental force from one's homeland . . . [Exile] is what makes remaining in one's homeland unbearable and untenable". Chancy, *Searching for Safe Spaces*, 2.
23. Davies, *Black Women*, 21.
24. Page, *Transnational Negotiations*, 15.
25. For discussions of the features of orality, see Ong, *Orality and Literacy*, and Warner-Lewis, "Orality in Caribbean Culture".
26. Edward Said uses the term "positional superiority" in *Orientalism: Western Conceptions of the Orient* (New York: Vintage, 1979), 7.
27. Edward Baugh, "Maps Made in the Heart: Caribbeans of Our Desire", *Journal of West Indian Literature* 18 no. 2 (2010): 7.
28. Ibid.

Afterword

1. Rohlehr, "Literature and the Folk", 68.
2. Nadia Ellis, "The Eclectic Generation", in Bucknor and Donnell, eds., *Routledge Companion*, 136.
3. See Ellis, "Eclectic Generation", 136–46.
4. Pamela Mordecai and Betty Wilson, introduction to *Her True-True Name: An Anthology of Women's Writing from the Caribbean* (Oxford: Heinemann, 1989), xi.
5. Simon Gikandi, "Merle Hodge" in *Caribbean Women Writers*, ed. Harold Bloom (Philadelphia: Chelsea House, 1997), 99.

6. See Carol Bailey, "Performing 'Difference': Reading Gossip in Olive Senior's Short Stories", in *Constructing Vernacular Culture in the Trans-Caribbean*, ed. Holger Henke and Karl-Heinz Magister (New York: Lexington Books, 2008), 123–38.
7. Charles H. Rowell, "An Interview with Olive Senior", *Callaloo* 11, no. 3 (Summer 1988): 480.
8. Olive Senior, "Lessons from the Fruit Stand: Or, Writing for the Listener", *Journal of Modern Literature* 20, no. 1 (Summer 1996): 42.
9. Bucknor, "'Grung'/ground(ed) Poetics", 85.
10. Merle Hodge, "The Language of Earl Lovelace", *Anthurium* 4, no. 2 (Fall 2006).
11. http://www.pearsonschoolsandfecolleges.co.uk/Secondary/Literature/14-16/CaribbeanWritersSeries/ISBN/PupilBooks/SongsofSilence.aspx
12. See Warner-Lewis, "Samuel Selvon's Linguistic Extravaganza", 60–69.
13. Michael Niblett, *The Caribbean Novel since 1945: Cultural Practice, Form, and the Nation-State* (Jackson: University Press of Mississippi, 2012), 204.
14. Warner-Lewis, "Samuel Selvon's Linguistic Extravaganza", 60.
15. Quoted in Ramchand, "Fate of Writing", 41.
16. See Senior, "Lessons from the Fruit Stand", 39–44.
17. Rohlehr, "Literature and the Folk", 68.
18. Ibid.
19. Rohlehr, "Construction of Masculinity", 355.

Selected Bibliography

Abrahams, Roger D. "A Performance-Centered Approach to Gossip". *Man* 5, no. 2 (1970): 290–301.

Abrams, M.H. *Doing Things with Texts: Essays in Criticism and Critical Theory*. New York: Norton, 1989.

Aidoo, Ama Ata. *No Sweetness Here and Other Stories*. New York: Feminist Press, 1970.

Aiyejina, Funso. "Decolonising Myth: From Esu to Bacchanal Aesthetics." Lecture, University of the West Indies, St Augustine, Trinidad and Tobago. http://sta.uwi.edu/uwitoday/archive/october_2009/article12.asp.

———. Introduction. *Growing in the Dark: Selected Essays* by Earl Lovelace, v–xxi. San Juan, Trinidad Lexicon, 2003.

———. "Unmasking the Chantwell Narrator in Earl Lovelace's Fiction". *Anthurium: A Caribbean Studies Journal* 3, no. 2 (2005): 1–10. http://scholarlyrepository.miami.edu/anthurium/vol3/iss2/8/.

Alleyne, Mervyn C. *A Linguistic Perspective on the Caribbean*. Washington, D.C.: Latin American Program, Woodrow Wilson International Center for Scholars, 1985.

Allsopp, Richard., ed. *Dictionary of Caribbean English Usage*. New York: Oxford University Press, 1996.

Ambursley, Fitzroy. "Grenada: The New Jewel Revolution". In *Crisis in the Caribbean*, edited by Fitzroy Ambursley and Robin Cohen, 191–222. New York: Monthly Review, 1983.

Austin, J.L. *How to Do Things with Words*. Cambridge, MA: Harvard University Press, 1975.

Bailey, Carol. "Performing 'Difference': Reading Gossip in Olive Senior's Short Stories". In *Constructing Vernacular Culture in the Trans-Caribbean*, edited by Holger Henke and Karl-Heinz Magister, 123–38. New York: Lexington Books, 2008.

Bakhtin, M.M. *The Dialogic Imagination: Four Essays*. Edited by Michael Holquist. Translated by Carryl Emerson and Michael Holquist. Austin: University of Texas Press, 1981.

———. *Rabelais and His World*. Translated by Hélène Iswolsky. Cambridge: MIT Press, 1968.

Baksh-Soodeen, Rawwida. "Issues of Difference in Contemporary Caribbean Feminism". *Feminist Review* 59 (Summer 1998): 74–85.

Baldrick, Chris. *The Concise Oxford Dictionary of Literary Terms*. Oxford: Oxford University Press, 1996.

Balutansky, Kathleen M., and Marie-Agnès Sourieau, eds. *Caribbean Creolization: Reflections on the Cultural Dynamics of Language, Literature, and Identity*. Kingston: University of the West Indies Press, 1998.

Banfield, Ann. *Unspeakable Sentences: Narration and Representation in the Language of Fiction*. Boston: Routledge and Kegan Paul, 1982.

Barber, Karin. "Literacy, Improvisation and the Public in Yoruba Popular Theatre". In *The Pressures of the Text: Orality, Texts and the Telling of Tales*, edited by Stewart Brown, 6–27. Birmingham: University of Birmingham Press, 1995.

Barrett, Leonard E. *The Sun and the Drum: African Roots in Jamaican Folk Tradition*. Kingston: Sangster's, 1979.

Barry, Peter. *Beginning Theory: An Introduction to Literary and Cultural Theory*. Manchester: Manchester University Press, 1995.

Baugh, Edward. *Derek Walcott*. Cambridge: Cambridge University Press, 2006.

———. "Maps Made in the Heart: Caribbeans of Our Desire". *Journal of West Indian Literature* 18, no. 2 (2010): 1–19.

———. "Tribute to Vic Reid". *Journal of West Indian Literature* 2, no. 1 (1987): 1–3.

———. "The West Indian Writer and His Quarrel with History". *Tapia* 7, no. 8 (20 February 1977): 6–7.

Bauman, Richard. "Performance". In *The International Encyclopedia of Communication* 3, edited by Erik Barnouw, 262–66. Oxford: Oxford University Press, 1989.

———. *Verbal Art as Performance*. Prospect Heights, IL: Waveland, 1977.

Beardsley, Monroe C. *Aesthetics from Classical Greece to the Present: A Short History*. Tuscaloosa: University of Alabama Press, 1975.

Beckles, Hilary McD. "Historicizing Slavery in West Indian Feminisms". *Feminist Review* 59 (Summer 1998): 34–56.

Benítez-Rojo, Antonio. *The Repeating Island: The Caribbean and the Postmodern Perspective*. 2nd ed. Translated by James E. Maraniss. Durham: Duke University Press, 1996.

———. "Three Words Toward Creolization". In *Caribbean Creolization: Reflections on the Cultural Dynamics of Language, Literature, and Identity*, edited by Kathleen M. Balutansky and Marie-Agnès Sourieau, 53–61. Kingston: University of the West Indies Press, 1998.

Benjamin, Walter. *Illuminations*. New York: Harcourt, 1995.

Bhabha, Homi. *The Location of Culture*. New York: Routledge, 1994.

Booker, M. Keith, and Dubravka Juraga. *The Caribbean Novel in English: An Introduction*. Kingston: Ian Randle, 2001.

Boxill, Anthony. "The Beginnings to 1929". In *West Indian Literature*, 2nd ed., edited by Bruce King, 27–37. London: Macmillan, 1995.

Boyce Davies, Carole. *Black Women, Writing and Identity: Migrations of the Subject*. New York: Routledge, 1994.

———. " 'Woman Is a Nation . . .' Women in Caribbean Oral Literature". In *Out of the Kumbla: Caribbean Women and Literature*, edited by Carole Boyce Davies and Elaine Savory Fido, 165–94. Trenton, NJ: Africa World Press, 1990.

Boyce Davies, Carole, and Elaine Savory Fido. "Women and Literature in the Caribbean: An Overview'. In *Out of the Kumbla: Caribbean Women and Literature*, 1–22. Trenton, NJ: Africa World Press, 1990.

Brand, Dionne. *Sans Souci and Other Stories*. Stratford, ON: Williams-Wallace, 1988.

Brathwaite, Kamau. "Creative Literature of the British West Indies During the Period of Slavery". *Savacou* 1, no. 1 (1970): 46–74.

———. *History of the Voice: The Development of Nation Language in Anglophone Caribbean Poetry*. London: New Beacon, 1984.

———. "The Love Axe/I: Developing a Caribbean Aesthetic". Pts. 1–3. *Bim* 16, no. 61 (June 1977): 53–56; no. 62 (December 1977): 100–106; no. 63 (June 1978): 181–92.

———. *Roots*. Ann Arbor: University of Michigan Press, 1996.

Brereton, Bridget. "The Trinidad Carnival, 1870–1900". *Savacou* 11–12 (1975): 46–57.

Broadhurst, Susan. *Liminal Acts: A Critical Overview of Contemporary Performance and Theory*. London: Cassell, 1999.

Brodber, Erna. "Fiction in the Scientific Procedure". In *Caribbean Women Writers: Essays from the First International Conference* edited by Selwyn R. Cudjoe, 164–68. Wellesley: Calaloux, 1990.

———. *Jane and Louisa Will Soon Come Home*. London: New Beacon, 1980.

———. *Louisiana*. London: New Beacon, 1994.

———. *Myal*. London: New Beacon, 1988.

———. "Re-engineering Black Space." *Black Renaissance/Renaissance Noire* 13 (1999): 153–66.

———. "Where Are All the Others?" In *Caribbean Creolization: Reflections on the Cultural Dynamics of Language, Literature and Identity*, edited by Kathleen M. Balutansky and Marie-Agnès Sourieau, 68–75. Kingston: University of the West Indies Press, 1998.

Brown, Stewart, ed. *The Pressures of the Text: Orality, Texts and the Telling of Tales*. Birmingham: University of Birmingham Press, 1995.

Bucknor, Michael A. "Olive Senior: 'Grung'/ground(ed) Poetics: 'The Voice from the Bottom of the Well'". In *The Routledge Companion to Anglophone Caribbean Literature*, edited by Michael A. Bucknor and Alison Donnell, 85–92. New York: Routledge, 2011.

———. "Staging Seduction: Masculine Performance or the Art of Sex in Colin Channer's Reggae Romance *Waiting in Vain?*". *Interventions: The International Journal of Postcolonial Studies* 6, no. 1 (2004): 67–81.

Bucknor, Michael A., and Alison Donnell, eds. *The Routledge Companion to Anglophone Caribbean Literature*. New York: Routledge, 2011.

Carlson, Marvin. *Performance: A Critical Introduction*. New York: Routledge, 1996.

Cebik, L.B. "Understanding Narrative Theory". *History and Theory* 25, no. 4 (1986): 58–81.

Chakrabarty, Dipesh. "Postcoloniality and the Artifice of History: Who Speaks for 'Indian' Pasts?" *Representations* 37 (Winter 1992): 1–26.

Chancy, Myriam. *Searching for Safe Spaces: Afro-Caribbean Women Writers in Exile*. Philadelphia: Temple University Press, 1997.

Channer, Colin. "How to Beat a Child the Right and Proper Way". In *Iron Balloons: Hit Fiction from Jamaica's Calabash Workshop* (Akashic Books, 2006).

Cobham-Sander, Rhonda. "The Background". In *West Indian Literature*, edited by Bruce King, 11–26. London: Macmillan, 1995.

———. "Revisioning Our Kumblas: Transforming Feminist and Nationalist Agendas in Three Caribbean Women's Texts". *Callaloo* 16, no. 1 (Winter 1993): 44–64.

———. "The Creative Writer and West Indian Society: Jamaica, 1900–1950". PhD dissertation, University of St Andrews, 1981

Collins, Merle. *Angel*. London: Women's Press, 1987.

———. *The Colour of Forgetting*. London: Virago, 1995.

———. *Rain Darling*. London: Women's Press, 1990.

———. "Writing and Creole Language Politics: Voice and Story". In *Caribbean Creolization: Reflections on the Cultural Dynamics of Language, Literature and Identity*, edited by Kathleen M. Balutansky and Marie-Agnès Sourieau, 87–100. Kingston: University of the West Indies Press, 1998.

Collins, R.G. *The Novel and Its Changing Form*. Winnipeg: University of Manitoba Press, 1972.

Connerton, Paul. *How Societies Remember*. Cambridge: Cambridge University Press, 2003.

Cooke, Michael. "V.S. (Vic) Reid". In *Dictionary of Literary Biography*, vol. 125, *Twentieth-Century Caribbean and Black African Writers*, edited by Bernth Lindfors and Reinhard Sander, 256–60. London: Bruccoli Clark Layman, 1993.

Cooper, Carolyn. *Noises in the Blood: Orality, Gender and the "Vulgar" Body of Jamaican Popular Culture*. London: Macmillan, 1994.

———. " 'Sense Make Befoh Book': Grenadian Popular Culture and the Rhetoric of Revolution in Merle Collins's *Angel* and *The Colour of Forgetting*". *Caribbean Quarterly* 41, no. 2 (1995): 57–70.

———. *Sound Clash: Jamaican Dancehall Culture at Large*. New York: Palgrave Macmillan, 2004.

Cooper, Carolyn, and Hubert Devonish. "A Tale of Two States: Language, Literature and the Two Jamaicas". In *The Pressures of the Text: Orality, Texts and the Telling of Tales*, edited by Stewart Brown, 60–74. Birmingham: University of Birmingham Press, 1995.

Croce, Benedetto. "Selections from 'Aesthetics'". In *Philosophies of Art and Beauty: Selected Readings in Aesthetics from Plato to Heidegger*, edited by Albert Hofstadter and Richard Kuhns, 556–76. Chicago: University of Chicago Press, 1976.

Cross, Wilbur L. Introduction to *The Development of the English Novel*. New York: Macmillan, 1920.

Daniel, Jack L., and Geneva Smitherman. "How I Got Over: Communication Dynamics in the Black Community". *Quarterly Journal of Speech* 62, no. 1 (February 1976): 26–39.

Davis, Lennard J. *Resisting Novels: Ideology and Fiction*. London: Methuen, 1987.

Dawes, Kwame. *Natural Mysticism: Towards a New Reggae Aesthetic in Caribbean Writing*. Leeds: Peepal Tree, 1999.

Donnell, Alison. *Twentieth-Century Caribbean Literature: Critical Moments in Anglophone Literary History*. London: Routledge, 2006.

Doyle, Laura. *Bordering on the Body: The Racial Matrix of Modern Fiction and Culture*. Oxford: Oxford University Press, 1994.

Edmondson, Belinda. *Caribbean Middlebrow: Leisure, Culture and the Middle Class*. Ithaca: Cornell University Press, 2009.

———. *Making Men: Gender, Literary Authority and Women's Writing in Caribbean Narrative*. Durham: Duke University Press, 1999.

Eliot, T.S. "Tradition and the Individual Talent". In *Selected Essays*. New York: Harcourt, 1950.

Esslin, Martin. *An Anatomy of Drama*. London: Temple Smith, 1976.

Fanon, Frantz. *Black Skin, White Masks*. New York: Grove, 1952.

———. *The Wretched of the Earth*. New York: Grove, 1963.

Fielding, Penny. *Writing and Orality: Nationality, Culture and Nineteenth-Century Scottish Fiction*. Oxford: Clarendon, 1996.

Finnegan, Ruth. *Oral Poetry: Its Nature, Significance and Social Context*. Cambridge: Cambridge University Press, 1977.

———. *Oral Traditions and the Verbal Arts: A Guide to Research Practices*. New York: Routledge, 1992.

Foley, John Miles, ed. *Oral Tradition in Literature: Interpretation in Context*. Columbia: University of Missouri Press, 1986.

Forbes, Curdella. *From Nation to Diaspora: Samuel Selvon, George Lamming and the Cultural Performance of Gender*. Kingston: University of the West Indies Press, 2005.

———. *Songs of Silence*. Oxford: Heinemann, 2002.

———. "Tropes of the Carnivalesque: Hermaphroditic Gender in Slave Society and West Indian Fictions." *Journal of West Indian Literature* 8, no. 2 (1999): 19–37.

Foucault, Michel. "Two Lectures". In *Power/Knowledge: Selected Interviews and Other Writings, 1972–1977*, edited by Colin Gordon, translated by Colin Gordon et al., 79–108. New York: Pantheon, 1980.

Francis, Donette. *Fictions of Feminine Citizenship: Sexuality and the Nation in Contemporary Caribbean Literature*. New York: Palgrave Macmillan, 2010.

Gates, Henry Louis, Jr. *The Signifying Monkey: A Theory of African-American Literary Criticism*. Oxford: Oxford University Press, 1988.

Glissant, Édouard. *Caribbean Discourse: Selected Essays*. Translated by J. Michael Dash. Charlottesville: University of Virginia Press, 1999.

Goodison, Lorna. *Selected Poems*. Ann Arbor: University of Michigan Press, 1992.

Halbwachs, Maurice. *On Collective Memory*. Translated by Lewis A. Coser. Chicago: University of Chicago Press, 1992.

Hall, Stuart M. "Lamming, Selvon and Some Trends in the W.I. Novel". *Bim* 6, no. 23 (1955): 173–78.

Hamilton, Bruce. Review of *The Lonely Londoners*. *Bim* 7, no. 25 (1957): 61–62.

Hardy, Barbara. "Towards a Poetics of Fiction: An Approach through Narrative". *Novel* 2 (Fall 1968): 5–14.

Harney, Stefano. *Nationalism and Identity: Culture and the Imagination in a Caribbean Diaspora*. Kingston: University of the West Indies Press, 1996.

Hassan, Ihab. "Queries for Postcolonial Studies". *Philosophy and Literature* 22, no. 2 (1998): 328–42.

Havelock, Eric A. *The Muse Learns to Write: Reflections on Orality and Literacy from Antiquity to Present*. New Haven: Yale University Press, 1986.

Hodge, Merle. *Crick Crack, Monkey*. Portsmouth, NH: Heinemann, 1981.

———. "Language Use and West Indian Literary Criticism." In *The Routledge Companion to Anglophone Caribbean Literature*, edited by Michael A. Bucknor and Alison Donnell, 470–79. New York: Routledge, 2011.

———. "The Shadow of the Whip: A Comment on Male-Female Relations in the Caribbean". In *Is Massa Day Dead? Black Moods in the Caribbean*, edited by Orde Coombs, 111–18. New York: Anchor, 1974.

Horne, Charles F. *The Technique of the Novel*. New York: Harper, 1908.

Hughes-Tafen, Denise. "Women, Theatre and Calypso in the English-Speaking Caribbean". *Feminist Review* 84 (2006): 48–66.
Hutcheon, Linda. *The Politics of Postmodernism*. New York: Routledge, 1989.
Iser, Wolfgang. "The Reading Process: A Phenomenological Approach". In *The Critical Tradition: Classic Texts and Contemporary Trends*, edited by David H. Richter, 955–67. Boston: Bedford, 1998.
James, C.L.R. "Discovering Literature in Trinidad: The Nineteen-Thirties". *Savacou* 2 (1970): 54–60.
James, Louis. *Caribbean Literature in English*. New York: Longman, 1999.
———. "Earl Lovelace". In *West Indian Literature*, 2nd ed., edited by Bruce King, 222–32. London: Macmillan, 1995.
James, Marlon. *The Book of Night Women*. New York: Riverhead, 2009.
John, Catherine A. *Clear Word and Third Sight: Folk Groundings and Diasporic Consciousness in African Caribbean Writing*. Durham: Duke University Press, 2003.
John, Marie-Elena. *Unburnable*. New York: Amistad, 2007.
Joyce, James. *A Portrait of the Artist as a Young Man*. New York: B.W. Huebsch, 1916.
Kacandes, Irene. *Talk Fiction: Literature and the Talk Explosion*. Lincoln: University of Nebraska Press, 2001.
Kellner, Hans. "Narrativity in History: Post-Structuralism and Since". *History and Theory* 26, no. 4 (December 1987): 1–29.
Kellogg, Robert. "Oral Literature". In *New Literary History* 5, no. 1 (1973): 55–66.
Khair, Tabish. "'Correct(ing) Images from the Inside': Reading the Limits of Erna Brodber's *Myal*". *Journal of Commonwealth Literature* 37, no. 1 (March 2002): 121–31.
Lamming, George. "The Negro Writer and His World". *Caribbean Quarterly* 5, no. 2 (1958): 109–15.
Laurence, Kemlin. "Trinidad English: The Origin of 'Mamaguy' and 'Picong'". *Caribbean Quarterly* 17, no. 2 (June 1971): 36–39.
Lazarus, Neil. "Introducing Postcolonial Studies". In *The Cambridge Companion to Postcolonial Literary Studies*, 1–15. Cambridge: Cambridge University Press, 2004.
Le Page, R.B. "Dialect in West Indian Literature". In *Critics on Caribbean Literature: Readings in Literary Criticism*, edited by Edward Baugh, 123–29. New York: St. Martin's Press, 1978.
Lewis, Linden. "Masculinity and *The Dragon Can't Dance*: Reading Lovelace Discursively". *Feminist Review* 59 (Summer 1998): 164–85.
Lima, Maria Helena. "Revolutionary Developments: Michelle Cliff's *No Telephone to Heaven* and Merle Collins's *Angel*". *Ariel* 24, no. 1 (1993): 35–56.

Lodge, David. "The Novel Now: Theories and Practices". *Novel* 21, nos. 2–3 (Winter/Spring 1988): 125–38.

Lovelace, Earl. *The Dragon Can't Dance*. London: Faber, 1979.

———. "Joebell and America". In *A Brief Conversion and Other Stories*, 111–24. Oxford: Heinemann, 1988.

———. *Salt*. London: Faber, 1996.

———. *The Schoolmaster*. Oxford: Heinemann, 1979.

———. *While Gods are Falling*. Port of Spain: Longman Caribbean, 1984.

———. *The Wine of Astonishment*. Oxford: Heinemann, 1986.

Lubbock, Percy. *The Craft of Fiction*. New York: Peter Smith, 1947.

Lyotard, Jean-François. *The Postmodern Condition: A Report on Knowledge*. Translated by Geoff Bennington and Brian Massumi. Minneapolis: University of Minnesota Press, 1979.

MacKenzie, Craig. "The Oral Style in the South African Short Story in English". In *Oral Tradition and Its Transmission: The Many Forms of Message*, edited by Edgard Sienaert, Meg Cowper-Lewis and Nigel Bell, 309–19. Durban: University of Natal, The Campbell Collections and Centre for Oral Studies, 1994.

Margolis, Joseph. "Literature and Speech Acts". *Philosophy and Literature* 3, no. 1 (1979): 39–52.

Mignolo, Walter D. *Local Histories/Global Designs: Coloniality, Subaltern Knowledges, and Border Thinking*. Princeton: Princeton Universtiy Press 2000.

Miller, James E., Jr. Introduction to *Henry James: Theory of Fiction*, 1–26. Lincoln: University of Nebraska Press, 1972.

Mohammed, Patricia. "The Future of Feminism in the Caribbean". *Feminist Review* 64 (Spring 2000): 116–19.

———. "Nuancing the Feminist Discourse in the Caribbean". *Social and Economic Studies* 43, no. 3 (1994): 135–67.

———. "Towards an Indigenous Feminist Theorizing in the Caribbean". *Feminist Review* 59 (1998): 6–33.

Mordecai, Pamela, and Betty Wilson, eds. *Her True-True Name: An Anthology of Women's Writing from the Caribbean*. Oxford: Heinemann, 1989.

Morris, Mervyn. Introduction to *New Day*, by V.S. Reid. London: Heinemann, 1973.

———. *Is English We Speaking*. Kingston: Ian Randle, 1999.

———. "Printing the Performance: 'Them' and 'Us'?" In *Us/Them: Translation, Transcription and Identity in Post-colonial Literary Cultures*, Cross/Cultures 6, edited by Gordon Collier, 241–47. Atlanta: Rodopi, 1992.

———. "Sounds and Sense: West Indian Poetry". *Journal of West Indian Literature* 8, no. 1 (October 1998): 10–19.

Myrie, Daisy. "Market Women". In *New Ships: An Anthology of West Indian Poems*, edited by D.G. Wilson, 29. Oxford: Oxford University Press, 1975.

Nanton, Philip. "Making Space for Orality on Its Own Terms". In *The Pressures of the Text: Orality, Texts and the Telling of Tales*, edited by Stewart Brown, 83–90. Birmingham: University of Birmingham Press, 1995.

Nazareth, Peter. Review of *The Dragon Can't Dance*. *World Literature Today* 56, no. 2 (1982): 394–95.

Nelson-McDermott, Catherine. "Myal-ing Criticism: Beyond Colonizing Dialectics". *Ariel* 24, no. 4 (1993): 53–65.

Niblett, Michael. *The Caribbean Novel since 1945: Cultural Practice, Form, and the Nation-State*. Jackson: University Press of Mississippi, 2012.

O'Callaghan, Evelyn. *The Lovelace "Prologue": Ideology in a Nutshell*. Coventry: Warwick University Press, 1989.

———. *Woman Version: Theoretical Approaches to West Indian Fiction by Women*. New York: St. Martin's Press, 1993.

Ochs, Elinor, and Lisa Capps. "Narrating the Self". *Annual Review of Anthropology* 25 (1996): 19–43.

Ong, Walter J. *Orality and Literacy: The Technologizing of the Word*. London: Routledge, 2002.

Page, Kezia. *Transnational Negotiations in Caribbean Diasporic Literature: Remitting the Text*. New York: Routledge, 2011.

Paine, Robert. "What Is Gossip About? An Alternative Hypothesis". *Man* 2, no. 2 (June 1967): 278–85.

Patteson, Richard F. "The Fiction of Olive Senior: Traditional Society and the Wider World". *Ariel* 24, no. 1 (January 1993): 13–33.

Pearse, Andrew. "Carnival in Nineteenth-Century Trinidad". *Caribbean Quarterly* 4, nos. 3–4 (1956) 175–93.

Philip, Marlene NourbeSe. *A Genealogy of Resistance and Other Essays*. Toronto: Mercury, 1997.

Philipsen, Gerry. "Cultural Communication". In *Handbook of International and Intercultural Communication*, edited by William B. Gudykunst and Bella Mody, 51–64. Thousand Oaks: Sage Publications, 2002.

Pollard, Velma. "An Introduction to the Poetry and Fiction of Olive Senior". *Callaloo* 36 (Summer 1988): 540–45.

Poovey, Mary. "What Is Cultural Economy?" *Connexions* module m34260. June 2010. http://cnx.org/content/m34260/1.4/.

Praeger, Michele. "Édouard Glissant: Towards a Literature of Orality". *Callaloo* 15, no. 1 (1992): 41–48.

Pratt, Mary Louise. *Imperial Eyes: Travel Writing and Transculturation*. New York: Routledge, 1992.

———. "The Short Story: The Long and Short of It". In *The New Short Story Theories*, edited by Charles E. May, 91–113. Athens: Ohio University Press, 1994.

Ramchand, Kenneth. "The Fate of Writing in the West Indies: Reflections on Oral and Written Literature". *Caribbean Review* 11, no. 4 (1982): 16–41.

———. "History and the Novel: A Literary Critic's Approach". *Savacou* 5 (June 1971): 103–13.

———. *The West Indian Novel and Its Background*. New York: Barnes and Noble, 1970.

Ramsay, Paulette. *Aunt Jen*. Oxford: Heinemann, 2002.

Reid, V.S. *New Day*. Chatham, NJ: Chatham Bookseller, 1972 [1949].

———. "The Writer and his Work". *Journal of West Indian Literature* 2, no. 1 (1987): 4–10.

Renk, Kathleen J. *Caribbean Shadows and Victorian Ghosts: Women's Writing and Decolonization*. Charlottesville: University of Virginia Press, 1999.

Roach, Joseph. *Cities of the Dead: Circum-Atlantic Performance*. New York: Columbia University Press, 1996.

Roberts, Peter A. *From Oral to Literate Culture: Colonial Experience in the English West Indies*. Kingston: University of the West Indies Press, 1997.

———. *West Indians and Their Language*. Cambridge: Cambridge University Press, 1988.

Robinson-Walcott, Kim. *Out of Order! Anthony Winkler and White West Indian Writing*. Kingston: University of the West Indies Press, 2006.

Rohlehr, Gordon. *Calypso and Society in Pre-independence Trinidad*. Port of Spain: Gordon Rohlehr, 1990.

———. " 'Man Talking to Man': Calypso and Social Confrontation in Trinidad, 1970 to 1984". *Caribbean Quarterly* 31, no. 2 (1985): 1–13.

———. *My Strangled City and Other Essays*. Port of Spain: Longman, 1992.

Rousseau, Jean-Jacques. *On the Origin of Language*. Chicago: University of Chicago Press, 1966.

Rowell, Charles H. "An Interview with Olive Senior". *Callaloo* 11, no. 3 (Summer 1988): 480–90.

Said, Edward W. *Orientalism: Western Conceptions of the Orient*. New York: Vintage, 1979.

Salinger, J.D. *The Catcher in the Rye*. Boston: Little, Brown, 1951.

Sander, Reinhard. "The Thirties and the Forties". In *West Indian Literature*, 2nd ed., edited by Bruce King, 38–50. London: Macmillan, 1995.

Sarup, Madan. "Lyotard and Postmodernism". In *An Introductory Guide to Post-structuralism and Postmodernism*, 129–60. New York: Harvester Wheatsheaf, 1993.

Schechner, Richard. *Between Theater and Anthropology*. Philadelphia: University of Pennsylvania Press, 1985.

Selvon, Samuel. *The Lonely Londoners*. New York: St. Martin's Press, 1956.

Senior, Olive. "Lessons from the Fruit Stand: Or, Writing for the Listener". *Journal of Modern Literature* 20, no. 1 (1996): 40–44.

Shakespeare, William. *The Two Gentlemen of Verona*. Edited by Roger Warren. Oxford: Oxford University Press, 2008.

Sharma, K.K. *The Tradition in Modern Novel-Theory: E.M. Forster, Somerset Maugham and Joyce Cary*. Atlantic Highlands, NJ: Humanities Press, 1981.

Shetty, Sandhya. "Masculinity, National Identity, and the Feminine Voice in *The Wine of Astonishment*". *Journal of Commonwealth Literature* 29, no. 1 (March 1994): 65–79.

Silko, Leslie Marmon. *Ceremony*. London: Penguin, 1977.

Simpson, Hyacinth. "'Voicing the Text': The Making of an Oral Poetics in Olive Senior's Short Fiction". *Callaloo* 27, no. 3 (2004): 829–43.

Sindoni, Maria Grazia. *Creolizing Culture: A Study on Sam Selvon's Work*. New Delhi: Atlantic, 2006.

Smith, Anthony D. *Theories of Nationalism*. New York: Harper Torchbooks, 1971.

Souvage, Jacques. "Towards a Definition of the Novel". In *An Introduction to the Study of the Novel, with Special Reference to the English Novel*, 3. Gent: E. Story-Scientia, 1965.

Sparshott, Francis E. *The Theory of the Arts*. Princeton: Princeton University Press, 1982.

Spivak, Gayatri Chakravorty. "Can the Subaltern Speak?" In *Marxism and the Interpretation of Culture*, edited by Cary Nelson and Lawrence Grossberg, 271–313. Chicago: University of Illinois Press, 1988.

Stam, Robert. *Subversive Pleasures: Bakhtin, Cultural Criticism, and Film*. Baltimore: Johns Hopkins University Press, 1989.

Stucky, Nathan, and Cynthia Wimmer, eds. *Teaching Performance Studies*. Carbondale: Southern Illinois University Press, 2002.

Tannen, Deborah, ed. *Spoken and Written Language: Exploring Orality and Literacy*. Norwood, NJ: Ablex, 1982.

Tarrant, Harold. "Orality and Plato's Narrative Dialogues". In *Voice into Text: Orality and Literacy in Ancient Greece*, edited by Ian Worthington, 129–47. Leiden: Brill, 1996.

Thiong'o, Ngũgĩ wa. "Borders and Bridges: Seeking Connections between Things". In *The Pre-occupation of Postcolonial Studies*, edited by Fawzia Afzal-Khan and Kalpana Seshadri-Crooks, 119–25. Durham: Duke University Press, 2000.

———. *Decolonising the Mind: The Politics of Language in African Literature*. London: J. Currey, 1986.

———. *A Grain of Wheat*. London: Heinemann, 1967.

———. Interview with Charles Cantalupo. In *Ngũgĩ wa Thiong'o Speaks: Interviews with the Kenyan Writer*, edited by Reinhard Sander and Bernth Lindfors, 333–52. Trenton, NJ: Africa World Press, 2006.

———. *Matigari*. Translated by Wangũi wa Goro. London: Heinemann, 1987.

———. "Postcolonial Politics and Culture". *Southern Review: Literary and Interdisciplinary Essays* 24, no. 1 (1991): 5–11.

Thomas, Rosalind. Introduction to *Oral Tradition and Written Record in Classical Athens*, 1–14. Cambridge: Cambridge University Press, 1989.

Torres-Saillant, Silvio. *Caribbean Poetics: Towards an Aesthetic of West Indian Literature*. Cambridge: Cambridge University Press, 1997.

Traugott, Elizabeth Closs, and Mary Louise Pratt. *Linguistics for Students of Literature*. New York: Harcourt, 1980.

Utley, Francis Lee. "Oral Genres as Bridge to Written Literature". *Genre* 2, no. 2 (June 1969): 91–103.

Veeder, William, and Susan M. Griffin, eds. *The Art of Criticism: Henry James on the Theory and the Practice of Fiction*. Chicago: University of Chicago Press, 1986.

Walcott, Derek. "The Muse of History". In *Is Massa Day Dead? Black Moods in the Caribbean*, edited by Orde Coombs, 1–27. New York: Anchor, 1974.

Walker, Warren S. "From Raconteur to Writer: Oral Roots and Printed Leaves of Short Fiction". In *The Teller and the Tale: Aspects of the Short Story*, edited by Wendell M. Aycock, 13–26. Lubbock: Texas Tech Press, 1982.

Warner-Lewis, Maureen. "Language Use in West Indian Literature". In *A History of Literature in the Caribbean*, vol. 2, *English- and Dutch-Speaking Regions*, edited by A. James Arnold, 25–37. Philadelphia: John Benjamins, 2001.

———. "The Oral Tradition in the African Diaspora". In *The Cambridge History of African and Caribbean Literature*, vol. 1, edited by F. Abiola Irele and Simon Gikandi, 117–36. Cambridge: Cambridge University Press, 2012.

———. "Samuel Selvon's Linguistic Extravaganza: *Moses Ascending*". *Caribbean Quarterly* 28, no. 4 (December 1982): 60–69.

Waters, Mary C. *Black Identities: West Indian Immigrant Dreams and American Realities*. Cambridge, MA: Harvard University Press, 2001.

Wilentz, Gay. *Binding Cultures: Black Women Writers in Africa and the Diaspora*. Bloomington: Indiana University Press, 1992.

Wilson-Tagoe, Nana. "Myth, Ritual and Song as 'Counter Texts' in Three Plays of Derek Walcott". In *The Pressures of the Text: Orality, Texts and the Telling of Tales*, edited by Stewart Brown, 28–36. Birmingham: University of Birmingham Press, 1995.

———. *Historical Thought and Literary Representation in West Indian Literature.* Gainesville: University Press of Florida, 1998.

Wynter, Sylvia. "Novel and History, Plot and Plantation". *Savacou* 5 (June 1971): 95–102.

Yerushalmi, Yosef Hayim. *Zakhor: Jewish History and Jewish Memory.* Seattle: University of Washington Press, 1982.

Zumthor, Paul. *Oral Poetry: An Introduction.* Translated by Kathryn Murphy-Judy. Minneapolis: University of Minnesota Press, 1990.

Index

activism
    anti-colonial resistance of women, 81, 191n16
    grassroots involvement in, 35
    by Indian women, 82, 192n21
    men as leaders myth of, 35, 93–94
    and political engagement, 75, 76
    women's involvement in 77–78, 102–3, 190n4, 190n5
Afro-Caribbean spirituality, 177
    Obeah, 40–41, 69, 154
    Pocomania, 2, 54
    and religious freedom, 83, 89, 94–95
    revivalist, 54
    Spiritual Baptists, 54, 83
    and warner women, 54–56
agency
    of the collective, 95–96
    and feminine perspectives, 20, 106–7
    and migrant subjectivity, 35–36
Aiyejina, Funso
    calypsonian as documenter, 129
    on chantwell/griot figure 88–89, 92, 193n34, 194n42
    on dance, 137–38
    novelypso, calypso aesthetic of, 12, 13
    on personhood, 121

Arrival of the Snake-Woman (Senior), 176
"At the Stelling" (Hearne), 27, 29, 30
audience
    call-and-response tradition, 5, 92
    demand of performance on, 14, 180
    participatory involvement of, 5, 13, 32–33
    and picong, 143, 197n2, 198n4
    reader-text interactions, 20–21, 31, 47, 189n14
    speaker-audience dynamic, 90–91
Aunt Jen (Ramsay), 177

Bakhtin, Mikhail
    anterior culture, 88
    carnival laughter, 124
    experimentation, and performing fiction, 4
Baksh-Soodeen, Rawwida, 80, 191n13
Barber, Karin, 42
Baugh, Cecil, 26
Baugh, Edward, 17, 178, 185n13
    history, and memory, 47
    "Maps Made in the Heart", 171, 172
    on *New Day*, 26, 28, 30, 34
    yard culture, 142
Bauman, Richard, 189n14
    performance as situated behaviour, 89, 193n38

Beckles, Hilary
   anti-colonial resistance of women, 81, 191n16
   colonialism, and womanhood, 79–80, 191n10
   male dominance, and nationalism, 77–78, 93–94, 190n4, 190n5

Benítez-Rojo, Antonio, 185n14
   calypso, and carnival celebrations, 139
   Caribbean identity, 171–72
   definition of poetics, 183n2
   on performativity of Caribbean fiction, 6, 11–12, 184n11

Bennett, Louise, 181, 198n7

Bishop, Maurice, 55

The Book of Night Women (James), 7, 88–93
   anti-slavery activities of women, 93, 94
   chantwell/griot figure, 88–89, 193n34
   constructions of womanhood, 82, 116–17
   cross-gender performances, 92–93
   female sexuality, and slavery, 112–14, 195n62
   feminist-womanist poetics of, 79
   framing device, 89–90
   gender constructions, 9, 18
   intersection of public and private realms, 105
   narrative strategies, 84, 88
   performances of multiple personas, 115–16
   as performing fiction, 90–91
   plantation power structure, 114–16
   representation of women, 104–5
   subversive resistance, 102–3
   womanist-feminist poetics, 101–2
   women as freedom workers, 101–2

Boxill, Anthony, 17

Boyce Davies, Carole, 126, 151, 159, 162, 190n5

Brand, Dionne, 146, 158

Brathwaite, Kamau
   masculinization of nation, 96–97
   nation language, 11, 39–40

The Brief Wondrous Life of Oscar Wao (Diaz), 178–79

Brodber, Erna, 174, 176–77
   Myal, 177, 190n27
   role of "secondary whites" in creole societies, 29
   use of dialect, 28

Bucknor, Michael
   "grung"/"grounded" poetics, 35, 176

Burning Spear, "Slavery Days", 37, 50

calypso
   anti-feminist calypsos, 119–20, 126, 195nn2–3, 196nn18–19
   Attilla the Hun, 119
   backhanded compliments in, 131
   Black Stalin, 120
   call-and-response tradition, 92, 126–27
   calypsonian as documenter, 129
   carnivalesque aspect of, 129, 139, 140, 181, 197n34
   constructions of womanhood, 82, 85–86, 193n28
   double entendre in, 130–31, 181
   evolution of, 123
   female voice in, 126–27
   in fiction of Lovelace, 12–13
   as male-dominated space, 85–86, 92, 125–26, 196n17, 196n18, 196n19
   Mighty Chalkdust, 20, 141, 142

Mighty Sparrow, 126
and performing fiction, 18–19, 76
and picong, 19–20, 127, 131, 143, 157, 181, 197n2, 198n4
Roaring Lion, 120
sexual exploitation in, 134–35
Singing Sandra. *See* Singing Sandra
"slackness", 108–9
as social commentary, 110–12, 124, 134
suppression of, 2, 183n1
themes of, 112, 195n61
and Trinidadian carnival, 123–24
as virtual opiate, 128–29
women as dangerous, 138–39, 197n31
Campbell, George, 26
capitalism, influence on folk culture, 67
Caribbean identity
anti-colonial "writing back", 6–7, 13
and "authentic" Caribbean culture, 41, 189n8
and cultural synergy, 185n14
and cultural valuables, 171–72
as cultural value system, 19–20
and diasporic consciousness, 149–55
and masculinity, 123–24
narrative voice, 17, 185n22
and nation language, 11, 39–40
picong, 19–20
self-definition in oral-performative systems, 6–7
yard storytelling, 19–20
Caribbean literature
and "authentic" Caribbean culture, 41
carnivalesque performance in, 11–12
credibility of dialect-speaking narrators, 27–29

creole voice, development of, 24–27, 187n6
development of by women writers, 174–75
female voice by male writers, 8
interdependence with oral-performance tradition, 3, 6, 7
migration experience, 158, 199n22
orature, and literature, 11–14
and orature, relationship between, 11–14
postcolonial characterization, credibility of, 27–29
women's literature in relation to men's writing, 12, 157–58, 174–75
writing of black men vs. black women 105
Caribbean Middlebrow (Edmondson), 41
Caribbean performance culture
Admiral Bailey, 141
Burning Spear, 37, 50
Lady Saw 87, 193n30
Michael "Ibo" Cooper, 1
Mighty Chalkdust, 20, 141, 142, 148, 149, 157
and migration, 141–42
picong, verbal sparring of, 143, 197n2, 198n4
Pluto Shervington, 141
protest music, 37–38
Queen Ifrica. *See* Queen Ifrica
Singing Sandra. *See* Singing Sandra
Tinga Stewart, 20, 141, 142, 148, 165
Vybz Kartel, 110
Carib people, 51–52
Carlson, Marvin, 184n10
carnival, 179
and calypso, 123–24
laughter of Trinidadian carnival, 124–25, 131
as means of self-assertion, 6

Chakrabarty, Dipesh, 47–48
Chancy, Myriam, 158, 162, 199n22
Channer, Colin. *See also* "How to Beat a Child the Right and Proper Way" (Channer)
    womanized performing fiction of, 8–9
chanté mas songs, 67
chantwell/griot figure
    The Book of Night Women (James), 85, 88–89, 92, 193n34, 194n42
    and stickfighters, 125–26, 196nn18–19
citizenship
    and migration, 9
    orature-performance as defensive strategy, 107
    sexual citizenship, 87
    of women, 9, 76
Clarke, Austin, 146
Clear Word and Third Sight (John), 142–43, 149–50
Cobham-Sander, Rhonda, 187n6
On Collective Memory (Halbwachs), 58, 59
Collins, Merle. See also *The Colour of Forgetting* (Collins)
    Angel, 60
    "Shame Bush", 10
colonialism
    anti-colonial "writing back", 6–7, 13
    and border thinking, 15–16
    and Caribbean identity, 6–7, 184n10
    constructions of womanhood, 79–80, 191n10
    marginalization of subaltern memory, 48–49, 68–70, 190n27
    and oral tradition, 68–70
The Colour of Forgetting (Collins), 17–18
    and Afro-Caribbean spirituality, 54–56
    comparison to *Unburnable*, 42–44, 73–74
    history as collaboration of orality and writing, 60–63
    internal monologues, 62
    oral tradition, and memory, 38–40, 49–53, 57–59
    orature as structuring device, 42–44
    repetition, 46–47
    representations of the past, 9–11, 185n13
    structural devices, 2–3, 38–40, 54–56
    use of colloquial expressions, 43–44
    warner woman, 2, 49, 54–56
community, rootedness in, 20
Connerton, Paul, 53
continuum theory, 39, 72, 188n1, 190n28
Cooke, Michael, 28
Cooper, Carolyn, 12, 39
    "slackness", and patriarchal gender ideology, 108–9, 110
Cooper, Michael "Ibo", 1
creole language, 9. *See also* language
    and Caribbean speaking voice, 17, 22–23, 90, 91–92, 169–70, 174–75
    in *The Colour of Forgetting*, 43–44
    creole voice, development of, 24–27, 187n6
    of dialect-speaking narrators, 27–29, 177–78
    as framing device, 89
    of informal storytelling, 91
    movement in Caribbean speech, 44
    orthography of, 26–27
    rhythms of, 25
creole performance tradition. *See also* performance modes

and artistic activism, 174
orature of, as discredited knowledges, 16, 186n27
as structuring device, 12–15, 185n22
Creolizing Culture (Sindoni), 13
Crick Crack, Monkey (Hodge), 175

dancehall performance culture
call-and-response tradition, 92
"cuss out", 92, 194n41
expressions of sexuality, 86–87, 193n30
forms of, 107
Lady Saw, 87, 193n30
as male-dominated space, 85–87, 92
pedophilia, 86, 109, 110, 194n57
Queen Ifrica, 18, 75
"slackness", 108–9, 110, 195n59
stereotypical female forms in, 92, 194n41
taboo subjects, treatment of, 109–10
Danticat, Edwidge, 146, 158
Davis, Sangie, 141
Dawes, Kwame
on creolized expression, 186n27
Natural Mysticism, 12
on reggae aesthetic, 11–12
decolonization, and nationalism, 7–8
The Dialogic Imagination (Bakhtin), 4
diasporic narratives, 19–20
inward turns of, 7–8
Diaz, Junot, 178–79
"Die with My Dignity", 18, 76, 82, 91–92, 102, 105–6, 108, 110–12, 117
Discerner of Hearts (Senior), 176
Donnell, Alison, 19, 41, 185n13, 189n8
The Dragon Can't Dance (Lovelace)
calypso as structuring device, 120–21, 131–33
calypso as virtual opiate, 128–29
dance, and dancing, 137–38
double entendre in, 130–31, 136–37
female sexuality, 133–36, 138–39, 197n31
feminist undercurrent in, 181
gender constructions, 9, 19, 127–28, 130–31
laughter of Trinidadian carnival, 124–25, 131
marginalization of urban poor, 127–28
nationalism, and masculinity, 121–22
as novelypso, 127–40
as performing fiction, 128–29, 140, 197n24
personhood, quest for, 130–31, 133, 136, 138, 139, 197n32
perspective of older women, 135–36
race relations, and internal racism, 128, 131–32, 133
self-actualization, 136–37
treatment of female subjectivity, 129–30, 132
validation of women's humanity, 139
as womanist-feminist discourse, 139–40

Edmondson, Belinda, 83
Caribbean Middlebrow, 41
on literary authority, 78
Making Men, 8, 78
masculinization of nation, 96–97, 100
education, formal
book sense, and life sense, 60
classroom as performance space, 20
marginalization of oral culture, 15, 39

education, formal (*continued*)
  marginalization of subaltern memory, 68, 190n27
  vs. oral tradition, 52–53
Ellis, Nadia, 174
Etana, 110
European culture, and subalternity, 15, 48–49, 163

feminine perspective
  and female agency, 20
  feminized vs. womanized performing fiction, 8–9
  woman-centred poetics, 8, 184n12
feminism
  constructions of womanhood, 79–80, 191n10, 191nn13–14
Fido, Elaine Savory, 190n5
folk tradition
  expressions of urban poor, 11
  improvisation in, 4–5
  orature of, as discredited knowledges, 16, 186n27
  in reggae music, 1–2
Forbes, Curdella, 177, 178
  calypso, and masculinity, 126–27
  hermaphroditic gender constructs, 94
  on *The Lonely Londoners*, 32, 35–36, 188n31
  on nationalist literature, 77, 190n4
  From Nation to Diaspora, 8, 76, 184n12
Foucault, Michel, 15
Francis, Donette, 87, 107

gender
  agency, and migrant subjectivity, 35–36
  and agency of the collective, 95–96
  anti-feminist calypsos, 119–20, 195nn2–3, 196nn18–19
  constructions of, 9
  definitions of Caribbean womanhood, 18–19, 76
  destabilizing of roles, 93–94, 99–101
  and feminine perspectives, 8, 184n12
  feminism, and cross-gender conversations, 77
  hermaphroditic gender constructs, 94
  inter-gender poetics, 76–77, 83
  and literary authority, 78
  in migration discourse, 147–48
  nationalism, and women's citizenship, 9, 77–78, 190n4, 190n5
  in nationalist discourse, 95–99
  patriarchal gender ideology, 108–9
  in performance traditions, 89
  and personhood, 84, 121–23, 192n26, 195n5
  personhood of women, 19
  in plantation society hierarchy, 103–5
  women-centred poetics, 18–19
  and women's literature, 12
Gikandi, Simon, 175
Glissant, Édouard
  on Caribbean national literature, 11
  oral tradition, and formal education, 39
globalization, and diasporic communities, 173–74
Goodison, Lorna, 178
  I Am Becoming My Mother, 1
  "Jah Music", 1–2, 3, 15
  use of Caribbean language, 1
gossip
  in creole performance tradition, 14

as form of storytelling, 47
as narrative strategy, 3, 18
in song form, 66–67
graphic novels, 179
Grenada
The Colour of Forgetting (Collins), 10
United States invasion of, 10, 55–56
"grung"/"grounded" poetics, 35, 176

Halbwachs, Maurice, 58, 59
Hall, Stuart, 26
Hamilton, Bruce, 30–31
Harriet's Daughter (NourbeSe Philip), 164
Harris, Wilson, 10
Hearne, John, "At the Stelling", 27, 29, 30
hearsay, as narrative strategy, 18, 46
Her True-True Name (Mordecai and Wilson), 174
history
    ancestral stories, active remembering of, 50–52
    as collaboration of orality and writing, 60–62
    colonial representations of, 70
    distortion of in reconstructing, 59
    engagement with the past, 34–35, 37–38
    Euro-American versions of, 10
    marginalization of subaltern memory, 15, 48–49, 163
    and memory, 17–18, 47–53, 59–61
    recollection of in oral tradition, 37–38
    representations of Caribbean history, 9–11, 51–52, 185n13
    revisionary history, 34–35
    suppression of, 10
Hodge, Merle

anti-feminist calypsos, 126
creole voice, development of, 24–27, 174–75
Crick Crack, Monkey, 175
moral authority of Caribbean women, 125
How Societies Remember (Connerton), 53
"How to Beat a Child the Right and Proper Way" (Channer), 7
    agency, and migrant subjectivity, 36
    authority, and cultural imposition, 159, 160, 161–63, 170, 182
    female protagonist as narrator, 158–59
    migration, and location of place, 9, 19–20
    monologue, as storytelling, 144–45
    as performing fiction, 160
    reshaping of migrant space 142, 143–45, 198nn6–7
    woman as narrator of nation, 147–48
    yard culture, 181–82
Hughes-Tafen, Denise, 85, 193n28
Huie, Albert, 26

I Am Becoming My Mother (Goodison), 1
improvisation, in folk tradition, 4–5
inner-city performance culture, 2
inter-gender poetics, 76–77, 83
inward turn
    of diasporic narrative, 7–8
    of selective remembering, 10
    as structuring device, 3
    of "writing back", 6–7

"Jah Music" (Goodison), 1–2, 3, 15
Jamaica
    political independence struggle, 35
    yard storytelling, 19–20

Jamaican dancehall. *See* dancehall performance culture
James, Marlon. See also *The Book of Night Women* (James)
   nationalism, and female activism, 77
   womanized performing fiction of, 8–9
Jane and Louisa Will Soon Come Home (Brodber), 177
"Jazz and the West Indian Novel" (Brathwaite), 11
"Joebell and America" (Lovelace)
   cultural valuables, 171
   "foreign" language, 152–53, 198n9
   inward turn of, 143
   male anti-hero, 147, 150, 154–55
   migration, and location of place, 9, 19–20, 142–43
   narrative strategy, 151
   picong, and yard culture, 150–51, 155–57
   structural devices, 149, 150
   yard culture, 145–46, 150–51
John, Catherine, 142–43
   "coming-to-consciousness", 155–57
   Negritude movement, 149–50, 199n17
John, Marie-Elena. See also *Unburnable* (John)
   on orality, 7
Joyce, James, 33

Kincaid, Jamaica, 25, 146
kinopoetics, 12
knowledge systems
   cultural knowledge, and performance, 156–57
   folk orature, as discredited knowledges, 16, 186n27
   and formal education, 20
   formal education vs. oral tradition, 52–53
   intersection of official and folk beliefs, 65–66
   memory, and academic discipline, 59–61
   overlapping of, 61–62
   spiritual knowledge system, 55–56
   storytelling, as knowledge system, 38–40, 49–53
   and subalternity, 15
   of warner women, 54–56
Kristeva, Julia, 88

Lamming, George, 8, 10, 78, 96–97
language. *See also* creole language
   Caribbean speaking voice, 17, 22–23, 90, 91–92, 169–70, 174–75
   creole voice, development of, 22–23, 24–27, 187n6
   movement in Caribbean speech, 44
   nation language, 11, 39–40, 91, 193–94n40
   picong, 19–20, 127, 131, 143, 197n2, 198n4
   Spanglish, 178
   use of colloquial expressions, 43–44
laughter
   as tool for mockery, 125, 131
   of Trinidadian carnival, 124–25
Laurence, Kemlin, 197n2
Le Page, R.B., 27, 28
Levy, Andrea, 146, 158
Lewis, Linden, 122
The Lonely Londoners (Selvon), 17
   creole as language of narration, 22–23, 30–31
   critical recognition of, 30–33
   female character, and subaltern points of view, 36
   immigrant transformation of space, 35–36

storytelling as structural device, 23
structure of, 30–31
stylistic comparison to *New Day*, 32–34
Lorde, Audre, 105
Louisiana (Brodber), 177
Lovelace, Earl, 12–13. *See also* "Joebell and America" (Lovelace); *The Dragon Can't Dance* (Lovelace); *The Wine of Astonishment* (Lovelace)
    anti-colonial "writing back", 6–7
    calypso aesthetic of, 120, 128–30
    feminized performing fiction of, 8–9
    intertextual relationship with Myrie, 130–31
    nationalism, and female activism, 77
    as nationalist writer, 84, 192n25
    personhood, concepts of, 84, 121–23, 192n26
    Salt, 177
    use of oral tradition, 150

Mair, Lucille Mathurin, 81, 192n19
Mais, Roger, 26
Making Men (Edmondson), 8, 78
male anti-hero, 147, 150, 154–55
male domination
    calypso performance tradition, 85–86, 125–26, 193n28, 196nn17–19
    critique of moral standards, 107–9
    destabilization of, 99–101
    and European patriarchy, 125
    female resistance to, 75
    and literary authority, 78
    male leader, myth of, 85, 93–101
    and nationalism, 77–78, 190n5
Manley, Edna, 26

Manley, Norman, 35
Manners and Customs of the Country a Generation Ago (Murray), 39
"Maps Made in the Heart" (Baugh), 171
Mckenzie, Shauna (Etana), 110
memory
    ancestral stories, active remembering of, 50–52
    associational loops, 57–58, 160–61
    collective memory and, 17, 49
    and cultural agency, 165–66
    and history, 17–18, 47–53
    importance of recollection, 37–38, 73
    incompleteness as characteristic of, 57–58, 63–64
    intersection of official and folk beliefs, 65–66
    marginalization of subaltern memory, 68–70, 190n27
    as perceptual phenomenon, 48–49
    as repository of history, 59–61
    as selective remembering, 38–39, 46–47, 52–53
    as social process, 58–59
    storytelling, as knowledge system, 38–40
    as structural device, 33, 160–61
Mighty Chalkdust, 20, 141, 142, 148, 149, 157
Mignolo, Walter, 15–16
migration
    as brain drain, 150–51, 157
    and Caribbean performance culture, 141–42
    and cultural loss, 141–42
    cultural negotiation as survival strategy 145–48, 152–53, 198n8, 198n14
    destination as controllable space, 163–64

migration (*continued*)
   and diasporic consciousness, 149–55, 155–57
   diasporic returning, 10–11
   as form of exile, 158, 199n22
   and hybrid homes, 146–47, 172
   as "imagigration", 157
   and location of place, 9, 19–20, 142–43, 159
   The Lonely Londoners, 35–36
   and male anti-hero, 147, 150, 154–55
   memory, and cultural agency, 165–66
   Other, constructions of, 169
   reshaping of migrant space, 143–45, 198n6, 198n7
   and self-representation, 148–49
migration literature
   in-betweenity of, 159–60
   recurring themes of, 146–47, 157–59
   representations of by women writers, 157–58
Mohammed, Patricia, 77, 79
Mordecai, Pamela, 174, 178
Morris, Mervyn, 5, 12, 23, 27
Morrison, Toni, 16
Murray, Henry G., 39
Myal (Brodber), 177, 190n27
Myrie, Daisy, "Market Women", 130
myth, 93–101

Naipaul, V.S., 10, 25, 187n6, 198n8
Nanton, Philip, continuum theory, 39, 188n1, 190n28
narrative strategies
   Caribbean speaking voice, 17
   creole voice, development of, 24–27
   dialect-speaking narrators, credibility of, 27–29
   episodic narrative structure, 179
   of female voice, 8
   gossip, 3, 18
   hearsay, 18, 46
   live performance as, 5–6
   memory as structural device, 33
   narrating techniques, 31, 44, 151
   narrators as performers, 5–6, 14
   oral storytelling, 17
   orature as, 3–4
   participatory involvement of audience, 5, 13, 32–33
   personal narrative, use of, 88
   repetition, 11, 29, 46–47, 95–96, 99, 130, 161, 185n14
   songs, 3, 46, 88, 177
   storytelling, 10, 17, 18, 38–40, 40–41, 73–74, 84, 88
   third-person narrative voice, 43, 177
   uncertainty, focus on, 45–46
   unmarked shifts of voice, 45–46
   woman-associated storytelling, 95
National Festival Song Competition, 141
nationalism
   and artistic activism, 174
   and black creole cultural tradition, 83
   and diasporic communities, 173–74
   in diasporic narrative, 7–8
   and female activism, 77–78, 94–95, 190nn4–5
   and male anti-hero, 147
   male leader, myth of, 85, 93–101, 121–22, 138
   nation as masculine, 95–98
   of *New Day*, 26, 29
   and performing fiction, 33–35
   and personhood of women, 19, 148
   suppression of women, 93
   and women's citizenship, 9, 76
national pride, shaming of, 10

nation language, 11, 39–40, 91,
    193–94n40
From Nation to Diaspora (Forbes), 8, 76,
    184n12
Natural Mysticism (Dawes), 12
Nazareth, Peter, 128
Negritude movement, and diasporic
    consciousness, 149–50, 199n17
neocolonialism, and Caribbean identity,
    6–7
New Day (Reid), 17
    creole as language of narration,
        22–23
    critical recognition of, 26–30
    engagement with the past, 34–35
    memory as structural device, 33
    storytelling as structural device, 32
    storytelling as structuring device, 23
    stylistic comparison to *The Lonely
        Londoners*, 32–34
Niblett, Michael, 179
Noises in the Blood (Cooper), 12, 39
Nora, Pierre, 48
NourbeSe Philip, Marlene, 12
    Harriet's Daughter, 164
novelypso, 12–13, 127–40
"Nuh Bwoy", 18, 75, 76, 82, 92, 105,
    106–7, 109–10, 117

Obeah, 40–41, 69, 154
O'Callaghan, Evelyn, 12, 198n8
orality
    and continuum theory, 72, 190n28
    definitions of, 2
    as essentialist concept, 42
    of historical representation, 10–11,
        72–73
    and oral culture, 39–40, 188n5
    in postcolonial Caribbean literature,
        39, 188n1
    relationship with writing, 64–66
    as source of trauma and healing,
        42, 70–71
    usage of, 21
    and written history, 60–62
    of yard storytelling, 160
oral-performance tradition
    audience participation in, 5
    cultural legitimacy of, 2–3
    features of, 29–30
    interdependence with writing, 3, 7
    as means of cultural transmission,
        14–15
    in performing fiction, 3–4, 11–14
    sounded voices of, 5
oral-scribal relationships
    creole as language of narration,
        22–23, 177–78
    in postcolonial Caribbean literature,
        12–13, 39–40, 173, 188n1
oral tradition(s)
    attempts at suppression of, 58, 73,
        190n27
    calypso, 122
    Carib people, 51–52
    deference to mothers, 126
    vs. formal education, 52–53
    of gossip in song form, 65, 66–67
    influence on Caribbean literature,
        175–76
    maroon community, 71–72, 73
    recovery of, 39–40, 188n5
    role of in activation of memory, 38
    and selective remembering, 10,
        38–39, 48–49, 57–59
    and spiritual knowledge system,
        55–56
    storytelling as knowledge system,
        38–40
    warner women, 2–3

oral traditions (*continued*)
  word of mouth, 66
orature
  compared to orality, 4
  critical recognition of, 13–14
  forms of in creole performance tradition, 14–15
  gender, and feminine perspectives, 8, 184n12
  and literature, relationship between, 11–14, 47, 189n14
  as narrative strategy, 3–4
  participatory involvement of audience, 5, 32–33
  and performance, 4, 183–84n5
  as structuring device, 23, 42–47
orature-performance
as defensive strategy, 107
  as structuring device, 12–13, 150, 183–84n5
  usage of, 21
Other, constructions of, 169

Page, Kezia, 147, 159, 198n6, 198n13
  Transnational Negotiations in Caribbean Diasporic Literature, 19
pedophilia, 86, 109, 194n57
performance modes. *See also* creole performance tradition
  as cultural trafficking, 147
  demands of on audience, 14
  as markers of belonging, 3–4
  orature-performance, 12–13, 21, 183–84n5
  reggae music, 1–2
  repeating pattern, 11, 185n14
  and resistance, 184n10
  subversive capacity of, 168–70
  verbal musics, 32, 188n31
  yard culture, 141–42, 144–45
performing fiction, 183n2
  and Caribbean performance culture, 38
  described, 3–6
  and experimentation, 4
  feminized vs. womanized performing fiction, 8–9
  inter-performative relationships, 18–19
  and literary criticism, 182
  of migrant Caribbean citizenship, 160
  and nationalism, 33–35
  oral-performance tradition in, 11–14
  oral-scribal relationships, 12–13, 22–23, 39–40, 173, 188n1
  participatory involvement of audience, 5
  performance poems, 5
  and poetics of performance, 3, 183n2
  reader-text interactions, 47, 180–81, 189n14
  as restored behaviour, 5–6
  speaker-audience dynamic, 90–91
personhood
  collective personhood, 138
  and double entendre, 130–31
  and gender, 84, 192n26
  recovery of, 121–23, 195n5
  subtextual anxiety of, 169
  of women, 19, 122–23, 197n32
personification imagery, 29
picong, 19–20, 127, 131, 181
  humour of, 153–54
  verbal sparring of, 143, 197n2, 198n4
  and yard culture, 150–51, 155–57
plantation society
  gender hierarchy, 103–5

hermaphroditic gender constructs in, 94
and post-slavery society, 15
power relations, 102–3
Pocomania, 2, 54
poetics of performance
elements of, 31
"grung"/"grounded" poetics, 35, 176
nationhood, and diasporic communities, 173–74
and performing fiction, 3, 183n2
political protest, in modes of performance, 3–4
positional superiority, 166–68, 199n26
Potter, Sally, 184n10
power relations
authority, and cultural imposition, 159, 161–63, 170
in calypso, 85–86, 193n28
in Caribbean performance culture, 85–87, 193n30
constructions of womanhood, 116–18
and marginalization, 70
"Nuh Bwoy", 106–7, 194n54
and orality, 66–67
in performance strategies, 159, 160
plantation society, 102–3
race, and positional superiority, 166–68
use of sexuality, 112–15
protest music, 37–38
proverbs
in creole performance tradition, 14
as narrative strategy, 3, 88

Queen Ifrica
"Nuh Bwoy", 18, 75, 76, 82, 86–87, 92, 106–7, 109–10, 117

racism
internal racism, 131–32, 133
and personhood of Caribbean peoples, 121, 195n5
race, and positional superiority, 199n26
Ramchand, Kenneth, 197n24
on *The Lonely Londoners*, 30, 31
on *New Day*, 23, 26, 29
reading vs. live performance, 180
on use of dialect, 24, 27, 30, 187n6
Ramsay, Paulette, 178
reading strategies
readers as interolocutors, 5
reader-text interactions, 20–21, 90–91
reading vs. live performance, 180–81
reggae
constructions of womanhood, 82
and dancehall performance culture, 87
as folk-generated performance mode, 1–2
oral-performance tradition, aesthetic of, 11–12
and performing fiction, 18–19, 76
suppression of, 183n1
Third World, 2
Tinga Stewart, 20, 141
Reid, Vic (V.S.), 10, 178
anti-colonial "writing back", 6–7
New Day, 17, 22, 23, 26–30
use of dialect, 28
repetition
and cadence of calypso, 130
of oral-performance tradition, 29, 46–47, 161
as rhetorical device, 99
resistance, performance as vehicle for, 6, 184n10

revivalists, 54
rhythms, of oral-performance tradition, 29, 31–32
Roach, Joseph, 49
Roberts, Peter, 15
Robinson-Walcott, Kim, 41–42, 189n9
Rohlehr, Gordon
    on anti-feminist calypsos, 119–20, 195n2
    on calypso, 139
    carnivalesque aspect of calypsos, 129
    evolution of calypsos, 123
    on *The Lonely Londoners*, 31
    oral-scribal relationship, 12–13, 173
    reader-text interactions, 180–81
    Trinidadian carnival, 124–25, 137
Rowell, Charles, 176

Said, Edward, 199n26
Salt (Lovelace), 177
Sander, Reinhard, 17
Schechner, Richard, 5
self-expression, performance as vehicle for, 6, 184n10
Selvon, Samuel, 8, 12–13, 146, 178, 179. See also *The Lonely Londoners* (Selvon)
    anti-colonial "writing back", 6–7
    calypso in performing fiction, 197n24
    comparison to Reid, 28
Senior, Olive, 174, 176, 177, 180
sexual abuse
    female resistance to, 75
    plantation society, 102
sexual exploitation
    and commodification, 134–35
    "Die with My Dignity", 18, 76, 82, 91–92, 102, 105–6

"Nuh Bwoy", 86–87, 92, 105
pedophilia, 86, 109, 110, 194n57
and social mobility, 86, 111–12
Shakespeare, William
    The Two Gentlemen of Verona, 133
Shepherd, Verene, 93
Shetty, Sandhya, 97
silence, impact of, 71–72
Sindoni, Maria Grazia
    Creolizing Culture, 13
    performative elements, 31–32
Singing Sandra
    "Die with My Dignity", 18, 76, 82, 85–86, 91–92, 102, 105–6, 108, 110–12, 117
slavery
    creole genealogy of, 9
    defeminizing of women, 80
    and female sexuality, 112–14, 195n62
    gender hierarchy of plantation society, 103–5
    memory of, 37–38
    modes of rebellion, 81, 192n19
    post-slavery society, 15
    resistance to, 6
social class
    and constructions of womanhood, 80, 191n14
songs, 76, 105–12. See also calypso; reggae
    "Brain Drain", 141, 145, 148
    chanté mas songs, 67
    in creole performance tradition, 14
    critique of moral standards, 107–8
    "Die with My Dignity", 18, 76, 82, 91–92, 102, 105–6, 108, 110–12, 117
    gossip in song form, 66–67
    "I Man Born Ya", 141

"Jean and Dinah", 119
"Mary Ann", 120
as narrative strategy, 3, 46, 88, 177
"No Way No Better Than Yard", 141, 145, 148
"No Woman No", 120
"Nuh Bwoy", 18, 75, 76, 82, 92, 117
  power relations between males and females, 106-7, 194n52
"Ramping Shop", 110
woman's "grumble", 86
"Women Will Rule the World", 119
Songs of Silence (Forbes), 178
song-stories, 67-68
Spiritual Baptists, 54
spiritual culture. *See* Afro-Caribbean spirituality
Stephens, Tanya, 87, 193n30
Stewart, Tinga, 20, 141, 142, 148, 165
storytelling, 188n5
  and African diasporic expression, 142-43
  ancestral stories, active remembering of, 50-52
  in creole performance tradition, 14
  gossip as form of, 47
  imrovisational characteristics of, 160
  as knowledge system, 38-40, 49-53
  multiple perspectives in, 44, 46
  as narrative strategy, 3, 10, 17, 18, 40-41, 73-74
  omissions and silences in, 53
  person-to-person style, 177
  as political action, 50
  ramifications of, 40-41
  as selective remembering, 38-39, 46-47, 52-53
  as structural device, 23, 32, 84
  uncertainty in, 63
  unreliability of, 42
  woman-associated storytelling, 95
  yard storytelling, 19-20, 163
structural devices
  calypso, 120-21
  carnival, 121
  creole performance tradition, 14-15, 185n22
  episodic narrative structure, 179
  female protagonist as narrator, 158-59
  inward turn, 3, 143
  "Joebell and America", 149
  The Lonely Londoners, 30-31
  memory, 33, 160-61
  monologue, as storytelling, 144-45
  orature, 23, 42-47
  orature-performance as, 12-13, 21
  storytelling, 23, 32, 84, 144-45
  warner woman as, 2, 54-56
Summer Lightning (Senior), 176

terms, usage of, 21
Thiong'o, Ngũgĩ wa, 4, 183-84n5
third-person narrative voice, 43
Thorpe, Marjorie, 83
Torres-Saillant, Silvio, 185n22
tracing, 103, 139, 197n34
transnationalism, in diasporic narrative, 7-8, 19-20
Trinidad. *See also The Dragon Can't Dance* (Lovelace)
  calypso performance tradition, 85-86
  carnival celebration, 123-24
  carnival laughter, 124-25
  picong, 19-20, 127, 131, 143, 157, 181, 197n2, 198n4
  Shouters Prohibition Ordinance, 83, 192n23

Trinidad *(continued)*
　urban poverty, 127–28
Twentieth-Century Caribbean Literature (Donnell), 19, 41, 189n8

Unburnable (John), 7, 63–74
　Afro-Caribbean spirituality, 40–41, 69
　comparison to *The Colour of Forgetting*, 42–47, 73–74
　diversity of oral modes, 42, 189n11
　history, and memory, 17–18, 63–64
　interplay of voices in, 45–46
　maroon community, oral culture of, 71–72, 73
　orality, relationship to sources of power, 66–67
　orality of historical representation, 10–11, 72–73
　orature, and denigration of culture, 40–41
　representations of orality, 64–66
　song-stories, 67–68
　uncertainty, in storytelling, 63, 71
　writing as marginalized mode of representation, 64–66
United States
　American myth vs. yard myth, 164
　invasion of Grenada, 10, 55–56
　migration to, 151–53
　Spanglish, 178

voice
　authoritative voice, diffusion of, 44, 45
　in Caribbean literature, 174–75
　in reclamation of culture, 175
　sounded narrative voice, 5
　third-person narrative voice, 43, 177
　unmarked shifts in, 45–46

Walcott, Derek, 10
　history, and memory, 47
Warner-Lewis, Maureen, 12
　on linguistic extravaganza, 13, 178
　national self-confidence, 33–34
　on *New Day*, 28–29
　on orality, 4
　standard English vs. dialect, use of, 24–25
　on works of Selvon, 179
warner women
　and Afro-Caribbean spirituality, 54–56
　oral tradition of, 2–3, 49
　selective remembering by, 10, 38–39
West Indian, usage of, 21
Wilson, Betty, 174
Wilson-Tagoe, Nana, 64
The Wine of Astonishment (Lovelace), 88–93
　constructions of womanhood, 82, 84, 116
　cross-gender performances, 92–93
　framing device, 89–90
　gender constructions, 9, 18
　male leadership in creole society, 93–94
　narrative strategies, 88
　nationalism, and feminine voice, 95–99
　nationalist theme, 105
　as performing fiction, 90–91
　personal narrative, use of, 83
　religion, and black creole cultural tradition, 83
　Shouters Prohibition Ordinance, 83, 192n23
　woman-centred poetics of, 78–79, 83–84
Winkler, Anthony, 41–42, 189n9

woman-centred poetics
    of calypso, 86
    constructions of womanhood,
        18–19, 76
    and subaltern worldview, 36
womanhood, 81
    constructions of, 79–82, 102–3,
        116–18, 191n10, 191nn13–14,
        192n22
    definitions of, 76
    European models of, 80
    expressions of sexuality, 85–87,
        193n30
    inter-gender poetics, 83
    language, and dominance of
        women, 91
    racial and ethnic constructions of,
        80
    and sexuality, 112–14
    as socially constructed category, 79
    stereotypes of, 106, 194n52, 194n53
    women's vision of, 75
womanist-feminist poetics
    The Book of Night Women (James),
        101–2
    The Dragon Can't Dance (Lovelace),
        139–40
women
    activism, and womanhood, 102–3
    anti-feminist calypsos, 119–20, 125–
        26, 195nn2–3, 196nn18–19
    anti-slavery activities, 80–82,
        93–94, 104–5, 191n15
    in calypso, 85–86, 131, 195n28
    as carriers of tradition, 85
    cultural negotiation as survival
        strategy, 145–48, 198n12

as dangerous, 138–39, 197n31
and female agency, 20, 75, 77,
    81–82, 85, 106–7, 176
as freedom workers, 8, 9, 13, 76,
    80–82, 94–95, 101–2, 191n15
marginalization of immigrant
    women, 163
moral authority of, 125
nationalism, and women's citizen-
    ship, 9, 77–78, 190n4, 190n5
oppression of, 110–12
personhood of, 19, 84, 122–23,
    196n26
religio-moral standards, rejection
    of, 107–9, 110, 195n59
sexuality of, 107–10
voicelessness of, 78, 190n5
yard-centred agency of, 144–45, 146,
    158–59
Woolf, Virginia, 33
Wynter, Sylvia, 4

yard, and yard culture, 19–20, 181
    age and agency, privileging of, 163
    cultural economy of, 148–49
    cultural valuables, 142, 148, 170–71,
        181–82, 198–99n15
    female agency of, 144–45, 146
    melodramatic tendencies of, 168
    in migrant experience, 141–42, 149,
        160
    as socio-cultural space, 149
    in storytelling, 19–20, 163, 170
Yerushalmi, Yosef Hayim, 48

Zirimu, Pio, 4

www.ingramcontent.com/pod-product-compliance
Lightning Source LLC
Chambersburg PA
CBHW031709230426
43668CB00006B/161